Psychology for Inclusive Education

D0322151

What can psychology offer inclusive education? Traditionally, special education has looked to psychology for many of its theoretical resources and practical strategies, while those seeking to promote more inclusive education have tended to see psychology and psychologists as part of the problem by providing a rationale for segregation. However, in practice many psychologists today are developing inclusive ways of working, and are paying attention to psychological theories that underpin inclusive education.

Psychology for Inclusive Education reframes the contribution of psychology in terms of its relevance to inclusion and will show how psychological theories of learning and human development are compatible with inclusive education. Part 1 explores psychological theories relevant to understanding inclusive education and Part 2 looks at how psychology can contribute to promoting more inclusive education in practice. Chapters cover:

- how psychologists can collaborate with teachers for inclusive solutions;
- Vygotsky's theories of learning and their significance for inclusion;
- the challenge of developing pedagogies for inclusion;
- sociocultural understandings of learning in inclusive classrooms;
- the role of emotion in learning and inclusion;
- cooperative learning and inclusion;
- the challenges and tensions of inclusion and high standards for schools;
- the practice of dynamic assessment as an inclusive alternative to IQ;
- social justice and inclusive psychology.

Bringing together a highly distinguished list of international contributors from the UK, USA and South Africa and including practising educational psychologists, this book will link theory to practice in schools and classrooms. International in focus and at the very cutting edge of the field, it is essential reading for all those interested in the development of inclusive education.

Peter Hick is Senior Lecturer in Inclusive Education at Manchester Metropolitan University, UK.

Ruth Kershner is Lecturer in Psychology of Education and Primary Education at the University of Cambridge, UK.

Peter T. Farrell is the Sarah Fielden Professor of Special Needs and Educational Psychology in the School of Education at the University of Manchester, UK and Past President of the International School Psychology Association, UK.

Psychology for Inclusive Education

New directions in theory and practice

Edited by Peter Hick, Ruth Kershner and Peter T. Farrell

Routledge
Taylor & Francis Group

LONDON AND NEW YORK

First published 2009
by Routledge
2 Park Square, Milton Park, Abingdon, Oxon, OX14 4RN

Simultaneously published in the USA and Canada
by Routledge
270 Madison Ave, New York, NY 10016

Routledge is an imprint of the Taylor & Francis Group, an informa business

© 2009 selection and editorial matter Peter Hick, Ruth Kershner and Peter T.
Farrell; individual chapters, the contributors

Typeset in Times New Roman by
GreenGate Publishing Services, Tonbridge, Kent

Printed and bound in Great Britain by
TJ International Ltd, Padstow, Cornwall

British Library Cataloguing in Publication Data
A catalogue record for this book is available from the British Library

Library of Congress Cataloging-in-Publication Data
A catalog record for this book has been requested

ISBN10: 0–415–39049–4 (hbk)
ISBN10: 0–415–39050–8 (pbk)
ISBN10: 0–203–89147–3 (ebk)

ISBN13: 978–0–415–39049–1 (hbk)
ISBN13: 978–0–415–39050–7 (pbk)
ISBN13: 978–0–203–89147–6 (ebk)

Contents

Contributors

Mel Ainscow is Professor of Education and Co-director of the Centre for Equity in Education at the University of Manchester. He is also the Government's Chief Adviser for the Greater Manchester Challenge, a £50 million initiative to improve educational outcomes for all young people in the region. Previously a head teacher, local education authority inspector and lecturer at the University of Cambridge, Mel's work attempts to explore connections between inclusion, teacher development and school improvement. A particular feature of this research involves the development and use of participatory methods of inquiry that set out to make a direct impact on thinking and practice in systems, schools and classrooms. Mel is a consultant for UNESCO, UNICEF and Save the Children; and is Marden Visiting Professor at the Hong Kong Institute of Education. He had two new books published in 2006: *Improving Urban Schools: Leadership and Collaboration* (with Mel West, Open University Press) and *Improving Schools, Developing Inclusion* (with Tony Booth, Alan Dyson and colleagues, Routledge).

Harry Daniels is Director of the Centre for Sociocultural and Activity Theory Research at the University of Bath. His current research is concerned with professional learning in the context of the formation of children's services. He has published extensively in the fields of post-Vygotskian theory and research as well as on SEN-related matters.

Alan Dyson is Professor of Education and Co-director of the Centre for Equity in Education at the University of Manchester. He researches widely in the fields of educational disadvantage, urban education and the development of equitable approaches to education. He has recently led the national evaluation of full service extended schools.

Petra Engelbrecht is Professor in Educational Psychology and was head of the Department of Educational Psychology and Senior Director: Research at Stellenbosch University. She is at present Executive Dean of the Faculty of Education Sciences at Northwest University in South Africa. Her own research focuses on inclusivity and diversity in educational psychology.

Peter T. Farrell is the Sarah Fielden Professor of Special Needs and Educational Psychology in the School of Education at the University of Manchester and Past President of the International School Psychology Association. He has carried out a number of research projects in the field of inclusive education and has published widely in this area. Much of the focus of this work has been on the contribution educational psychologists can make towards promoting inclusive practice.

Lani Florian is Professor of Social and Educational Inclusion at the University of Aberdeen. Her research interests include teaching practice and pupil achievement in inclusive schools, and issues of categorisation of children. She has written extensively on inclusive education and recently co-authored *Achievement and Inclusion in Schools* (Routledge, 2007).

Peter Hick is Senior Lecturer in Inclusive Education at Manchester Metropolitan University. He was a lecturer at the University of Birmingham, the University of Manchester, the Open University and the University of Bolton, and previously worked as an educational psychologist. His research interests focus on inclusive learning mediated with ICT and on race, ethnicity and disproportionality in the identification of special educational needs.

Andrew Howes is a senior lecturer in Education at the University of Manchester, with current interests in inclusive education and science at secondary level, and the related design of contexts for teacher learning through action research. He is currently co-director of an ESRC TLRP research project, 'Facilitating Teacher Engagement in More Inclusive Practice', in which educational psychologists are key facilitators in schools.

Ruth Kershner is a lecturer in the psychology of education in the Faculty of Education at the University of Cambridge. She has particular interests in the areas of teaching children identified with learning difficulties, the development of teachers' pedagogical knowledge through school-based research, and the uses of technology such as interactive whiteboards in the primary classroom environment. She is currently an Associate Director of the Primary Review (directed by Professor Robin Alexander, 2006–8), an independently funded review of primary education in England.

Ingrid Lunt is Professor of Education in the Department of Education at the University of Oxford. From a background in secondary school teaching and educational psychology practice, she moved to the Institute of Education at the University of London where she carried out a number of research projects on special educational needs and inclusive education. She has a particular interest in the role of educational psychologists in promoting more inclusive practice.

Ian McNab is currently the Assistant Principal Educational Psychologist with the Staffordshire Educational Psychology Service. He is currently working on projects to do with encouraging multi-disciplinary collaborative work, service provision for looked-after children and continuing professional development for educational psychologists. He maintains his long-time interest in solution-focused work.

Brahm Norwich is Professor of Educational Psychology and Special Educational Needs in the School of Education and Lifelong Learning at the University of Exeter. He has researched and published widely in these fields. His most recent books are *Moderate Learning Difficulties and the Future of Inclusion* (Routledge, 2005) and *Dilemmas of Difference, Disability and Inclusion: International Perspectives* (Routledge, 2007).

JoAnne W. Putnam is Professor in the School of Education at the University of Maine Presque Isle. She consults and has authored books on cooperative learning and inclusive education. She is developing an indigenous curriculum with the Gesgapegiag Mi'kmaqs of Quebec, Canada and directed the Inupiat Teacher Education program at Ilisavik College, Barrow, Alaska.

Phil Stringer is an educational psychologist working for Hampshire Children's Services Department, where he is County Services Manager, with a responsibility for the educational psychology service, the behaviour support teams and the school counselling service. He has played a significant role in promoting dynamic assessment in the UK.

Gary Thomas is Professor of Inclusion and Diversity at the University of Birmingham. His books include *Deconstructing Special Education and Constructing Inclusion* and *The Making of the Inclusive School*.

Isobel Urquhart is currently a member of Homerton College, University of Cambridge, where she is the Assistant Director of Studies for Psychology. She is an affiliate member of the British Psychological Society and a qualified psychoanalytic psychotherapist. Previously, she was Head of Special Educational Needs in a large comprehensive school. Her research interests include the emotional aspects of learning and teaching, literacy teaching in developing countries and pedagogical responses to literacy difficulties.

Keith Venables convenes the UK-based Educational Psychologists for Inclusion, an organisation committed to promoting the inclusion of all children and young people into their local community mainstream schools. Educational Psychologists for Inclusion runs seminars to increase the skills of educational psychologists, school staff and others to ensure that schools are rich and diverse environments. He has worked in a number of local authorities and seen the best and worst of inclusive practices.

Foreword

The publication of this book could not be more timely. It comes at a time when education systems around the world are struggling to find more effective ways of reaching out to all children and young people in the community. In economically poorer countries this is mainly about the estimated 72 million children who are not in school. Meanwhile, in wealthier countries – despite the resources that are available – many young people leave school with no worthwhile qualifications, others are placed in various forms of special provision away from mainstream educational experiences, and some simply choose to drop out since the lessons seem irrelevant to their lives.

Faced with these challenges, there is evidence of an increased interest in the idea of *inclusive education*. However, the field remains confused as to what actions need to be taken in order to move policy and practice forward. In some countries, inclusive education is still thought of as an approach to serving children with disabilities within general education settings. Internationally, however, it is increasingly seen more broadly as a reform that supports and welcomes diversity amongst all learners. It presumes that the aim of inclusive education is to eliminate social exclusion that is a consequence of attitudes and responses to diversity in race, social class, ethnicity, religion, gender and ability. As such, it starts from the belief that education is a basic human right and the foundation for a more just society.

Fourteen years ago the UNESCO Salamanca World Conference on Special Needs Education endorsed the idea of inclusive education. Arguably the most significant international document that has ever appeared in the field of special education, the Salamanca Statement argued that regular schools with an inclusive orientation are 'the most effective means of combating discriminatory attitudes, building an inclusive society and achieving education for all'. Furthermore, it suggested that such schools can 'provide an effective education for the majority of children and improve the efficiency and ultimately the cost-effectiveness of the entire education system'.

It is worth noting that the Salamanca event followed soon after the groundbreaking Jomtien Conference of 1990, which committed almost all the countries in the world to achieve the goal of *Education for All*. This was particularly significant because it acknowledged that large numbers of vulnerable and marginalised groups of learners were excluded from education systems worldwide. However, despite the apparent unequivocal nature of the Jomtien declaration, the decision to hold the Salamanca conference would seem to imply that the phrase 'education for all' really meant 'almost all', accepting the historical assumption that a small percentage of children have to be seen as 'outsiders', whose education must be catered for by a separate, parallel system, usually known as special education.

As we consider possible ways forward, then, it is important to recognise that the field of inclusive education is riddled with uncertainties, disputes and contradictions. Yet throughout the world attempts are being made to provide more effective educational responses for all children, whatever their characteristics, and, encouraged by the Salamanca Statement, the overall trend is towards making these responses within the context of general educational provision. As a consequence, this is leading to a reconsideration of the future roles and purposes of practitioners throughout education systems, including those who work in special education provision and services. And, of course, this has major implications for the direction of national policies and the development of practice in the field.

Within this complex policy context, as the editors of this book note, those seeking to promote more inclusive forms of education have often seen psychology and psychologists as part of the problem, rather than as a source of helpful guidance. It is, therefore, refreshing to see the way the authors of the chapters in this book throw new light on how psychology can offer important resources to support the development of more inclusive practices in education.

Mel Ainscow
Professor of Education
University of Manchester

Chapter 1

Introduction

Peter Hick, Ruth Kershner and Peter T. Farrell

Teachers and educationalists have traditionally looked to psychology as a source of ideas and evidence about how best to support children's learning, especially for those who may experience difficulties in learning in school. However the rationale for inclusive education has tended to be sociological, philosophical, political or educational – in fact anything but psychological. Those seeking to promote more inclusive education have often seen psychology and psychologists as part of the problem rather than the solution, referring to the roles of psychology in providing an IQ-based rationale for separating children into special schools (Thomas and Loxley, 2001), or in ascribing difficulties in learning to individual child deficit. Yet psychology can offer important resources to support the development of more inclusive practices in education.

This book examines the possibilities for developing a psychology for inclusive education, by drawing on a variety of relevant theoretical perspectives and practical strategies. This involves exploring some of the psychological aspects of what is understood to be inclusive practice both in schools and in professional educational psychology services. It also means thinking about whether there are resources in psychological theory for promoting inclusive education. The intention is to open up critical discussion about psychology and inclusive education and help formulate an agenda for research and development in the field, in the knowledge that we may be heading towards a diverse collection of relevant 'psychologies' rather than a single psychological framework. To provide some background to the chapters which follow, we first review current definitions of inclusion and then consider how psychology may be seen as relevant, or even essential, for developing more inclusive education.

What do we mean by inclusion?

For many the principle of 'inclusion' has become a cornerstone of the development of policy and practice for the education of all pupils. This general movement was strongly influenced by the Salamanca Statement (UNESCO, 1994) which had a major impact on shaping policy developments in many different countries. In England this is evident in various government initiatives since the late 1990s, including, for example, the statutory Inclusion Guidance (DfES, 2001a), the Special Educational Needs and Disability Act (DfES, 2001b), and the 'Removing Barriers to Achievement' strategy (DfES, 2004), each providing a further impetus towards inclusion.

Despite these policy developments, inclusion remains a complex and controversial issue, with continuing uncertainty about its definition and implications. There remain pressures to maintain separate special schools, for example from some parents who have immediate concerns about their own children's educational experiences and available school choices. It is hard to point to convincing research evidence that can inform policy and practice in the face of often opposing assumptions and preferences. Furthermore, in the UK, schools are under more pressure than ever to raise academic standards for all their pupils. In this climate some teachers are expressing increasing reluctance to admit more pupils identified with special needs, fearing that their presence may have a negative effect on the attainments of other pupils. In addition, the recent emphasis on beacon and specialist schools and the 'threat' of returning to forms of selection in some areas (e.g. in the new Academies) suggests that there is a growing movement in education that values 'elitism' – hardly values that are compatible with an inclusive philosophy.

Until the early 1990s the term 'inclusion' was rarely used in this context. Instead we referred to 'integration' or 'mainstreaming', meaning the placement of pupils with disabilities or special needs in mainstream schools. There were of course different degrees of integration, from full-time placement of a child with disabilities in a mainstream class in his/her local school (functional integration), to the placement of a pupil in a special class or unit attached to a mainstream school (locational integration) – see Hegarty (1991). However there was often little difference between locational integration and a traditional special school, which can be seen as equally segregating experiences (Jupp, 1992). Indeed, even pupils placed in a mainstream class may be isolated from their peers, particularly if they work with a support worker in one-to-one sessions for the majority of each day. 'Integrated' placements, therefore, still leave many pupils 'segregated' (Harrower, 1999).

Partly for these reasons, the term 'inclusion' came to describe the extent to which a school or community welcomes pupils identified with special educational needs (SEN) as full members of the group and values them for the contribution which they make. This implies that for inclusion to be 'effective', all pupils must actively belong to, be welcomed by and participate in a mainstream school and community. Their diversity of interests, abilities and attainment should be welcomed and be seen to enrich the life of the school. In this sense, as Ballard (1999) argues, inclusion is about valuing diversity rather than assimilation.

Arguably, this understanding of inclusion questions the familiar approaches to identifying particular pupils with SEN, and in the late 1990s definitions of inclusion have broadened to reflect this (see, for example, Booth and Ainscow, 1998). These writers take the view that policies on inclusion should not be restricted to the education of pupils thought to have special needs. Inclusion, they argue, is a process in which schools, communities, local authorities and governments strive to reduce barriers to participation and learning for all citizens.

This broader view of inclusion is reflected in guidance from the UK Government for inspectors of schools in England and Wales (Ofsted, 2000), which states:

> An educationally inclusive school is one in which the teaching and learning, achievements, attitudes and well being of every young person matters. Effective schools are educationally inclusive schools. This shows, not only in their performance, but also in their ethos and their willingness to offer new opportunities to pupils who may have experienced previous difficulties ... The most effective schools do not take educational inclusion for granted. They constantly monitor and evaluate the progress each pupil makes. They identify any pupils who may be missing out, difficult to engage, or feeling in some way apart from what the school seeks to provide.

In addressing what they refer to as 'educational inclusion', the document focuses attention on a wide range of vulnerable groups and it draws attention to the need for inspectors to go beyond an analysis of aggregate performance scores in order to determine the extent a school is supporting the learning of all individuals within a school.

One influential strand of research has developed this *organisational paradigm* for understanding inclusive practice in terms of school development, in contrast to an earlier *special needs paradigm,* focused on individuals with identified disabilities or special needs. Perhaps the best known product of this approach is the 'Index for Inclusion' (Booth and Ainscow, 2002) which was circulated to all schools in England by the DfES. This tool for school self-evaluation has stimulated the development of a range of materials, including a distillation of a definition of inclusive practice around the dimensions of 'presence, participation and achievement'. This approach has been adopted for example by the Audit Commission (2003) and incorporated in a more recent definition of inclusion as:

- the processes of increasing the participation of students in, and reducing their exclusion from, the curricula, cultures and communities of local schools;
- restructuring the cultures, policies and practices in schools so that they respond to the diversity of students in their locality;
- the presence, participation and achievement of all students vulnerable to exclusionary pressures, not only those with impairments or those who are categorised as 'having special educational needs'.

Ainscow *et al.* (2006: 25)

The contributors to this book explore a range of understandings of inclusion, however the approach described above is offered as a point of reference. It is a definition that embraces all learners, and despite the challenges it presents, offers a way forward for all involved in the education of children and young people. So can psychology add anything useful?

Is psychology useful?

The fact that connections between psychology and inclusive education are in need of clarification, may partly be seen as symptomatic of longstanding doubts about the broad social and practical value of psychology itself. Cole and Valsiner (2005: 288–9) point out with reference to a 1926 essay by Vygotsky on 'The Historical Sense of Psychology's Crisis' that '… psychology is a discipline where the creation of crises is a regular pastime'. They argue that the social usefulness of psychology, as with other sciences, is hindered by clashes between different ways of knowing in society and by the integration of scientific with current ideological discourses. This can lead to the over-generalisation and over-simplification of discoveries and concepts, and this process is notable today in the field of education. For many teachers in England, relevant psychological knowledge now commonly comes through school-based training on specific concepts and approaches, such as 'multiple intelligences', 'learning style', 'circle time' and 'phonics teaching' – often received and implemented in school without direct examination of any related research evidence. In these contexts, the concepts themselves may gain a meaning, status and practical use which seem independent of the original psychological argument and evidence base. The educational 'usefulness' of psychology comes to be determined by the success of 'non-psychologists' in applying snippets of psychological knowledge and procedures that have somehow gained cultural value.

One solution to this apparent fragmentation could be to focus on devising cross-disciplinary research approaches which are sufficiently complex for studying human thinking and activity in social and cultural contexts, often with an emancipatory aim. For instance Barker and Pistrang (2005) outline the characteristics of pluralistic methodology in psychology from the perspective of community psychologists. The use of multiple research methodologies is one of several values and principles which underpin their work, including sensitivity to people's contexts, respect for diversity among people and settings, addressing competencies (as well as problems), promoting empowerment, giving voice to traditionally under-represented populations, and promoting social justice (pp. 205–6). This explicitness about purposes and values is also evident in the field of critical psychology which focuses on social change and social justice, often drawing out the implications for policies on child care, welfare reform, education, equal opportunities legislation, etc. (Walkerdine, 2002; Sloan, 2000). Critical approaches in psychology apparently challenge what may have been seen or claimed in the past as a neutral scientific activity. For example even a light reading of the early development of intelligence testing reveals a strong (and often eugenicist) aim for social and educational engineering. Questions about psychology's usefulness inevitably require cultural values to be made explicit – as evident in relation to the development of inclusive education.

It is not always clear in discussions of psychology and education whether reference is being made to psychological knowledge and ways of thinking or to practising professional psychologists, and both positions are represented in this book. Some psychologists have loosened their ties with psychology as a discipline, while others have sought to retain this academic and psychological identity in their daily work and their professional affiliations. Borders have become blurred between the theory and practice of psychology and education, and it is not always clear that the use of psychology in the education system requires the presence of psychologists. Yet there would seem to be a need for the critical evaluation of psychological evidence without necessarily rejecting the less easily digestible elements. As Cole and Valsiner (2005: 309) suggest from a sociocultural perspective, psychology can incorporate culture and everyday practice in a way that allows psychological knowledge to be constantly re-constructed, and therefore co-constructed, by people engaged in purposeful, culturally meaningful activity.

In the end, the development of inclusive education is a radical challenge to schools and education systems. Olson (2003: 288) suggests that 'schooling is a bold and risky means of pursuing education' and he argues that in developing a psychology that can contribute to educational reform, the school institution itself requires attention, together with the meanings and goals of all concerned:

> schools are successful to the extent that they, through their teachers and programs, return these responsibilities to the learners by negotiating goals acceptable to both and by allowing students to recruit the resources and energy to achieve them. Understanding how persons and institutions negotiate these responsibilities for learning may be the first step in explaining what schools are, what they do, why they are virtually universal, and why they are resistant to fundamental change. (pp. 288–9)

This may be a useful starting point for developing a psychology, or a set of psychologies, that will have real value for inclusive education. The writers in this book each make a distinctive contribution to an interesting and developing field.

Part 1: Understanding inclusive learning

The first part of the book focuses on key theoretical issues in understanding how psychology can offer resources to support the development of more inclusive practices in education. In Chapter 2, Gary Thomas explores the epistemological basis for a psychology for inclusive education, starting from a critical examination of claims often made for psychology as producing 'scientific' knowledge. He exposes some influential myths about the 'scientific method' and illustrates the dangers of a simplistic application of this approach to education. Thomas traces the discursive construction and socially situated nature of knowledge through the history of special education. He suggests that by privileging psychological knowledge we may have disempowered teachers in addressing the needs of their pupils.

Thomas concludes by calling for psychologists to rely more on social values and for a 'reinstatement of the personal knowledge of teachers' as reflective practitioners.

In Chapter 3, Harry Daniels introduces key aspects of Vygotsky's theories in relation to inclusion. He deals with linguistic and cultural barriers which sometimes hinder an understanding of Vygotsky's arguments and their implications for pedagogy today. When Vygotsky's writing on concept formation is placed alongside his view of 'primary' (organically influenced) and 'secondary' (socially influenced) disability, a familiar educational dilemma emerges: how to intervene in a way that addresses children's particular strengths, while minimising secondary, social effects on children's lives. Daniels concludes that this dilemma remains unresolved in our current systems of either special or mainstream education, including much that is called 'inclusive'.

In Chapter 4, Lani Florian challenges the assumption that learners with identified special educational needs require a 'specialist pedagogy'. She argues that, while some 'special education knowledge' can be useful to teachers, research evidence suggests the need to develop pedagogy inclusive of all learners, focusing on general processes of learning and teaching rather than on the specialised remediation of perceived learning deficits. She presents an English secondary school case example of what this might comprise, drawing on teachers' views of their own practice. Florian concludes that one of the key features of inclusive pedagogy is teachers' adaptation to pupils' individual differences in the context of whole-class teaching, focusing on responsiveness to the kinds of difficulties some children may experience in learning but rejecting deterministic, categorical beliefs about fixed ability and potential.

In Chapter 5, Ruth Kershner writes from a social constructivist perspective to discuss the contribution of sociocultural approaches to understanding inclusion. She focuses on 'children's engagement in the social activities associated with learning', drawing attention to the 'collective experience of classroom learning'. Kershner reviews the sociocultural literature on learning as participation in schools and classrooms as activity systems. She goes on to examine the notions of 'situated cognition', 'distributed intelligence', 'dialogic teaching' and 'multimodal communication', and comments critically on simplistic notions of fixed individual learning styles. Kershner concludes that diverse learners themselves become the embodiment of inclusive educational activity in practice.

In Chapter 6, Isobel Urquhart writes about the emotional dimension to inclusion, employing a psychodynamic perspective to understand the emotional repercussions of particular practices and dilemmas at the personal, interpersonal and structural levels of education. She warns against the romanticisation of a narrow focus on emotion as an 'antidote' to exclusionary practices, particularly in the form of self-contained initiatives and programmes. She concludes, in contrast, that we need seriously to address the affective context and processes of education at all levels, while bearing in mind that it is the day-to-day communication and the quality of care for children in school that may most immediately represent a truly inclusive educational system to children and parents.

Part 2: Promoting inclusive learning

In Part 2, the contributors address the contributions of psychology to the development of more inclusive practices in a range of contexts. These include both teachers and schooling, and the profession of educational psychology itself.

In Chapter 7, JoAnne Putnam reviews a core concept for the development of inclusive learning: cooperative group activities. Writing as a researcher on cooperative learning in the US tradition, she introduces the legislative context for inclusive education in the USA. She describes the basic principles of cooperative learning and shows how students with disabilities can be included in cooperative learning activities. Putnam outlines the basis for cooperative learning in psychological theory and reviews the research evidence on the benefits of cooperative learning for inclusion. She concludes by addressing the challenges of implementing cooperative group activities and suggests that there is much to be gained by further developing this approach.

In Chapter 8, Ingrid Lunt and Brahm Norwich write about the 'challenges and tensions' involved in combining policies for increasing school 'effectiveness' with those aimed at greater 'inclusiveness'. They refer to empirical studies of schools which appear to combine inclusiveness with effectiveness, including their own work. They conclude from their case studies that while certain common features can be identified, any notion of recipes for school development is hindered by multiple and conflicting value positions and by local contexts and priorities. Lunt and Norwich conclude that focusing on the process of becoming more inclusive, not just on the outcomes, requires interdisciplinary research encompassing contributions from psychology.

In Chapter 9, Petra Engelbrecht discusses inclusion in a context of social change, offering the example of South Africa where the implementation of inclusive education remains a challenge in most schools. Since 1994, the constitutional principle of 'substantive equality' emphasises the restoration of human rights to all marginalised groups. Engelbrecht points out that in this situation, the development of psychology in South Africa has had to cast aside the myth of scientific and political neutrality. The profession of educational psychology has moved towards an ecosystemic model, promoting the values of sustainability and partnership in an inclusive democratic society. However, Engelbrecht notes that the potential to cross divides in community settings, depends on the courage to move away from safe professional boundaries and deal with the ambivalence of acknowledging the continuing legacy of apartheid.

In Chapter 10, Peter T. Farrell and Keith Venables examine the contradictory demands faced by educational psychologists (EPs) aiming to develop more inclusive practices, whilst playing a central role in the formal assessment of pupils' special educational needs that supports a segregated system of educational provision. They note that whilst EPs may often be reluctant to change their practice – in spite of a wealth of literature criticising IQ testing and the medical model of SEN – there are many examples of EPs working to promote inclusive practices in schools and local authorities. Farrell and Venables conclude, however, that recent English initiatives in the training of educational psychologists, in integrated children's services and government policy may hinder this apparent progress in working towards inclusion – unless the EP role can be redefined to incorporate this agenda.

In Chapter 11, Phil Stringer focuses on the strategy of dynamic assessment as a means of responding to the 'individual children with individual differences' who may need support to participate, learn and develop in any learning community. Stringer presents dynamic assessment as an interactive process of assessment and intervention, that involves asking a series of questions about how learners learn. Feuerstein's notion of mediated learning experience is seen as central to understanding differences in learning in this way, assuming that learning and intelligence are modifiable through experience rather than predictable and fixed. Stringer notes the different traditions in dynamic assessment, focusing either on the psychometric properties of interactive testing, or on learning processes. As a practising educational psychologist concerned with including children in learning, Stringer advocates more use of dynamic assessment as an empowering process for all involved.

In Chapter 12 Ian McNab writes about how psychologists and teachers can work together to support the development of more inclusive practices, through an approach he describes as 'collaborative consultation'. McNab characterises the nature of the collaborative relationship as one of 'respectful not-knowing', subverting the 'expert' role typically assigned to the psychologist. He posits collaborative consultation as a transformational process, engaging parents and pupils as active partners. Rather than donating or imposing solutions, the psychologist offers alternative constructions which teachers, parents and pupils may choose to adopt in reframing issues to arrive at more inclusive ways forward.

Part 3: Challenges and possibilities

The concluding section reflects on possible research agendas for the development of inclusive education and on how the contributions of psychology can be located in relation to these. In Chapter 13, Alan Dyson and Andrew Howes consider interdisciplinary research on inclusive education, starting with an account of competing perspectives or paradigms for understanding inclusion. Drawing on accounts of their own research, they explore the limitations of working within one perspective alone. Dyson and Howes describe the processes of 'deconstruction and reconstruction' in theorising inclusive education and identify a 'bio-psycho-social' model as an example of an interdisciplinary approach. They point to an enduring 'dilemma of difference' created by competing demands on educational systems, which cannot necessarily be resolved in the field of inclusive education. Dyson and Howes conclude by calling for a more systematic process of critique; a more programmatic approach to researching inclusion; and for 'bridge building' research that crosses boundaries between perspectives.

They offer a critique of a research project they were both involved with, as an example of how a productive interdisciplinary dialogue could be developed.

In the final chapter, Peter Hick draws together the themes of the book, and explores how psychology for inclusive learning can be reframed within a social justice agenda. There is a sense in which theory lags behind practice in relation to psychology and inclusive education, and there is a need to examine approaches that pose alternatives to traditional paradigms and pedagogies. Hick reviews elements of Vygotsky's writings to highlight theoretical resources that may be relevant to understanding inclusive learning today. He suggests that the practice of inclusive education must be framed in its broader social context and that the contributions that psychology can offer to the development of more inclusive practices in education need to be located within an interdisciplinary frame.

References

Ainscow, M., Booth, T., and Dyson, A. with Farrell, P., Frankham, J., Gallannaugh, F., Howes, A. and Smith, R. (2006) *Improving Schools, Developing Inclusion*. Abingdon, Oxon: Routledge.

Audit Commission (2003) *Special Educational Needs: A Mainstream Issue*. London: Audit Commission.

Ballard, K. (1999) *Inclusive Education: International Voices on Disability and Justice*. London: Falmer Press.

Barker, C. and Pistrang, N. (2005) Quality criteria under methodological pluralism: Implications for conducting and evaluating research. *American Journal of Community Psychology*, 36(3/4), 201–212.

Booth, T. and Ainscow, M. (1998) *From Them to Us: An International Study of Inclusion in Education*. London: Routledge.

Booth, T. and Ainscow, M. (2002) *Index for Inclusion: Developing Learning and Participation in Schools*. Bristol: Centre for Studies on Inclusive Education.

Cole, M. and Valsiner, J. (2005) Actualizing potentials: Learning through psychology's recurrent crises. In D.B. Pillemer and S.H. White (eds), *Developmental Psychology and Social Change: Research, History, and Policy*. (pp. 283–313) Cambridge: Cambridge University Press.

DfES (2001a) *Inclusive Schooling: Children with Special Educational Needs*. London: DfES.

DfES (2001b) *Special Educational Needs and Disability Act*. London: The Stationery Office.

DfES (2004) *Removing Barriers to Achievement: The Government's Strategy for SEN*. London: DfES.

Harrower, J. (1999) Educational inclusion of children with severe disabilities. *Journal of Positive Behavioral Interventions*, 1, 215–230.

Hegarty, S. (1991) Toward an agenda for research in special education. *European Journal of Special Needs Education*, 6(2), 87–99.

Jupp, K. (1992) *Everyone Belongs: Mainstream Education for Children with Severe Learning Difficulties*. London: Souvenir Press.

Ofsted (2000) *Evaluating Educational Inclusion: Guidance for Inspectors and Schools*. London: OFSTED.

Olson, D. (2003) *Psychological Theory and Educational Reform: How School Remakes Mind and Society.* Cambridge: Cambridge University Press.

Sloan, T. (2000) *Critical Psychology: Voices for Change.* Basingstoke, Hants: Macmillan Press.

Thomas, G. and Loxley, A. (2001) *Deconstructing Special Education and Constructing Inclusion.* Buckingham: Open University Press.

UNESCO (1994) *Final Report: World Conference on Special Needs Education: Access and Quality.* Paris: UNESCO.

Vygotsky, L.S. (1926/1982) Istoricheskii smysl psykhologicheskogo krizisa. In L.S. Vygotsky *Sobranie sochinenii,* Vol 1 (pp. 291–346). Moscow: Pedagogika (Original published in 1926).

Walkerdine, V. (2002) *Challenging Subjects: Critical Psychology for a New Millennium.* Basingstoke, Hants: Palgrave.

Part I

Understanding inclusive learning

Chapter 2

An epistemology for inclusion

Gary Thomas

How can we know about inclusion? How can we know that it is the right thing to do or that we can rely on any of the evidence that we think we have as to its benefits? More particularly, how can the kind of knowledge that we collect and analyse as psychologists inform our endeavours to promote inclusive education?

It is the last of these questions with which I have wrestled most in writing this chapter. The first questions raise some interesting issues, but these are general: they concern everyone interested in education, not just psychologists. The reason that I have wrestled with the question about psychology is that I feel that much of psychology's influence on education has been destructive – not constructive – when it comes to practical, workaday contribution. I am not alone in this view. Take what some highly respected psychologists have had to say about psychology as a field. The American experimental psychologist J.J. Gibson (1967: 142) concluded, after a lifetime's work in the field, about the gains made by psychologists that '... these gains seem to me puny, and scientific psychology seems to me ill-founded'. Rom Harré (1985: 14) goes even further in saying that it is a 'tragedy' that so many able people waste their time on the methods and products of a field which is 'disappointing in content and quality'. Will Swann (1985: 35) concluded that 'much knowledge derived from scientific psychology is not applicable in any straightforward sense. Psychology and education are enterprises guided by radically different ground rules. Much confusion has been wrought, much of it unrecognised, by the failure to understand this'.

It seems to me that much of the problem about which these commentators speak here is psychology's allegiance to what it takes to be science. Psychology, an infant discipline as the nineteenth century turned into the twentieth, was unsure of its epistemological status and attached itself to what it considered to be the rock-solid epistemology of the natural sciences. The successes of science meant that its methods were looked upon increasingly favourably by the intelligent layperson. The influential philosopher-sociologist Herbert Spencer was able to promote the notion, in a reification of science's methods that has come to be known as 'scientism', that the only reliable knowledge of the universe was that found in the sciences.

And this has continued. For the best part of the twentieth century, there has been the optimistic assumption that the path of progress in scientific knowledge would be a smooth one – that progress would follow naturally out of scientific advance, and science would broaden its virtuous ambit to advance and enrich study in fields other than the natural sciences. It was assumed that the methods of investigation that had been so successful for physics and chemistry would be appropriately employed not just in those sciences but also in social inquiry.

There are two problems with this worldview. One, appreciated only relatively recently, is that scientific methods may be useful for looking at the behaviour of physical and chemical phenomena, but are less productive when examining human behaviour. Scientific methods may be valuable in answering some questions (and their success with certain kinds of question is palpable), but whether it is valuable for all questions – and in our case, educational questions – is far less certain. I share Berlin's (1979) view that the sciences represent the major achievement of the human mind. But the problem arises, as he proceeds to note, from the assumption that 'the world is a single system which can be described and explained by the use of rational methods' (p. 81). The problem comes from the twentieth century assumption – held *par excellence* by psychologists at the beginning of the century – that scientific method, 'while it may not lead to absolute certainty, attains to a degree of verisimilitude or probability quite sufficient for human affairs' (p. 88).

The second central problem is that the methods of science are difficult to put one's finger on, with many mistaken ideas about what 'scientific method' actually comprises. This uncertainty grew during the later part of the twentieth century. Let us look at what a few prominent scientists and philosophers of science have said about it.

> The essence of scientific method is in seeking 'in whatever manner is suitable, a simplified and lucid image of the world … There is no logical path, but only intuition'.
>
> Einstein, in Holton (1995: 168)

> There is no scientific method as such, but the vital feature of the scientist's procedure has been merely to do his utmost with his mind, *no holds barred* [original emphasis].
>
> Percy Bridgman (Nobel Prize-winning physicist),
> in Wright Mills (1970: 69)

> Most [discoveries] enter the mind by processes of the kind vaguely called 'intuitive' … this is seldom apparent from scientific writings because scientists take pains to ensure that it should not be.
>
> (Medawar, 1982: 88)

> Science is not a method. Doing science is not a matter of 'applying' or 'using' a method, but of using the proper methods to answer particular questions about particular phenomena.
>
> (Egan, 1984: 132)

> The only principle that does not inhibit progress is *anything goes*.
>
> Feyerabend (1993: 14)

What is clear from these statements is that science is not characterised by the kinds of processes imagined by psychologists of a certain generation to characterise science. Indeed, one could say that psychology always seems to be a bit behind the times when it comes to assumptions about guiding principles on methodology and epistemology. Koch's (1964) summary about psychology and epistemology is as true today as when it was written. It is speaking of the way that psychology rooted itself in what it presumed to be limited kinds of 'legitimate' data, namely the kinds prescribed by the logical positivists:

> In every period of our history we psychologists have looked to external sources in the scholarly culture – especially natural science and the philosophy of science – for our sense of direction. And typically we have embraced policies long out of date in those very sources ... Psychology is thus in the unenviable position of standing on philosophical foundations which began to be vacated by philosophy almost as soon as the former had borrowed them. (pp. 4–5)

Koch was talking in particular about the destructive influence of logical positivism, a branch of philosophy popular in the early twentieth century which influenced a generation of psychologists – and, in fact, still has its influence on the way that some think about epistemology and method. Logical positivists asserted that the only data worth looking at were 'observable'. To examine thought, thinking or any of the woolly, unseeable phenomena psychologists had hitherto examined would result in psychology producing no findings of any interest, as it perpetually concerned itself with issues that could not be verified by the kind of data that natural scientists used.

This epistemological stance had huge consequences for the field of psychology. For example, the behaviourists who promulgated behavioural objectives insisted on the observability of the behaviour which was being promoted. This insistence owes a lineage directly to logical positivism via Skinner's behaviourism. It led, in the study of learning, to an insistence that a child be seen to *do* something, rather than merely be noted vaguely to *enjoy* it, and the pedigree of this absurdity is traceable with no difficulty at all to the logical positivists' insistence on the verification of meaningfulness through observation. Carnap (leader of the logical positivists' Vienna Circle) would no doubt have turned in his grave at the knowledge that the philosophical school which he helped to form had, fifty years later, provided the intellectual lead for a system of teaching which involved breaking down learning into dozens of 'behavioural objectives'. The consequences are now plain for all to see: a host of teaching innovations and behaviour modification procedures that resulted in a kind of curricular desertification as educational principles evaporated in the heat of the confidence conferred by what was assumed to be rock-solid scientific epistemology.

It is worth noting that confidence in what was assumed to be scientific episte-mology had other consequences for educational psychology. It is perhaps no coincidence that one of the most notorious scientific frauds of the twentieth cen-tury was perpetrated by an educational psychologist in the shape of Sir Cyril Burt. So keen was Burt to appear scientific that he was prepared to fabricate results (and personnel) to prove to the world that his ideas were right. The inter-esting intellectual genealogy of his fraud is that his belief (in the shape of the primarily genetic determination of intelligence) itself lay in the distortion by social scientists of actual scientific knowledge and theory. Social Darwinists had – without evidence – twisted Darwinian theory to promote eugenics and heredi-tarian views about the inheritance of ability and Burt's allegiance to this notion lay in the fact that it was – or appeared to be – scientific. Insult had been added to injury: false belief in the easy transferability of epistemology and method from one paradigm to another led to attempts to use those methods again, as though this was an unproblematic operation. The fact that it could not be done so simply led to the fraud which Burt is now known to have perpetrated (see Kamin, 1977; Hearnshaw, 1979). For educational psychology, and for the social sciences generally, the consequence of this attempt to borrow epistemology inappropri-ately has been a loss of confidence in the status and credibility of the fields' methods and findings.

Epistemology post-scientism

Inquiry in educational psychology has tended to follow the methods of science, or at least what has been taken to be those methods (see Chambers, 1992, for a fuller cri-tique than that given above). At the heart of these methods has been experimental study used to advance theory. It was assumed that theory would, refined and improved, go on to explain and predict more effectively, that theory would stimulate research, and theory and research hand in hand would inform practice. The model is deeply flawed for education generally, as I have tried to indicate elsewhere (see Thomas, 1997), and in special education it has had particularly unfortunate effects (Thomas and Loxley, 2001). Academic special educators during the twentieth cen-tury regarded the theoretical products of psychology – Piagetian, psychoanalytic, psychometric and behavioural theoretical models – almost as a kind of pick'n'mix. The result has been, in educational psychology, an epistemic jumble, an agglomera-tion of bits and pieces from many and varied theoretical provenances, often contradictory in their tenets and widely different in their recommendations.

It is only of late that there has been recognition of the limits of supposedly sci-entific inquiry in determining the ways in which we should examine education. It has come to be recognised that in education foci for analysis do not usually lend themselves to the analytical instruments borrowed from the major disciplines. A position increasingly taken of late is that far too much has been made of the potential contribution of these schools of thought and that they have exercised a disproportionate influence on special education, on our understanding of why children fail at school, and on our prescriptions for action when they do. Too much has been invested in their significance. Their status as frameworks within which thinking can be usefully constructed has been overplayed and the extent to which practice can usefully follow from research generated within their parameters has been exaggerated.

The problem comes in claiming some *special* status for one's work because it has the label 'scientific'. For verification of the (albeit healthily self-questioning) hankering after 'scientific knowledge', note that the 2005 annual meeting of the Division of Educational and Child Psychology focused on the educational psychologist as 'scientist-practitioner' (see Belar, 2000, for a discussion). At least one keynote speaker at the meeting called for the '… development of systematic and rigorous approaches to practice which complement and are congruent with the scientific tradition' (see BPS, 2006). As the sociologist Leonard Schatzman (1991) notes, we are constantly using 'common interpretive acts' (p. 304) and using these to help us order and comprehend the world. We all see links, discover patterns, make generalisations, create explanatory propositions all the time, emerging out of our experience, and this is all in a sense scientific. The question is: what can a specially labelled 'scientific' approach offer in a field of human practice such as education or psychology?

The weapons of a scientific psychology, in other words, have to offer more than natural everyday analytic skill, yet one cannot be confident that they will ever do this. We have to avoid proffering what the anthropologist Clifford Geertz (1975) called 'clever simulations' (p. 11) – clever simulations, in other words, of what appears in the common imagination to be a 'scientific approach' – in our work with teachers.

It's not *un*scientific to develop and use one's own insights and intuitions as a teacher or educational psychologist. One could in this sense paraphrase Schatzman and talk of a 'common epistemology'. For we all find pieces of evidence, make links between them, discover patterns, make generalisations, create explanatory propositions all the time, emerging out of our experience, and this is all 'empirical'. All practitioners do this: engineers, medics, teachers and educational psychologists. The question is, how far should other kinds of supposed evidence be privileged over this everyday knowledge? I don't think they should – certainly in education – be so privileged. They should be examined and assessed next to the tacit knowledge that we have as part of our professional experience. In this sense we should be what the anthropologist Lévi-Strauss called 'bricoleurs' – in other words not fussy about method but using evidence from wherever it might emerge, from here, there and everywhere, assessing its value as part of an emerging tapestry of evidence. We should, in Einstein's words be 'unscrupulous opportunists' in our scientific method.

All professionals will seek knowledge, collect evidence deliberately and tacitly in ways described by Donald Schön in his book *The Reflective Practitioner* – and he emphasises the interconnectedness of professional knowledge and the importance of the ability to reflect on experience. The evidence will be reviewed, talked about with colleagues, new things will be tried out as a consequence and informally evaluated.

Epistemology post-Foucault

In the last quarter of a century the philosopher-historian Michel Foucault has had a significant influence on way that epistemology was considered in the social sciences. In two of his works, *The Archaeology of Knowledge* (1972) and *The Order of Things* (1970), he makes it clear that knowledge is never constituted in objective terms but rather is defined in a particular place and in a particular era by sets of habits, rules and expectations about what can and cannot be said. The ways we think, and the things we know are, for Foucault, products of our cultural, institutional, professional and personal histories and the intellectual environments that those histories have framed. Foucault uses the words *episteme* and *archive* to describe these intellectual environments. McNay (1994: 66) puts it thus: 'Like the episteme, the archive is defined as the general condition of possibility – the system of discursive regularities – which determines what can and cannot be spoken in a given historical era'.

The key words here are not only 'episteme' and 'archive', but perhaps more importantly 'discursive regularities'. For Foucault, much of what defines ways of knowing lies in *discourse* – patterns of contact and communication – and the *discursive* is central for Foucault's analysis of knowledge. Discourse, in other words, defines what counts as knowledge, and epistemology – the study of what we know and how we know it – centres in the human sciences around cultural, institutional and personal communications, all of these being constructed in an historical context. The foregrounding of discourse thus suggests that knowledge is *located* socially and historically.

Foucault's analyses help one to understand that social structures – in our case special schools, special assessments and special pedagogy – far from being God-given are made by people acting intentionally. The interesting insight which Foucault provides is that the intellectual apparatus which has emerged ostensibly to add objectivity, humanity and disinterested 'science' to an analysis of social structures in fact does nothing of the kind. In the highly complex world of human beings and human relations, this intellectual apparatus does little other than provide in new words and garb what we already recognise and know. The real knowledge, in other words, lies in the discourses permitted by the cultures that we live in, albeit that these are given added legitimacy by being reframed in the context of educational psychology in the language of science and in the 'officialese' of professionals. Philp (1990: 67) puts it thus: 'The normal child, the healthy body, the stable mind ... such concepts haunt our ideas about ourselves, and are reproduced and legitimated through the practices of teachers, social workers, doctors, judges, policemen and administrators'. This is all relevant for our examination of educational psychology and its knowledge, for this knowledge displays particular characteristics that have changed according to the predominant discourses of the time (see also Reid and Valle, 2004; Thomas and Loxley, 2005). It is important to remember that special education is a product of social and political frameworks – the ways people think at a particular time frame their views about what is good for children and how education should be made to happen. It is a product of Foucault's 'archive'.

So, in examining the knowledge of special education it is worth looking briefly at the history of the subject and at the intellectual currents that appear to have shaped its development since its institutional beginnings. It is worth looking at the discourses that have moulded the field as it exists today.

A case in point

Following Foucault, Giddens suggests that phenomena as we 'discover' them are shaped by our methods of discovery. Let us give an example in special education: in the UK the Warnock Committee (DES, 1978) – an influential governmental committee examining 'special educational needs' in the late 1970s – used supposedly highly reliable and objective forms of information to arrive at its conclusions and recommendations. Empirical and epidemiological information was painstakingly drawn on by the committee to show that one in five children had 'special educational needs' at school. It was almost as though the committee members assumed that the empirical instruments that they had drawn upon provided a magic machine through which messy reality could be poured, with neatly packaged findings emerging for the perusal of interested policy-makers and educators.

But what was really happening was that these analytic methods and the discourses surrounding them were actively generating a 'reality' – which then had to be lived up to by practitioners. An instance of this phenomenon of 'reality generation' can be seen in the way that reading difficulty was taken to exist in schools following Warnock's report. The Warnock Committee had decreed after its deliberations (having examined all the relevant empirical literature) that one in five children had special educational needs. It therefore came as no surprise that following these recommendations, teachers, rather too consistently, seemed to 'discover' that one in five children in their classes had special educational needs (in this case, special needs concerning reading difficulty). Thomas and Davis (1997) showed that this happened even when the schools were situated in affluent suburbs. In other words, teachers in different schools would construct their children with reading difficulty depending on their local experience: the children with whom they worked were viewed through and talked about from the point of view of a particular discourse. It was the discourse that constructed the 'difficulty' – the defined difficulty did not rest in some objective reality.

To suggest that this was happening is not to suggest that some children do not have difficulty with reading. Rather, it is to say that one's views about the provenance of those difficulties and the best ways of tackling them are based in discourses, and that these discourses are rooted in notions of normality and abnormality, of success and failure, of the functional and the dysfunctional. The reality is constructed around and within these discourses; it does not exist in some inert empirical universe. The construction of a reality in this way means that practitioners will seek ways of conforming to it and confirming it. In this sense, the absorption of 'theoretical insights' into the day-to-day practices of schools are revealed in the categories that are used to 'mark out' pupils as being similar or different.

Can there be an epistemology for inclusion?

None of this is to say that the power of discourses can be diminished or legislated for. It is rather to say that educational psychologists have become entangled in inappropriate kinds of discourse and discursive formation. The ones that have been so appealing have led in the wrong direction. For example, the legacy of positivistic science when transplanted to a focus on human beings was that we should deny what we know, as people, and put faith in a certain kind of putatively disinterested knowledge. B.F. Skinner (1972: 160) exemplified this denial and showed his contempt for our own knowledge of others when he said: 'What, after all, have we to show for nonscientific or prescientific good judgment, or common sense, or the insights gained through personal experience? It is science or nothing'. Fifty years of behavioural 'science' enable that question to be turned on its head: What has the supposedly scientific approach to human behaviour given us that we didn't already know? What has it caused us to disregard and to suppress?

Indeed, it is worse than this, for this discourse and our faith in it hasn't merely suppressed: it has distorted what educators know and has, in the process, relegated our own personal knowledge. Take, for example, the notions of deficit and deprivation, which were (and sometimes still are) at the forefront of educational psychologists' analyses of school failure, presenting us with what Labov (1973: 154) – in discussing the educational problems of children in ghetto schools – called 'the illusion of verbal deprivation'. The analytic frames constructed by educational psychologists, in their fascination with deficit and disease, have distracted thought from more straightforward ways of explaining difference. As Labov continues, 'In the writings of many prominent educational psychologists, we find very poor understanding of the nature of language' (ibid.) – very poor understanding of 'the logic of nonstandard English' (ibid.).

Especially rooted in the analytical systems of psychology and educational psychology, the methods and predilections of special education provide an exemplary case of how certain discourses can be misleading. Especially worrying is how these frameworks can seem to make us lose confidence in ourselves as teachers, and indeed, as people. The Canadian educator Frank Smith's (1992) powerful narrative of his work teaching at a South African university documents the resilience of belief among his teaching colleagues there in the canons of teaching and research method, and the way in which this belief had subverted their own self-confidence as teachers, and as people.

Reid and Valle (2004) make the point that these basic forms of knowledge – personal, tacit knowledge – that teachers possess must be reinstated over those that owe their lineage to scientistic thinking of one kind or another. They say that teachers need to approach their work as scholar practitioners and that they need to again pick up the tools of critical inquiry – 'observation, conferencing, and interviewing; generating anecdotal records; taking and analyzing field notes; constructing sociograms, analyzing student work and portfolios'. This reinstatement of the personal knowledge of teachers is vital for the development of inclusive education.

Practitioners can use their reflective ability, though, only if they feel confident in the knowledge that using it does not restrict their understanding – only if they feel that they are not missing out on some important empirical knowledge or missing some key theoretical insight. And it is most unlikely that anyone will have missed out on such knowledge or insight, for the models, theories and intellectual castles created in the discourses of special pedagogy have helped little in improving learning – helped little in understanding why children fail at school. This is unfortunate enough in itself, but the even more unfortunate corollary is that the existence of this kind of supposedly privileged knowledge has persuaded teachers in ordinary schools across the globe that they may not be sufficiently knowledgeable or sufficiently expert to help children who are experiencing difficulty: that they do not have sufficient technical expertise or theoretical knowledge to teach all children.

If Reid and Valle are right, the knowledge available to us as educational psychologists is literally staring us in the face as we work. Guided by our principles and values we gather and develop personal knowledge both as professionals and laypeople. This kind of personal, tacit, everyday knowledge should not be ritually slaughtered on an altar of 'scientific rigour'.

Remember what two prominent philosophers of science have said about scientific knowledge. Ziman (1991) has said merely that it is 'reliable knowledge', while Canguilhem (1994: 41) has said that it is the 'elimination of the false by the true'. Such comments give credence to what Joynson (1974: 2) has said about the kinds of knowledge psychologists can use. They can use their own knowledge, as people, of human nature and ability, and they can trust what others say. As he puts it: 'Human nature is not an unknown country, a terra incognita on the map of knowledge. It is our home ground. Human beings are not, like the objects of natural science, things which do not understand themselves'. We can use our understanding of these facets of being human, though, only if we feel confident in the knowledge that using them does not restrict our understanding – only if we feel that we are not missing out on some important empirical knowledge or missing some key theoretical insight.

For an inclusive education system there should be more reliance by educational psychologists on ideals of equity, social justice and opportunity for all. In pursuing these ideals educational psychologists should accept rather than deny the insights which emerge by virtue of being human – insights which emerge from our own knowledge of learning; our own knowledge of failure, success, acceptance or rejection. There is nothing to be lost in so doing, for the evidence is that there are no magic fixes or startling insights to emerge from the traditional knowledge-base of special education or educational psychology (see Thomas and Loxley, 2001). Indeed, there is a great deal to be regained through recourse to our common humanity. Joynson (1974) begins his book *Psychology and Common Sense* with a précis of a G.K. Chesterton story that makes an appropriate end to this chapter:

> … a man dreams of emulating the great explorers. One day he sets sail from the West Country and heads out into the Atlantic, confident that he is destined to discover an unknown land. For many weeks he wanders across the ocean, buffeted by storms and uncertain of his position. At last, a coastline comes in view and, as he approaches, he sees the towers and domes and minarets of a strange civilisation. Greatly excited, he makes his way ashore. To his astonishment, the natives speak English. He has landed at Brighton.
>
> (Joynson, 1974: 1)

References

Belar, C.D. (2000) Scientist-practitioner not equal to science + practice. Boulder is bolder. *American Psychologist,* 55(2), 249–50.

Berlin, I. (1979) The divorce between the sciences and the humanities, in I. Berlin, *Against the Current.* London: Hogarth Press.

BPS (2006) Division of Education and Child Psychology Annual Conference, 2006. Available online at: http://www.bps.org.uk/conferences-&-events/event-listing/events$/2006/january/decp-06/decp-06_home.cfm

Canguilhem, G. (1994) The various models, in F. Delaporte (ed.) *A Vital Rationalist: Selected Writings from Georges Canguilhem.* New York: Zone Books.

Chambers, J.H. (1992) *Empiricist Research on Teaching: A Philosophical and Practical Critique of its Scientific Pretensions.* Dordrecht: Kluwer Academic Publishers.

DES (1978) *Special Educational Needs.* Report of the Committee of Enquiry into the Education of Handicapped Children and Young People, Cmnd 7212. London: HMSO.

Egan, K. (1984) *Education and Psychology.* London: Methuen.

Feyerabend, P. (1993) *Against Method*, 3rd edn. London: Verso/New Left Books.

Foucault, M. (1970) *The Order of Things: An Archaeology of the Human Sciences.* London: Tavistock.

Foucault, M. (1972) *The Archaeology of Knowledge.* London: Tavistock Publications.

Geertz, C. (1975) *The Interpretation of Cultures.* London: Hutchinson.

Gibson, J.J. (1967) in E.G. Boring and G. Lindzey (eds) *A History of Psychology in Autobiography,* Vol. 5. New York: Appleton Century Crofts.

Harré, R. (1985) Foreword in G. Claxton, W. Swann, P. Salmon, V. Walkerdine, B. Jacobsen and J. White, *Psychology and Schooling: What's the Matter?* London: Bedford Way Papers.

Hearnshaw, L.S. (1979) *Cyril Burt: Psychologist.* London: Hodder and Stoughton.

Holton, G. (1995). The controversy over the end of science. *Scientific American,* 273(4), 168.

Joynson, R.B. (1974) *Psychology and Common Sense.* London: Routledge and Kegan Paul.

Kamin, L.J. (1977) Burt's IQ data. *Science,* 195, 246–8.

Koch, S. (1964) Psychology and emerging conceptions of knowledge as unitary, in T.W. Wann (ed.) *Behaviourism and Phenomenology.* Chicago: University of Chicago Press.

Labov, W. (1973) The logic of nonstandard English, in F. Williams (ed.) *Language and Poverty.* Chicago: Rand McNally.

McNay, L. (1994) *Foucault: A Critical Introduction.* Cambridge: Polity Press.

Medawar, P. (1982) *Pluto's Republic.* Oxford: Oxford University Press.

Philp, M. (1990) Michel Foucault, in Q. Skinner (ed.) *The Return of Grand Theory in the Human Sciences.* Cambridge: Canto.

Reid, D.K. and Valle, J.W. (2004) The discursive practice of learning disability: implications for instruction and parent–school relations. *Journal of Learning Disabilities,* 37(6), 466–481.

Schatzman, L. (1991) Dimensional analysis: notes on an alternative approach to the grounding of theory in qualitative research, in D.R. Maines (ed.) *Social organisation and Social Process: Essays in Honor of Anselm Strauss* (pp. 303–314). New York: Aldine.

Schön, D.A. (1991) *The Reflective Practitioner: How Professionals Think in Action.* Aldershot: Avebury.

Skinner, B.F. (1972) *Beyond Freedom and Dignity.* London: Jonathan Cape.

Smith, F. (1992) *To Think: In Language Learning and Education.* London: Routledge.

Swann, W. (1985) Psychological science and the practice of special education, in G. Claxton, W. Swann, P. Salmon, V. Walkerdine, B. Jacobsen and J. White, *Psychology and Schooling: What's the Matter?* London: Bedford Way Papers.

Thomas, G. (1997) What's the use of theory? *Harvard Educational Review,* 67(1), 75–105.

Thomas, G. and Davis, P. (1997) Special needs: objective reality or personal construction? Judging reading difficulty after the Code. *Educational Research,* 39(3), 263–270.

Thomas, G. and Loxley, A. (2001) *Deconstructing Special Education and Constructing Inclusion.* Buckingham: Open University Press.

Thomas, G. and Loxley, A. (2005) Discourses on bad children and bad schools. *Journal of Learning Disabilities,* 38(2), 175–182.

Wright Mills, C. (1970) *The Sociological Imagination.* London: Pelican.

Ziman, J. (1991) *Reliable Knowledge.* Cambridge: Canto.

Chapter 3

Vygotsky and inclusion

Harry Daniels

In this chapter I will discuss the implications for inclusion of the theoretical framework which has been developed on the basis of the work of the Russian social theorist L.S. Vygotsky. In so doing I will draw on terminology which may seem, at best, to be inappropriate in contemporary debates. I will attempt to draw on the original meanings of these now 'strange' culturally and historically located terms to try and bring a relatively unfamiliar perspective to bear on current debates. This chapter falls into three sections. First, I will discuss some of the difficulties of 'reading' work which was written more than seventy years ago in a radically different culture from that which obtains today in almost any national context. Second, I will outline aspects of his general social theory which are relevant to his writings on disability, educational difficulty and pedagogy. Last, I will identify the core issues and implications that such writing has for debates concerning inclusion.

Reading Vygotsky

Vygotsky was charged with developing a state system for the education of 'pedagogically neglected' children in post-revolutionary Russia (Yaroshevsky, 1989, p. 96). This group included the homeless, of which there were a very large number, and those with certain categories of special need. The recently published Volume 2 of the Collected Works, *The Fundamentals of Defectology* (Vygotsky, 1993) is one of the relatively few sources of Vygotsky's writing on disability and special needs available in English. Many Western attempts to interpret Vygotsky have been marked more by enthusiasm for Western pedagogical preoccupations than for the concern to understand the range and depth of his arguments.

Wertsch in the foreword to Asmolov (1998) notes the difficulty that exists in translating Russian terms. By way of illustration he discusses the transformation through translation of the Russian word *lichnost* into English. The standard translation is from *lichnost* to *personality*. Wertsch's concern is with the received set of understandings associated with the term personality in western psychology. Valsiner (1988) suggests that personality is often thought of as a phenomenon that 'belongs inherently to the person and is not causally related to the social context'.

His own sociocultural position on the meaning of personality is that it should be viewed as something which is created socially. Thus reading/understanding the legacy of the early Russian psychologists is in itself both a problem for and of cultural psychology. In his discussion of Asmolov's handling of *lichnost*, Wertsch uses the following quote from Bakhtin (1981) to try and construct a sociocultural theoretical base for the problems of translation in a very general way:

> The word in language is half someone else's. It becomes 'one's own' only when the speaker populates it with his own intention, his own accent, when he appropriates the word, adapting it to his own semantic and expressive intention. Prior to this moment of appropriation, the word does not exist in a neutral and impersonal language, but rather it exists in other people's mouths, in other people's context, serving other people's intentions; it's from there that anyone must take the word and make it one's own.
>
> (Bakhtin, 1981, pp. 293–294)

Wertsch encourages the reader of Asmolov's work on *lichnost* to treat its translation as *personality* as *strange* by mentally ascribing quotation marks to the text thus – 'personality'. In order to benefit from Asmolov's writing, Wertsch suggests that the reader must acknowledge the problematic nature of the translation.

Bearing these factors in mind, Wells (1999) argues that we should certainly read Vygotsky's texts and try to understand what he had to say; but, in appropriating his ideas and putting them to use, we should also be willing to transform those ideas so that they can be of greatest use to us in meeting the demands of our own situations (p. 334). When we come to 'read' Vygotsky we are faced with a complex task. Wertsch suggests that we should try and remember the complexity or strangeness of the task and gradually work our way in to *an* understanding which as Wells reminds us is appropriate in our own circumstances. This is true of the term *defectologia*. The Russian word is probably best translated as 'study of defect'. The term defectology understandably carries many negative connotations to English ears, although its use persist in some sectors of post-Soviet states. In this chapter I will attempt to lever meanings which are relevant to current concerns about inclusion from Vygotsky's writing on defectology. In order to do this I will discuss aspects of Vygotsky's general theory of social formation of mind and make specific reference to what Gindis (2003) has called his special theory of 'disontogenesis' or 'distorted development'.

Vygotsky's general theory of the social formation of mind

Vygotsky discussed his well known notion, the Zone of Proximal Development (ZPD), in terms of assessment and instruction. Within both frames of reference he discussed the relationship between an individual learner and a supportive other or others even if that other was not physically present in the context in which learning was taking place. The second, instructional, account of the ZPD is to be found in *Thinking and Speech* (1934/1987), and is embedded in chapter 6, in which he discussed 'The Development of Scientific Concepts in Childhood'.

> We have seen that instruction and development do not coincide. They are two different processes with very complex interrelationships. Instruction is only useful when it moves ahead of development. When it does, it impels or awakens a whole series of functions that are in a stage of maturation lying in the zone of proximal development. This is the major role of instruction in development. This is what distinguishes the instruction of the child from the training of animals. This is also what distinguishes instruction of the child which is directed toward his full development from instruction in specialized, technical skills such as typing or riding a bicycle. The formal aspect of each school subject is that in which the influence of instruction on development is realized. Instruction would be completely unnecessary if it merely utilized what had already matured in the developmental process, if it were not itself a source of development.
>
> (Vygotsky, 1987, p. 212)

As Chaiklin (2003) reminds us, the reference made by Vygotsky was to instruction that is designed to support the development of psychological functions as they are transformed and reconfigured through particular age periods. He suggests that much of what has been discussed under the rubric of the ZPD misses the central insistence on instruction leading *development*. The distinction between microgenesis and ontogenesis is missed in, what for Chaiklin, are misinterpretations of the original formulation of ZPD in its instructional frame of reference. He suggests that terms such as scaffolding should be reserved for practices which are designed to teach specific skills and subject matter concepts as against instruction designed to serve explicitly developmental purposes (p. 59). The conception of the teaching and learning process that lies at the heart of any particular form of schooling is itself derived from beliefs about the relationship between instruction and development. Should the teacher wait for development to take place before teaching and thus be looking for signs of instructional readiness as indicated by developmental markers? Should the teacher take no account of development whatsoever and proceed to develop instructional packages on the basis of analyses of specific tasks?

The diagram in Figure 3.1 identifies three positions. The first, a crude behaviourist position, is one in which instruction and development proceed together. In one sense this is a model in which development and instruction are synonymous. In this case task analysis in teaching may be viewed as a determinant of developmental sequence. The second is a version of the Piagetian position in which teaching comes to view the characteristics of the child's thinking as a lower threshold for instruction. Here the possibilities for instruction are thought of as trailing after development as shown in the middle section of Figure 3.1. Instruction must

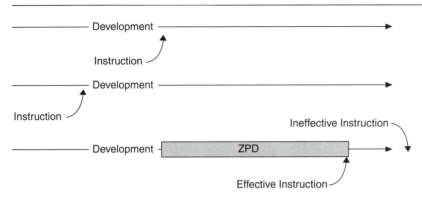

Figure 3.1 The relationship between learning and development in Skinner, Piaget and Vygotsky

wait for development to have done its work before it can be effective. Vygotsky's (1978) position was that instruction actually creates the possibilities for development rather than being seen as subordinate and incidental to developmental processes. The organisation and content of teaching implied by this suggestion is directed towards the formation of developmental possibilities rather than trailing behind developmental inevitabilities. This is the ZPD which was originally defined as the distance between the actual developmental level of the child as determined by independent problem solving and the level of potential development as determined through problem solving under adult guidance, or in collaboration with more capable peers (Vygotsky, 1978, p. 86). For Vygotsky the ZPD embodies a concept of readiness to learn that emphasises upper levels of competence. These upper boundaries are not immutable, however, but constantly changing with the learner's increasing independent competence. What a child can perform today with assistance she will be able to perform tomorrow independently, thus preparing her for entry into a new and more demanding collaboration. These functions could be called the 'buds,' rather than the fruits of development. The actual developmental level characterises mental development retrospectively, while the ZPD characterises mental development prospectively (Vygotsky, 1978, pp. 86–87).

If we accept the Vygotskian position then we have to accept a notion of a complex relationship between teaching and development. The first two positions shown in Figure 3.1 have been associated with practices which assume that instructional sequences are to some extent unproblematic and universal. In the first position the sequence of teaching arranges the sequence of development. In the second the sequence of development predicts the sequence of teaching. It is in the third position that teaching must be responsive to the individual within a specific curriculum context. A discussion of the post Vygotskian principles that may be employed in the selection of curriculum content is beyond the scope of this chapter. It is, perhaps, sufficient to note that these would be designed to guide the development of the structured systematic concepts which Vygotsky termed 'scientific' and would introduce general principles and seek to explore their implications in a variety of contexts.[1]

In schooling the first model of the relationship between learning and development may result in the view of the child as the passive recipient of educational transmissions. The second leads to the view of the child as the active constructor of understanding along pre-established paths. In the third the learner becomes an active participant in a project which is socially negotiated. Vygotsky developed a conception of the teaching and learning process based on dialogue. For example the teacher and child start out doing the task together. The teacher may initially take the major part of the responsibility for executing the task and the child may play a relatively small part. The teacher's intention will be to gradually transfer control of progress in task completion to the learner. The transfer is negotiated in dialogue. This dialogue may be mediated by a variety of tools and signs which Vygotsky referred to as 'psychological tools' or more recently, cultural artefacts. These cultural products, such as speech or symbol and sign systems, are human products which are seen as the means which humans employ in their own development. The social influence becomes individual not through a process of simple transmission. Individuals construct their own sense from socially available meanings. Vygotsky argued that it was through the use of whatever cultural artefacts and tools (e.g. speech, braille, Makaton, form boards, Paget Gorman, etc.) that were accessible to the child and were made available socially that they are able to 'master themselves from the "outside" through symbolic, cultural systems' (Knox and Stevens, 1993, p. 15). Crucially, he stated that it is the *meaning* that is or could be encoded in such cultural artefacts that is important. For him the type of symbolic system does not matter.

> All systems (Braille for the blind and for the deaf, dactylology or finger spelling, mimicry or a natural gesticulated sign language) are tools embedded in action and give rise to meaning as such. They allow a child to internalise language and develop those higher mental functions for which language serves as a basis. In actuality, qualitatively different mediational means may result in qualitatively different forms of higher mental functioning.
>
> (Knox and Stevens, 1993, p. 15)

---

1 For example a circle would be introduced through the examination of the shapes that may be drawn by placing one end of a piece of string at a fixed point and drawing with a pencil fixed to the other end whilst the string was taut. This contrasts with the introduction of a variety of shapes and sizes of circles to a pupil who is expected to understand the essence of the circle on the basis of this empirical 'everyday' experience. In the Vygotskian model the 'scientific' concept informs the design of the instruction.

The emphasis is thus on meaningful communication irrespective of means. For the teacher this becomes a matter of making meaningful connection between the concepts that the child has formed on the basis of their everyday experiences and the concepts that are being introduced through schooling. This approach to teaching not only involves the acquisition of new teaching skills, such as interpreting when a child is operating within the ZPD, it also involves a major attitude shift. The dimensions of this shift may be couched in terms of difference rather than deficiency, informed and supported acquisition rather than transmission, and transfer of control.

The period 1927–34 was when Vygotsky was particularly interested in two types of concepts: the scientific and the everyday or spontaneous. By 'scientific concepts', Vygotsky referred to concepts introduced by a teacher in school; spontaneous concepts were those that were acquired by the child outside contexts in which explicit instruction was in place. Scientific concepts were described as those which form a coherent, logical, hierarchical system. For Vygotsky scientific concepts are characterised by a high degree of generality and their relationship to objects is mediated through other concepts. According to Vygotsky (1987) children can make deliberate use of scientific concepts; they are consciously aware of them and can reflect upon them. The editors of the most recent translation of *Thinking and Speech* (1987) suggest that when Vygotsky uses the terms 'spontaneous thinking' or 'spontaneous concepts' he is referring to a context of formation which is that of immediate, social, practical activity as against a context of instruction in a formal system of knowledge. Scientific concepts are through their very systematic nature open to the voluntary control of the child.

For Vygotsky cooperation and collaboration are crucial features of effective teaching.

> The development of the scientific ... concept, a phenomenon that occurs as part of the educational process, constitutes a unique form of systematic co-operation between the teacher and the child. The maturation of the child's higher mental functions occurs in this co-operative process, that is, it occurs through the adult's assistance and participation. ... In a problem involving scientific concepts, he must be able to do in collaboration with the teacher something that he has never done spontaneously ... we know that the child can do more in collaboration that he can independently.
>
> (Vygotsky, 1987, pp. 168–9, 216)

Vygotsky argued that the systematic, organised and hierarchical thinking that he associated with scientific concepts becomes gradually embedded in everyday referents and thus achieves a general sense in the contextual richness of everyday thought. Vygotsky thus presented a model of an interdependent relationship between scientific and everyday or spontaneous concepts in the process of true concept formation. He argued that everyday thought is given structure and order in the context of systematic scientific thought. Vygotsky was keen to point out the relative strengths of both as they both contributed to each other:

> the formation of concepts develops simultaneously from two directions: from the direction of the general and the particular ... The development of a scientific concept begins with the verbal definition. As part of an organised system, this verbal definition descends to concrete; it descends to phenomena which the concept represents. In contrast, the everyday concept tends to develop outside any definite system; it tends to move upwards toward abstraction and generalisation ... the weakness of the everyday concept lies in its incapacity for abstraction, in the child's incapacity to operate on it in a voluntary manner ... the weakness of the scientific concept lies in its verbalism, in its insufficient saturation with the concrete.
>
> (Vygotsky, 1987, pp. 163, 168, 169)

Vygotsky argued that scientific concepts are not assimilated in ready-made or pre-packaged form. He insisted that the two forms of concept are brought into forms of relationship within which they both develop. An important corollary of this model of conceptual development is the denial of the possibility of direct pedagogic transmission of concepts:

> pedagogical experience demonstrates that direct instruction in concepts is impossible. It is pedagogically fruitless. The teacher who attempts to use this approach achieves nothing but a mindless learning of words, an empty verbalism that stimulates or imitates the presence of concepts in the child. Under these conditions, the child learns not the concept but the word, and this word is taken over by the child through memory rather than thought. Such knowledge turns out to be inadequate in any meaningful application. This mode of instruction is the basic defect of the purely scholastic verbal modes of teaching which have been universally condemned. It substitutes the learning of dead and empty verbal schemes for the mastery of living knowledge.
>
> (Vygotsky, 1987, p. 170)

In *Educational Psychology* he uses the analogy of a gardener trying to affect the growth of a plant by tugging directly at its roots with his hands from underneath the plant when criticizing teachers who attempt to directly influence concept development in the student (Vygotsky, 1997, p. 49). If it is to be effective in the formation of scientific concepts instruction must be designed to foster conscious awareness of conceptual form and structure and thereby allow for individual access and control over acquired scientific concepts. It must also foster the interaction and development of everyday concepts with scientific concepts. One of his better known examples is that of learning a foreign language, where he posits raising the level of development of mother tongue speech through the development of conscious awareness of linguistic forms. Similarly, he suggests that by learning algebra, the child comes to understand arithmetical operations as partic-ular instantiations of algebraic operations. The scientific concepts of grammar and algebra are seen as means by which thought is freed from concrete instances of speech or numerical relations and raised to a more abstract level (1987, p. 180). In this feature of his work Vygotsky argued that instruction must be designed to connect everyday concepts with the formal structures of scientific concepts. In this way he distances himself from the practices of empirical induction which have been so influential in curriculum design in the West.

Disability and pedagogy: implications of Vygotsky's writing

One of the great dangers with early interpretations of this work was the sugges-tion that children whose elementary, and supposedly natural, psychological functions were damaged or deficient were beyond the reach of education. Children would be assessed to see if they could benefit from education. This assessment would consist of a means of scrutinising those functions deemed elementary. Those who 'failed' the assessment were removed from the educa-tional community. The work of early years developmentalists and Russians such as Davydov gives ground for rejecting the sharp delineation between higher, culturally mediated functions, and lower, natural functions and the practices that were associated with the demarcation. The development of Vygotsky's own thinking on this matter was incomplete. He certainly changed his views on sev-eral occasions. He was also working at a time when the cultural artefacts of the late twentieth century were not even imagined. He had no access to tape recorders, freeze-frame video recorders, etc. and was not in a position to 'see' the data on development that those who followed him have examined. A modern position such as that of Nelson (1995) seems more appropriate. Her depiction of three levels of conceptual development yields a suggestion that the first level is constructed by individuals on the basis of direct experience with the world with-out the mediational effects of language; at the second level knowledge is a product of the 'language using community' and at the third level it is that of a formally organised cultural system – theoretical knowledge. Thus she proposes the transitions from the natural to the sociohistorical; and from spontaneous to scientific.

In summary, Vygotsky asserts the importance of the formative effect of social, cultural and historical influences. The notion of the ZPD establishes his position on the way in which instruction (which embodies social, cultural and historical influence) can lead development. Importantly, he acknowledges that not all instruction will serve a developmental function. It may, for example, only serve to promote skill acquisition. With the distinction between scientific and everyday concepts he outlines his views on the complexities of true concept development. These ideas can be deployed in arguments which attempt to justify particular approaches to the formulation of the 'what' and 'how' of teaching.

We should not only be concerned about responding in face-to-face teaching but we should also organise our institutions in such a way that they are learning systems which are themselves responsive to feedback. This suggestion accords with the recent development in interpretations of the term ZPD. The early 'scaffolding' definition of the distance between problem-solving abilities exhibited by a learner working alone and that learner's problem-solving abilities when assisted by or collaborating with more experienced people reflects Vygotsky's view of the role of instruction. This is refined in the 'cultural' interpretation which draws on Vygotsky's distinction between scientific and everyday concepts. Here the emphasis is on the distance between the cultural knowledge, usually made accessible through instruction and the active knowledge, as owned by individuals in their everyday experience. More recently a 'collectivist', or 'societal', perspective has emerged. The focus tends to be on processes of social transformation and on what can be done together that cannot be done alone. It places the study of learning beyond the context of face to face pedagogical structuring, and includes the structure of the social world in the analysis.

Whilst there are surprisingly few references to the ZPD in his own writing there is no doubt that in many ways the concept lies at the heart of Vygotsky's social account of learning. He emphasised this in one of his relatively rare published discussions of the education of children with Severe Learning Difficulties:

> The developmental path for a severely retarded child lies through collaborative activity, the social help of another human being, who from the first is his mind, his will, his activities. This proposition also corresponds entirely with the normal path of development for a child. *The developmental path for a severely retarded child lies through relationships and collaborative activity with other humans.* For precisely this reason, the social education of severely retarded children reveals to us possibilities which might seem outright Utopian from the viewpoint of purely biologically based physiological education.
>
> (Vygotsky, 1993, p. 218)

This, again, raises questions about the nature of the 'social' in the pedagogic relationship alongside questions concerning the nature of the relationship itself.

Vygotsky (1993) drew a distinction between a 'primary' disability, which he referenced to organic impairment due to biological factors, and a 'secondary' disability refering to distortions of higher psychological functions due to social factors. For Vygotsky the way in which the child with a primary disability is positioned in the social world can itself give rise to 'secondary' disabilities. Thus one level of intervention is at the social level: 'Changing negative societal attitudes towards the individuals with disabilities should be one of the goals of special educators' (Vygotsky, 1995).

In a way that is familiar to many modern educators he also called for a focus on strength rather than weakness and was very critical of what he termed the 'arithmetical concept of handicap' in which children are viewed as the sum of their negative attributes.

> Each child's resources and strengths must be the deciding factors in establishing an educational programme. … [rather than look for weaknesses] we would do better to look for strengths and recognise that these will be different for different children. Differences offer hope because they provide the possibility of alternative routes for development, educational and personal fulfillment. We would rejoice in them and capitalise on them. They are after all, the very stuff of life.
>
> (Connolly, 1993, p. 942)

Vygotsky's term for this approach was 'positive differentiation'. He was concerned with the 'secondary' handicapping conditions that may result where the person with the 'primary disability' is acting in a social world which has negative formative effects on development. In essence he was suggesting that the child with an impairment may suffer the effects of social deprivation which arise as a consequence of the way in which the social world responds to that impairment.

Whilst it is also inescapable that Vygotsky did account for biological factors and individual differences, in his work on 'defectology' he insists that individual differences in patterns of communication give rise to differences in patterns of social mediation and hence development.

> Any physical handicap … not only alters the child's relationship with the world, but above all affects his interaction with people. Any organic defect is revealed as a social abnormality in behaviour. It goes without question that blindness and deafness per se are biological factors. However, the teacher must deal not so much with these biological factors by themselves, but rather with their social consequences. When we have before us a blind boy as the object of education, then it is necessary to deal not so much with blindness by itself, as with those conflicts which arise for a blind child upon entering life.
>
> (Vygotsky, 1983, p. 102)

However it is in the manner of social engagement that differences may arise and form their own dynamic. Hence the following statement about the implications of cultural difference for the psychological implications of impairment: 'The blindness of an American farmer's daughter, of a Ukrainian landowner's son, of a German duchess, of a Russian peasant, of a Swedish proletarian – these are all psychologically entirely different facts' (Vygotsky, 1983, p. 70).

Vygotsky was concerned that social responses to people with disabilities should not create problems of their own. Given that he argues that cultural tools and practices have a formative effect on development, then barriers to participation are a cause for concern. Barriers may be both social and biological. Specific forms of impairment may give rise to difficulty in participation in a society where most participants do not experience similar difficulties. The solution could be to seek alternate forms of participation either through transforming social practices in such a way as not to marginalise those with the impairment or through specific interventions such as supplementary forms of communication such as braille. In the past, and to a slightly lesser extent now, many people with disabilities removed themselves or are removed from certain aspects of society. Gallaudet University is an example of a setting where deaf people are educated with other deaf people. This setting is usually regarded as positive (Ramsey, 1997). There are many examples of social responses to people with disabilities where satisfactory communities are not the outcome. Vygotsky's suggestion is that transformations in patterns of participation carry with them implications for cognitive development. Exclusion may carry cognitive consequences.

Vygotsky's distinctions between primary and secondary disability give rise to a question as to the nature of development in the case of a child with a primary disability. He certainly objected to the terms 'developmental disability' or 'developmental delays'. 'A child whose development is impeded by a disability is not simply a child less developed than his peers; rather, he has developed differently' (Vygotsky, 1983, p. 96). His argument is that intervention, including teaching, should be oriented to the differences that had arisen along with interventions which sought to minimise the development of secondary disabilities.

When placed alongside his writing on concept development a familiar dilemma emerges. The 'difference' or particularity of a child's 'different development' may require forms of intervention that are distinctive to particular sets of strengths. However, the child should be placed in a setting in which social complications of the disability are minimised. The challenge is, as ever, to provide appropriate forms of developmental teaching in settings which do not lead to the formation of additional secondary disabilities. This kind of teaching would lead to the formation of what Vygotsky termed 'compensatory strategies' which enable the child to acquire the 'psychological tools' necessary for the development of the competences in circulation in particular cultures. Vygotsky was interested in creating 'disability-specific' approaches. For him the efficient compensation for the loss or weakness of natural functions can be achieved through the development of the higher psychological functions.

Objects of rehabilitation are the cultural processes of abstract reasoning, logical memory, voluntary attention, goal-directed behaviours, etc. Vygotsky pointed to the limitations of traditional sensory-motor training, saying that pure biological compensation (e.g., superior hearing in individuals who are blind) has been an exception rather than the rule, while the domain of higher psychological activities has no limits: 'Training sharpness of hearing in a blind person has natural limitations; compensation through the mightiness of the mind (imagination, reasoning, memorization, etc.) has virtually no limits' (Vygotsky, 1983, p. 212).

In Vygotsky's view, special education programs should have the same social/cultural goals as general education programs. Their specificity is in addressing the 'secondary' disability syndrome, that is in countering the negative social consequences of the 'primary' disability (Gindis, 2003). Different 'tools' (e.g. various means of communication) may convey essentially the same educational information, the same meaning. 'Different symbolic systems correspond to one and the same content of education ... Meaning is more important than the sign. Let us change signs but retain meaning' (Vygotsky, 1983, p. 54).

However, as is so often the case there are multiple readings of Vygotsky's work on this issue. In a text that has become very influential it is argued that the greatest difficulties for children with special needs are created not by their particular special needs, but by isolation from typically developing peers (Berk and Winsler, 1995). Their emphasis is on ensuring that children with disabilities and difficulties have the opportunity of learning new ideas on the social level with more capable peers and adults. This account lacks the emphasis on the creation of a learning environment in which specific instructional needs can be met. It celebrates the interactional benefits of a mainstream location without reference to the specific needs for developmental teaching that may have arisen as a consequence of 'the primary disability' and its secondary consequences.

Here lies the enduring problem. The theory generates two particular foci: one on particular and 'non-distorting' forms and patterns of interaction and another on the need for instruction that is tailored to meet developmental needs. Segregated special education has often, and rightly, been criticised for the social isolation which it engenders and weakness in curriculum provision associated with lowered expectations. Mainstream provision has also been criticised for the lack of attention to individual needs and for the potential social damage that can arise as a result of inappropriate forms of social relation. The challenge is to meet both the demands of the Vygotskian theoretical position. Some very recent research ventures to claim that there is remarkably little that is pedagogically special about much special provision (Lewis and Norwich, 2001). If this is the case then one has concerns about the likelihood of young people with disabilities being placed in a social position where they can acquire the 'psychological tools' that are most appropriate to compensate for their particular disability. Although Vygotsky did at one time call for 'normalization through mainstreaming' he was also critical of both 'unlawful segregation' of the disabled and 'mindless mainstreaming' (Gindis, 2003). As I argued above, one has to view Vygotsky's contribution in its cultural and historical context. His comments on inclusion are not informed by the organisational and pedagogic advances of the late twentieth century. However strange the terminology that flows from his work may appear in the current context it is clear that his thinking on primary and secondary disabilities and scientific and everyday concepts offer much to our current thinking.

In 1980 World Health Organization (WHO) published the first version of the ICIDH (International Classification of Impairments, Disabilities, and Handicaps). This has been revised as ICIDH-2 which is based on a model of human functioning in which functioning and disablement are viewed as outcomes of an interaction between a person's physical or mental condition and a social and physical environment. It has been designed for use at individual, institutional and social policy levels. It helps to characterise the kind and level of intervention that is appropriate to the actual disablement needs of the individual, and lists:

- impairment interventions;
- activity limitation interventions;
- participation restriction interventions.

Here the emphasis is on activity instead of disability and participation rather than handicap.

Arguably this may give rise to practices which are commensurate with Amartya Sen's (1992) capability- and rights-based approach to social exclusion which calls for efforts to ensure that people have equal access to basic capabilities. This approach to work on social exclusion which has informed aspects of the current administration's policy making (Bentley, 1997) is important in that:

- it emphasises that the inability to participate in, and be respected by, mainstream society is a violation of a basic right that should be open to all citizens;
- it does not demand uniformity of outcomes, but instead calls for equal freedoms to enjoy all aspects of citizenship;
- it recognises the diversity of people in their ability to make use of opportunities.

From this point of view placement in a mainstream setting which does not offer either appropriate instruction or respectful forms of social relation is unlikely to support eventual participation in mainstream society. Schools which demand uniformity of outcome and fail to respond to diversity do not constitute inclusive settings. Conversely special segregated settings which do not promote 'compensatory strategies' fail by the same criteria. Vygotskian theory calls for a much more detailed examination of the pedagogic and social relations of schooling wherever it is located. There is much to be gained from a consideration of those measures which lead to the prevention of social exclusion.

If social exclusion is defined as the loss of access to the most important life chances that a modern society offers, where those chances connect individuals to the mainstream of life in that society then we must ask whether all our 'inclusive schooling' really does serve this purpose. I fear that much that is presented under this banner remains an account of placement not provision.

References

Asmolov, A. (1998) *Vygotsky Today: On the Verge of Non-classical Psychology.* New York: Nova Science Publishers.

Bakhtin, M.M. (1981) *The Dialogic Imagination: Four Essays by M.M. Bakhtin.* Austin: University of Texas Press. (Edited by M. Holquist; translated by C. Emerson and M. Holquist.)

Bentley, T. (1997) Learning to Belong, in *The Wealth and Poverty of Networks.* Demos Collection 12. London: Demos.

Berk, L. and Winsler, A. (1995) *Scaffolding Children's Learning: Vygotsky and Early Childhood Education*. Washington, DC: National Association for Young Children.

Chaiklin, S. (2003) The Zone of Proximal Development in Vygotsky's Analysis of Learning and Instruction, in A. Kozulin, B. Gindis, V. Ageyev and S. Miller (eds) *Vygotsky's Educational Theory in Cultural Context*. Cambridge: Cambridge University Press.

Connolly, K.J. (1993) In praise of difference. *Developmental Medicine and Child Neurology*, 35(11), 941–943.

Gindis, B. (2003) Remediation through Education: Sociocultural Theory and Children with Special Needs, in A. Kozulin, B. Gindis, V. Ageyev and S. Miller (eds) *Vygotsky's Educational Theory in Cultural Context*. Cambridge: Cambridge University Press.

Knox, J.E. and Stevens, C. (1993) Vygotsky and Soviet Russian Defectology: An Introduction, in Vygotsky, L.S (1993) *The Collected Works of L.S. Vygotsky, Volume 2: Problems of Abnormal Psychology and Learning Disabilities*. New York: Plenum Press.

Lewis, A. and Norwich, B. (2001) A critical review of evidence concerning teaching strategies for pupils with special educational needs. *British Educational Research Journal*, 27(3), 313–329.

Nelson, K. (1995) From Spontaneous to Scientific Concepts: Continuities and Discontinuities from Childhood to Adulthood, in L.M.W. Martin, K. Nelson and E. Tobach (eds) *Sociocultural Psychology: Theory and Practice of Knowing and Doing*. Cambridge: Cambridge University Press.

Ramsey, C. (1997) *Deaf Children in Public Schools: Placement, Context, and Consequences*. Washington DC: Gallaudet University Press.

Sen, A. (1992) *Poverty Re-examined*. Cambridge, Mass: Harvard University Press.

Valsiner, J. (1988) *Developmental Psychology in the Soviet Union*. Sussex: Harvester Press.

Vygotsky, L.S. (1978) *Mind in Society: The Development of Higher Psychological Processes*. Cambridge, Mass: Harvard University Press. (Edited by M. Cole, V. John-Steiner, S. Scribner and E. Souterman.)

Vygotsky, L.S. (1983) *Sobraniye Sochinenii* [Collected Works], volume 5. Moscow: Pedagogika Publisher.

Vygotsky, L.S. (1987) *Thinking and Speech*, in *L.S. Vygotsky, Collected works*, Volume 1 (pp. 39–285). New York: Plenum. (Edited by R Rieber and A Carton; translated by N. Minick.)

Vygotsky, L.S. (1987–1998) *The Collected Works of L. S. Vygotsky. Volume 1: Problems of General Psychology. Volume 2: The Fundamentals of Defectology. Volume 3: Problems of the Theory and History of Psychology. Volume 4: The History of Development of Higher Mental Functions. Volume 5: Child Psychology*. New York: Plenum Press. (Edited by R. Rieber.)

Vygotsky, L.S. (1993) *The Collected Works of L. S. Vygotsky. Volume 2: The Fundamentals of Defectology (Abnormal Psychology and Learning Disabilities)*. New York: Plenum Press. (Edited by R. Rieber and A.S. Carton; translated and with an introduction by J.E. Knox and C.B. Stevens.)

Vygotsky, L.S. (1995) *Problemy Defectologii* [Problems of Defectology]. Moscow: Prosvecshenie Press.

Vygotsky, L.S. (1997) *Educational Psychology*. Boca Raton, Fla.: St. Lucie Press. (Originally written 1921–1923).

Wells, G. (1999) *Dialogic Inquiry: Toward a Sociocultural Practice and Theory of Education*. Cambridge: Cambridge University Press.

Yaroshevsky, M. (1989) *Lev Vygotsky*. Moscow: Progress Publishers.

Chapter 4

Towards an inclusive pedagogy

Lani Florian

Introduction

In recent years, much has been written about efforts to include pupils identified as having special educational needs (SEN) in mainstream schools and class-rooms. Three main strands can be seen in this literature. One is about equal opportunities and the right to education for all. It argues that any form of segregated or separate education on the basis of disability or learning difficulty is morally wrong (Jordan and Goodey, 1996). A second strand is based on a re-conceptualisation of the special needs task as part of the process of school improvement (Ainscow, 1991). This idea is based on the argument that it is the structure of schools as organisations rather than differences between individual pupils that creates special educational needs (Tomlinson, 1982; Skrtic, 1988). The third strand of the literature has been concerned with questions of pedagogy. Though some have focused on the development of inclusive practice from the outset (e.g. Forest and Pearpoint, 1992), others have considered whether or not the teaching practices and methods associated with meeting special educational needs can be implemented in mainstream schools and classrooms in order to meet the challenge of inclusive education (see for example, Cook and Schirmer, 2003).

Thus, 'inclusion' or 'inclusive education' can be conceptualised in terms of a rights-based process of 'increasing participation and decreasing exclusion from the culture, curriculum and community of mainstream schools' (Booth *et al.*, 2000). 'Inclusive practice' is concerned with actions and activities, the things staff in schools *do* that give meaning to the concept of inclusion. This chapter focuses on teaching practice. The first part of the chapter considers the notion of specialist pedagogy and the research that has investigated this notion. The second part of the chapter considers some of the lessons learned about practice from a study of the strategies used by teachers in English secondary schools committed to the concept of inclusion.

The notion of specialist pedagogy

The line of research that is concerned with how methods developed by special educators can be applied in mainstream classrooms is based on an assumption that there is a specialist pedagogy for children with special educational needs that teachers need to know about in order to include these children in mainstream schools. This view is rooted in the difference position in the longstanding 'development vs. difference' debate in the psychological literature (e.g. Zigler, 1982). The deficit position views children with various types of disabilities and/or learning difficulties as qualitatively different as learners and therefore in need of educational responses that are uniquely tailored to respond to those differences. The opposing position assumes development follows a sequence that is the same for all learners but at a slower rate. Differences are explained in terms of when rather than whether learners pass through stages of development.

Though this debate is far from settled, there is a presumption that the identification of impairments in individuals has direct implications for educational interventions. This notion of *label-treatment interaction* or *diagnostic-prescriptive teaching* reflects historical attempts to understand the nature of a particular disability and its implications for treatment. The idea is that the kind of diagnostic precision so useful in medicine should also underpin psychological and educational assessments in order to match within-child characteristics with particular remedial or compensatory interventions. Depending on whether so-called impairments were thought to be the result of deficits or developmental lags, interventions were intended to help children 'catch up' by stimulating 'development' or overcoming 'deficits'.

Based on this view, special education provision has come to mean educational provision which is 'additional to', or otherwise 'different from', that which is made generally for children of similar age in mainstream schools (§312 Education Act, 1996). For many years this has been provided in specialist facilities based on disability categories of special need (such as schools for pupils who have physical or sensory impairments, and so on). However, recent legislation in England and Wales (e.g. the Special Educational Needs and Disability Act, SENDA, 2001) has strengthened the right to a mainstream school place for pupils identified as having SEN. Together with other developments, such as the revised OFSTED framework for the inspection of inclusion, the DfES (2001a) guidance *Inclusive Schooling: Children with Special Educational Needs (SEN)*, the inclusion statement in the National Curriculum and the *Special Educational Needs Code of Practice* (2001b), SENDA provides a firm legislative context for further developments in inclusive education. These developments require new ways of thinking about and responding to individual differences.

Responding to these kinds of policy imperatives requires a consideration of how the teaching practices and methods developed within special education settings and based upon individual learning differences could be transferred to mainstream schools and classrooms in order to extend inclusive education. This literature documents many implementation problems and often attributes resistance or implementation failure to a lack of mainstream teacher preparation for the inclusion of pupils considered to have special educational needs (SEN) (e.g. Giangreco, 1997; Scott *et al.*, 1998; Jorgensen, 1998). In other words, many teachers are thought to have negative attitudes about including pupils identified as having special educational needs resulting from a lack of knowledge about teaching such children. However, a review of the research on the question of specialist pedagogy, along with careful consideration of psychological theories of learning and the pedagogical practices they have given rise to, offer an interesting new way of helping teachers to think differently about what they need to know about including children with special needs in their classrooms.

Research on specialist pedagogy

There is no shortage of literature reviews on teaching pupils with SEN. In England for example, there is the Audit Commission review of SEN (Dockrell *et al.*, 2002), the EPPI-Centre review of effectiveness of school-level actions for promoting participation by all students (Dyson *et al.*, 2002) and the Lewis and Norwich (2000, 2005) research on specialist pedagogy. In the USA, there have been substantial recent reviews including Gersten *et al.*'s (2001) study produced for the *Handbook of Research on Teaching* and McDonnell *et al.*'s (1997) report on students with disabilities and standards-based reform carried out for National Research Council. Additional literature reviews on teaching pupils with the full range of SEN are to be found in Davis and Florian (2004); Scott *et al.* (1998); and McGregor and Vogelsberg (1998).

Researchers in the USA have been interested in the efficacy of special education. Kavale (2007) has reviewed the use of meta-analysis in answering questions about what works in special education. In his review Kavale shows how early beliefs about the 'altered learning functions' or deficits of disabled children gave rise to a pedagogical emphasis on cognitive processes or process training (e.g. corrective perceptual-motor training, psycholinguistic training, etc.) which proved to be very modest in their effectiveness. It is only when research which investigates the teaching-learning process in general is 'interpreted' for special education 'by modifying the way in which instruction is delivered' that we find significant effect sizes (p. 212). Kavale is clearly pointing to the power of teaching strategies based on psychological principles of teaching and learning, and the differentiation that may be necessary to respond to individual differences.

Though Kavale is sceptical of inclusive education as a model for meeting special educational needs (for a discussion, see Kavale and Forness, 2000), he argues that the efficacy of special education practice is due to a change in emphasis from strategies that emphasise the remediation of learning deficits to those that focus on teaching and learning. When 'instructional techniques originating in general education were adapted to assist students with disabilities in acquiring and assimilating new knowledge, the efforts demonstrated significant success and much improved academic outcomes' (p. 12).

Researchers in the UK (Lewis and Norwich, 2000, 2005) have investigated whether 'differences between learners (by particular SEN group) could be identified and systematically linked with learners' needs for differential teaching' (p. 10). Their review was organised by types of learning difficulties (low attainment, specific learning difficulties, moderate learning difficulties and severe, profound and multiple learning difficulties). Lewis and Norwich found that though the evidential base was problematic, the trend was away from SEN-specific pedagogies. Two central findings emerged from their review:

- the available evidence does not support the qualitative difference position and
- while it does not fully endorse the developmental difference position there was some support for the argument that what works for most pupils works for all pupils though there might be differences in application for various types of difficulties.

As a result Lewis and Norwich advocated the notion of a 'continua of teaching or pedagogic approaches' and argued that arguments for separate provision cannot be based on distinctive teaching approaches but 'on better opportunities to provide appropriate adaptations to common teaching approaches to meet unusual individual needs' (p. 59). More recently, Lewis and Norwich (2005) have elaborated on their notion of a continuum of teaching approaches by suggesting that strategies can be arranged along such a continuum from high to low intensity. Here again, the focus is on the application of a general strategy rather than the use of a different kind of strategy.

Davis and Florian (2004) undertook a study commissioned by the DfES as part of the agenda to raise the achievement of pupils with special educational needs. The aim of the study was to examine the relevant published literature in order to 'map out and assess the effectiveness of the different approaches and strategies used to teach pupils with the full range of special educational needs' (p. 7). The review of literature that informed this study was structured in terms of the four 'areas of need' identified in the SEN Code of Practice (language and communication, cognition and learning, physical and sensory, and emotional and behavioural difficulties). The review found that:

> certain teaching strategies and approaches are associated with, but not necessarily related directly to specific categories of SEN (such as autism, learning difficulty, etc). However the teaching strategies and approaches identified in the review were not sufficiently differentiated from those which are used to teach all children to justify a distinctive SEN pedagogy. It was clear that sound practices in teaching and learning in both mainstream and special education literatures were often informed by the same basic research, and that certain teaching strategies developed for one purpose

could be effectively applied to other groups of children with different patterns of educational need (e.g. co-operative learning). This does not, however, diminish the importance of what might be construed as 'special education knowledge' as an element of pedagogy applying to all learners.

Here it is helpful to clarify what is meant by the use of the term pedagogy. Alexander (2004) defines it as

> what one needs to know, and the skills one needs to command, in order to make and justify the many different kinds of decisions of which teaching is constituted ... [including]
>
> - *children*: their characteristics, development and upbringing
> - *learning*: how it can best be motivated, achieved, identified, assessed and built upon
> - *teaching*: its planning, execution and evaluation, and
> - *curriculum*: the various ways of knowing, understanding, doing, creating, investigating and making sense which it is desirable for children to encounter, and how these are most appropriately translated and structured for teaching.
>
> (p. 11)

Davis and Florian (2004) argued that it is not the differences between children, their characteristics or upbringing that is problematic, but when the magnitude of these differences exceeds what schools can accommodate that children are considered to have special educational needs. The process of providing this support, the provision of something 'additional to' in and of itself, does not constitute pedagogy but is an element of it. This does not diminish the importance of knowledge about individual differences but highlights it as an essential component of pedagogy. Davis and Florian concluded that questions about special education pedagogy are unhelpful, and that the more important agenda is about how to develop pedagogy that is inclusive of all learners.

Towards an inclusive pedagogy

There is limited research that has been carried out on pedagogy in inclusive classrooms and much of this work tends to focus on the primary years. In an extensive review of the research on inclusive practice, McGregor and Vogelsberg (1998) reported that only seven studies specifically focused on secondary school practice. In the remainder of this chapter, Florian and Rouse's 2001 study of inclusive practice in English secondary schools is offered as a case study that may provide some insights into the development of a pedagogy that is inclusive of all learners.

Schools in England have been subjected to the major structural reforms of education that have dominated the international education scene for the past twenty years. These reforms, which stress accountability, choice, achievement and excellence, coexist with other reforms that encourage the development of inclusive education. This presents a particular dilemma for teachers in English schools because the right to a place in a mainstream school for children with special educational needs is qualified on the grounds that it is not disruptive to other pupils. If, by definition, children with special needs require something 'additional to' or 'different from' that which is available to other children, how can teachers provide for such children without 'disrupting' that which is available to others?

Florian and Rouse (2001) were interested in understanding what happens in secondary schools when subject-specialist teachers attempt to create the conditions for inclusive learning in their classrooms. This research was designed to examine the extent to which classroom practice in the various subjects of the national curriculum was consistent with that which is promoted as effective by the literature on inclusion. It also sought to identify any other strategies that were being used which seemed successful in extending inclusive practice and whether or not there might be differences between teachers of various subjects. A questionnaire was designed to examine possible relationships between subject taught and teaching strategy used. Data from classroom observations, interviews and analysis of teachers' inclusion journals supplemented the questionnaire data and permitted a consideration of the kind of contextual information not generally permitted by survey research.

Schools from a network of secondary schools from around England that met regularly to share experiences and ideas about how to develop more inclusive practice were invited to participate in the study (further details of the network and the work of the schools can be found in Ainscow, 1999). Four schools volunteered to participate in the full study and a fifth school agreed to administer the questionnaire. Nominations from senior staff and the special educational needs coordinator (SENCO) at the four case study schools were used to identify subject-specialist teachers considered skilled in including pupils designated as SEN in their classes. Each teacher was observed for the equivalent of two full teaching days and participating teachers also kept 'Inclusion Journals' for a period of five weeks. The journal guidelines asked the teachers to make one entry each day, paying particular attention to their own thoughts and feelings about the commitment to inclusive practice, how subject area knowledge informs their teaching, how they account for individual differences, and 'what works'.

Questionnaires were distributed to all teachers in the four case study schools plus one additional network school. A total of 268 teachers completed the questionnaire for an overall response rate of 66 per cent. The questionnaire contained a list of 44 teaching strategies mentioned in the literature as helpful in promoting inclusive practice. These were derived from a review of the literature carried out by Scott *et al.* (1998). The strategies were organised under the following broad headings: differentiation strategies; cooperative learning strategies; classroom management strategies and social skills. Teachers were asked to rate their familiarity with these strategies. They were also asked to rate the strategy as appropriate or inappropriate to the teaching of their subject. If teachers thought the strategy was appropriate they were asked to indicate if it was a teaching technique that they 'typically used' or something 'additional' that was used specifically to ensure the inclusion of pupils with special educational needs. If they thought the strategy was inappropriate they were asked if this was because it was unhelpful or too difficult to manage. A glossary defining ambiguous terms was appended to the questionnaire.

With few exceptions, teachers overwhelmingly reported they were familiar with and used all of the strategies listed in the questionnaire. The most frequent response was that the teacher was very familiar with the strategy and used it typically (i.e. with all pupils). Only two strategies (consult with pupil on preferred learning style, and the use of learning support assistants for one-to-one teaching) were identified as being used additionally (i.e. specifically because a pupil was designated as having SEN). Teachers were evenly divided as to the use of team teaching as a typical or additional strategy. Importantly, a number of teachers noted in written comments that they did not differentiate between teaching strategy and whether a pupil had a special educational need.

There were numerous differences between teachers of different subjects and their use of particular strategies. For example, teachers of English were more likely than maths teachers to provide abridged or modified texts, use drama or role play, allow alternative responses, and explicitly teach social and group skills. Maths teachers were more likely than English teachers to make use of mnemonic devices. There were also differences between English and modern foreign language teachers with English teachers more likely to consult with pupils on preferred learning style, use jigsawing, peer tutoring, or scaffolding and teaching meta-cognitive strategies. Differences were also found between maths and science teachers. Maths teachers were more likely than science teachers to use mnemonic devices while science teachers were more likely to use drama or role play, jigsawing, and peer collaboration. There were no differences between history and geography teachers in their reported use of any of the strategies.

The differences that were found between subjects in the use of the various strategies could be a function of any number of factors including the nature and status of the knowledge in a particular subject domain and whether the teachers perceive learning their subject as being related to prior learning. Maths and modern foreign languages tend to be seen as sequential; the humanities and English much less so (Hallam and Ireson, 1999). The training of teachers is organised on a subject basis (Cooper and McIntyre, 1996) and most secondary schools are organised into subject departments that have different histories, varying degrees of autonomy and different priorities. All these factors produce a range of subject and department 'cultures' that may have an impact upon teachers' practice and their views about what works in promoting inclusion.

The open-ended comments sections of the questionnaire enabled the identification of intervening variables that aided the interpretation of the data: one was that teachers commented that the use of some strategies was resource-dependent (e.g. use of computer-assisted instruction), while others depended on administrative arrangements and support (e.g. 'team teaching and co-teaching are difficult to organise but they work'). Some teachers went out of their way to comment that they made no distinction between pupils with SEN and others when it comes to teaching strategy although others made very specific comments about how they included pupils with SEN (i.e. 'give the pupil a responsibility vital to the lesson') suggesting that the teachers individualised on the basis of their knowledge about individuals rather than whether a pupil had a special educational need in a formal sense.

When asked about strategies that were not included in the questionnaire, teachers' responses fell into three categories: affective strategies, conferring with others, and more detailed and specific versions of the listed strategies. Affective strategies included such things as using humour as a teaching strategy, and providing discreet support to pupils so they wouldn't feel singled out. Teachers most frequently mentioned the importance of developing pupils' self-esteem and sense of belonging by establishing relationships with pupils outside of class, being involved with pupils on an extra-curricular basis, offering supplementary sessions at mutually convenient times, running homework clubs, mentoring, and offering what one teacher called a 'careful mix of praise and criticism'. It is interesting to note that teachers considered conferring with colleagues and regularly circulating information about pupils to be as important as teacher knowledge about individual pupil characteristics.

Jordan and Stanovich (1998) found that though models of expert teaching do little more than give passing reference to the importance of knowledge of individual student characteristics, teachers in inclusive classrooms draw on this knowledge as a means of challenging pupils as learners. In addition, they found that the specific adaptations made by these teachers were not readily apparent to observers because the teachers applied the adaptations to all pupils in the classroom, a finding supported by the questionnaire data. With this in mind, classroom observations were followed by semi-structured interviews to home in on how the teachers were responding to individual pupils who were experiencing learning difficulties as well as specific information about the nature of those difficulties. The resulting field notes were then reviewed to identify strategies the teachers were using. This was accomplished by searching for evidence of strategy utilisation (what was observed or became apparent during discussion) matched to the questionnaire data, or emerging from the dialogue between the teacher and the interviewer. This procedure for analysing field notes enabled the teacher's self-reports on the use of strategies to be verified. It also permitted the identification of a number of additional strategies including:

- volunteering to work in a pastoral role as a means of increasing capacity for inclusion;
- an emphasis on providing a rationale for why pupils are doing what they are doing and relating learning to everyday life;
- preparing schemes of work and work packs which include a range of materials;
- taking the initiative to approach members of learning support teams for advice;

- making use of personal planners to give pupils feedback or commendations; and
- circulating information about pupils' needs including special educational needs.

The teachers observed in this study were skilled in whole-class teaching, presenting one lesson but offering a choice of tasks and varying expectations with respect to individual pupils as is traditionally understood and promoted as good practice. What enabled these teachers to include pupils with a wide range of learning abilities seemed to be the way in which they embedded a responsiveness to individual need within the process of whole-class teaching, a finding consistent with other studies on inclusive practice (e.g. Jordan and Stanovich, 1998). In addition, there was an awareness that certain strategies may be associated with particular kinds of special educational need. As a result, circulating information about individual special educational needs and disabilities was seen as very important. All the schools in this study had devised mechanisms for doing this. Although teachers spoke and wrote about their concerns about their own capacity with respect to mixed-ability teaching, they viewed the learning support departments in their respective schools as sources of knowledge and support for teaching and learning.

An analysis of the inclusion journals was undertaken to gain a deeper understanding of teachers concerns regarding inclusion. Teachers wrote about their responses to individual differences in a 'holistic' manner as indicated in the following journal extract:

> A very *mixed ability group*, but also very *mixed in motivation* and *attendance*. The motivation does not always match ability and achievements. It is the difficult time of the term with year 11 when they are beginning to get weary and increasingly eager for it all to be over. I can see *GCSE grades slipping away before my eyes. The structure of the course is part of the problem, not enough variety of task and focusing on only two of the four attainment targets*. The problem is to avoid the staleness that is almost bound to creep in by constant repetition and practice. Although a modular course is of benefit to mixed ability in some respects, allowing them to focus on smaller areas of work, *it does take the spontaneity out of teaching*. It also creates an *'exclusion zone' for pupils who are poor at tenders or long term sick, as there is less time to catch up and pupils feel there is a defeating mountain to climb.*

In this extract we see a concern for the limits of mixed-ability teaching, and a shift in teacher concern from individual pupil progress in the curriculum at the end of Key Stage 3 to group performance on examinations in Key Stage 4 (14–16 years). Because the GCSE examination requires a high standard of reading, teachers often find it difficult to know at which level of the examination to enter pupils: foundation or higher. The pressure comes from knowing that pupils who are entered into foundation-level examinations cannot get grades higher than a D while pupils entered into the higher level can only get an A, B, C or fail. This leads teachers to gear their practice towards preparation for examinations. That teachers shift their concern from individual pupil progress through the curriculum to group performance on examinations was clearly evident in their practice, discussions, and reflections. As one teacher stated: 'the GCSE requires a lot of essays so a lot of teaching is focused on how to write an essay'. In this school, the department had developed a procedure called The Stick, which teachers introduce in Year 8. The Stick is a stick figure representing the three main parts of an essay: the introduction (head), main body and conclusion (feet). The teacher described the strategy as 'a good structure for getting borderline kids a C'. The study found that when coupled with a school policy on setting at Key Stage 4, the focus on examination results makes it difficult to sustain inclusive practice.

Overall, there were no apparent differences between schools with respect to teachers' knowledge about practice although teachers in schools with more experience in mixed-ability teaching made more suggestions about what works. That they may not be able to engage in a practice is different from not knowing how to do it, and some teachers made this comment when filling out the questionnaire. Organisational arrangements and resource constraints were factors that determined whether certain strategies were used. For instance, it would not be possible to make use of information communication technology if the hardware was not available. Notably, teachers tended not to differentiate between types of students. Though they found the support of colleagues with specialist knowledge invaluable, they did not view the pupil designation of SEN as particularly helpful when thinking about teaching strategies.

Whether or not these findings would be replicated in other schools is not clear. Indeed many subject teachers may not recognise themselves or their practice in the above descriptions. What is important to note is that there were differences between subjects that need to be considered when thinking about how to include pupils who experience difficulties in learning in those subjects. It is not simply a matter of placement. Different subjects will make different demands on learners and teachers of those subjects will use different strategies in teaching the various subjects of the curriculum.

Discussion

Research on school improvement has produced a more refined understanding of how to enhance the capacity of schools to make them more effective for increasingly heterogeneous groups of pupils (for a review, see Creemers, 1996). However, as this line of research has not specifically addressed the problem of pupils identified as having special educational needs its relevance to the education of *all* pupils has been questioned by those who argue that high standards for all are unlikely to be achieved because of the limitations of current knowledge about effective inclusive practice (e.g. McDonnell *et al.*, 1997).

The extent to which teachers who are committed to extending inclusive practice need to have knowledge about special education practice is central to resolving the debate about what mainstream teachers need to know about 'special educational needs' in order to include pupils who experience difficulties in learning. Clearly it is impractical for all teachers to know about the educational implications of all types of disabilities and learning difficulties. Moreover, what they need to know is not entirely clear as specific teaching strategies do not map neatly onto disability categories of special educational needs (Davis and Florian, 2004; Ysseldyke, 2001). Equally, the often quoted view that good teaching is good teaching wherever it occurs (e.g. Babbage et al., 1999) may not stand up to close scrutiny when differences in the use of various teaching strategies across the various subjects of the secondary curriculum and the limits of so called 'mixed ability' teaching are probed.

Proponents of inclusive schooling have attempted to develop practice in two ways. One has been to build on the work of those in the school improvement field by extending the definition of 'all' pupils to include pupils with learning difficulties, disabilities and other special educational needs (e.g. Ainscow, 1997). A second way forward has involved reconceptualising difficulties in learning as dilemmas for teaching that provide insights into ways in which practice might be improved for the benefit of all (Hart, 1996; Clark et al., 1999; Ainscow, 1999). Susan Hart and her colleagues (2004) have persuasively argued that this reconceptualisation depends on a rejection of psychological notions of fixed ability that assume intelligence is normally distributed. Their work shows what is possible when teachers stop seeing children as points along a continuum in a positive or negative direction from an average point.

Questions of biodeterminism are very much in the forefront of psychology today. Great advances in scientific knowledge have led to new collaborations and new fields in psychology such as cognitive neuroscience. While these advances have rekindled interest in old debates about the structure of the brain and how the mind works, they have also led to new understandings about learning and new ideas about how to facilitate it (for a discussion see for example, Bransford et al., 2000; Child, 2004). While psychologists may be divided in their views about how learning occurs, there is deeper understanding about how to facilitate and support it. Educational psychologists are key agents in supporting teachers to make the necessary adjustments to the *strategies they already know to be effective* in supporting the learning of children who experience difficulty.

Though it is often argued that a lack of knowledge on the part of mainstream classroom teachers, attributed to a lack of training is one of the main barriers to inclusion, careful consideration of the evidence does not support this argument. First, the *label-treatment interaction* or *diagnostic-prescriptive teaching* approach to individual differences in learning has not shown that interventions are differentially effective with different kinds of learners (Keogh and MacMillan, 1996). Second, meta-analyses of 'what works' in special education shows that the teaching strategies used in mainstream education can be adapted to assist students identified as having SEN in learning. It is the process of adaptation that defines the special education knowledge teachers need. This adaptation depends on a responsiveness to individual differences within the context of whole-class teaching (Jordan and Stanovich, 1998) though it does not depend on the identification of SEN (Florian and Rouse, 2001).

Responsiveness to individual differences includes knowledge about the kinds of difficulties children experience in learning but it also suggests that medical categories of disability have not proved to be particularly relevant in developing effective teaching strategies (Lewis and Norwich, 2000, 2005; Ysseldyke, 2001). A pedagogy that is inclusive of all learners is based on principles of teaching and learning that reject deficit views of difference and deterministic beliefs about ability (Hart, 1998; Hart *et al.*, 2004), but see individual differences as part of the human condition.

References

Alexander, R. (2004) Still no pedagogy? Principle, pragmatism and compliance in primary education. *Cambridge Journal of Education,* 34(1), 7–33.

Ainscow, M. (1997) Towards inclusive schooling. *British Journal of Special Education,* 24(1), 3–6.

Ainscow, M. (1999) *Understanding the Development of Inclusive Schools.* London: Falmer Press.

Ainscow, M. (ed.) (1991) *Effective Schools for All.* London: David Fulton.

Babbage, R., Byers, R. and Redding, H. (1999) *Approaches to Teaching and Learning: Including Pupils with Learning Difficulties.* London: David Fulton.

Booth, T., Ainscow, M., Black-Hawkins, K., Vaughan, M. and Shaw, L. (2000) *The Index for Inclusion.* London: Centre for Studies on Inclusive Education.

Bransford, J.D., Brown, A.L., and Cocking, R.R. (2000) *How People Learn: Brain, Mind Experience and School.* Washington, DC: National Academy Press.

Child, D. (2004) *Psychology and the Teacher, 7th edition.* London: Continuum.

Clark, C., Dyson, A., Milward, A. and Robson, S. (1999) Inclusive education and schools as organisations. *International Journal of Inclusive Education,* 3(1), 37–51.

Cook, B.G. and Schirmer, B.R. (2003) Special series: What is special about special education? *The Journal of Special Education,* 37(3), 200–204.

Cooper, P. and McIntyre, D. (1996) *Effective Teaching and Learning: Teachers' and Pupils' Perspectives.* Buckingham: Open University Press.

Creemers, B. (1996) The goal of school effectiveness and school improvement. In D. Reynolds, R. Bollen, B. Creemers, D. Hopkins, L. Stoll, and N. Lagerweij (eds) *Making Good Schools: Linking School Effectiveness and School Improvement.* London: Routledge.

Davis, P. and Florian, L. (2004) *Teaching Strategies and Approaches for Children with Special Educational Needs. A Scoping Study* [Research Report 516]. London: DfES.

DfES (2001a) *Inclusive Schooling: Children with Special Educational Needs.* London: DfES.

DfES (2001b) *Special Educational Needs Code of Practice.* London; DfES.

Dockrell. J., Peacey, N. and Lunt, I. (2002) *Literature Review: Meeting the Needs of Children with Special Educational Needs.* London: Institute of Education.

Dyson, A., Howes, A. and Roberts, B. (2002) *A systematic review of the effectiveness of school-level actions for promoting participation by all students.* Inclusive Education Review Group for the EPPI Centre. Available online at: http://eppi.ioe.ac.uk.

Florian, L. and Rouse, M. (2001) Inclusive practice in secondary schools. In R. Rose and I. Grosvenor (eds) *Doing Research in Special Education.* London: David Fulton.

Forest, M. and Pearpoint, J. (1992) Putting all kids on the MAP. *Educational Leadership,* 50(2), 26–31.

Gersten, R., Baker, S., Pugach, M. with Scanlon, D., and Chard, D. (2001) Contemporary research on special education teaching, in V. Richardson (ed.) *Handbook of Research on Teaching, 4th edition.* Washington DC: AERA.

Giangreco, M.F. (1997) Key lessons learned about inclusive education: summary of the 1996 Schonell Memorial Lecture. *International Journal of Disability, Development and Education,* 44(3), 194–206.

Hallam, S. and Ireson, J. (1999) Pedagogy in the secondary school. In P. Mortimore (ed.) *Understanding Pedagogy and its Impact on Learning.* London: Paul Chapman.

Hart, S. (1996) *Beyond Special Needs: Enhancing Children's Learning through Innovative Thinking.* London: Paul Chapman.

Hart, S. (1998) A sorry tail: Ability, pedagogy and educational reform. *British Journal of Educational Studies,* 46(2), 153–168.

Hart, S., Dixon, A., Drummond, M.J. and McIntyre, D. (2004) *Learning Without Limits.* Berkshire: Open University Press.

Jordan, L. and Goodey, C. (1996) *Human Rights and School Change: The Newham Story.* Bristol: Centre for Studies in Inclusive Education.

Jordan, A. and Stanovich, P. (1998) Exemplary Teaching in Inclusive Classrooms. Paper presented at the Annual Meeting of the American Educational Research Association, San Diego, California, April.

Jorgensen, C.M. (1998) *Restructuring High Schools for All Students: Taking Inclusion to the Next Level.* Baltimore: Paul H. Brookes.

Kavale, K. and Forness, S. (2000) History, rhetoric and reality: an analysis of the inclusion debate. *The Journal of Special Education,* 21(5), 279–296.

Kavale, K. (2007) Quantitative research synthesis: Meta-analysis of research on meeting special educational needs. In L. Florian (ed.) *Handbook of Special Education.* London: Sage.

Keogh, B.K. and MacMillan, D.L. (1996) Exceptionality. In D.C. Berliner and R.C. Calfee (eds) *Handbook of Educational Psychology.* New York: Simon & Schuster Macmillan.

Lewis, A. and Norwich, B. (2000) *Mapping a Special Educational Needs Pedagogy.* Exeter: University of Exeter and University of Warwick.

Lewis, A. and Norwich, B. (eds) (2005) *Special Teaching for Special Children? Pedagogies for Inclusion.* Maidenhead: Open University Press.

McDonnell, L., McLaughlin, M. and Morrison, P. (eds) (1997) *Educating One and All: Students with Disabilities and Standards-based Reform.* Washington DC: National Academy Press.

McGregor, G. and Vogelsberg, R.T. (1998) *Inclusive Schooling Practices: Pedagogical and Research Foundations.* Baltimore: Paul H. Brookes.

Scott, B.J., Vitale, M.R. and Masten, W.G. (1998) Implementing instructional adaptations for students with disabilities in inclusive classrooms: a literature review. *Remedial and Special Education,* 19(2), 106–119.

Skrtic, T. (1988) The organizational context of special education. In E.L. Meyen and T.M. Skrtic (eds) *Exceptional Children and Youth: An Introduction.* Denver: Love.

Special Educational Needs and Disability Act 2001 (2001 c 10).

Tomlinson, S. (1982) *A Sociology of Special Education.* London: Routledge/Kegan Paul.

Ysseldyke, J.E. (2001) Reflections on a research career: Generalizations from 25 years of research on assessment and instructional decision making. *Exceptional Children,* 67(3), 295–309.

Zigler, E. (1982) MA, IQ, and the developmental difference controversy. In E. Zigler and D. Balla (eds) *Mental Retardation: The Developmental-difference Controversy.* Hillsdale, NJ: Lawrence Erlbaum.

Chapter 5

Learning in inclusive classrooms

Ruth Kershner

Introduction

In this chapter, the pragmatic starting position for discussing learning and teaching in inclusive classrooms is 'where we are now' in England, a context in which a concept of inclusion is broadly supported in national policy documents (DfES, 2004) but where a role is retained for special schools and local policies and procedures vary widely. In a situation where educational resources are limited and educational aims and values differ, the development of a more consistently inclusive education system with children learning together in mainstream schools becomes a matter of balancing certain opposing demands and goals – at least in the short-term future. It depends on identifying the cluster of values, beliefs and activities that succeeds in maximising children's engagement in learning while minimising the marginalisation or exclusion of certain groups or individuals in the school system. This cluster includes what we understand and want learning to be. At the very least, inclusive education involves schools in welcoming children to participate as pupils, without setting arbitrary boundaries based on previous attainment, social characteristics, behaviour, linguistic proficiency, sensory and physical skills, or assumptions about intellectual potential. However, inclusive education also implies that the children are not just present in classrooms, but that they learn and succeed in this context.

Day-to-day experience with children and psychological research studies of children's mathematical problem-solving, reasoning, memory, language and conceptual understanding (e.g. Siegler, 1996) show that there is wide variability in how children of the same age think and behave. This can apply to the same child at different points of an activity, or in different contexts, as well as to differences between peers. So grouping school pupils by age or by 'ability' oversimplifies the educational task (Ireson and Hallam, 2001). Organisational decisions like pupil grouping do not work as strategies for inclusion in themselves unless they are informed by an understanding of how children learn. The main line of thinking in this chapter draws on social constructivist models of learning which emphasise the inherently social nature of learning, involving an interplay between the individual learner and the sociocultural context of learning which transforms both over time (Palincsar, 2005; Wertsch and Kanner, 1992). As part of this process learning is supported by the use of material and symbolic 'tools' such as writing materials, measuring devices, pictures and diagrams, mathematical formulae, teamwork guidelines, assessment devices, subject-related vocabularies and language in general – all of which are so culturally embedded that human activity and education cannot easily be imagined without them. In adopting this approach to understanding learning, the psychological focus is not, for example, on how the brain processes information or on the structure of memory. While it is important to know about these and other areas of psychological research, the aim here is to consider learning at the level that seems to be most directly related to inclusive education, i.e. children's engagement in the social activities associated with learning in school and the implications of this for their developing knowledge and understanding as members of society. This interest in how school-based activity connects with children's learning is not just to do with finding the most appropriate unit of analysis or descriptive framework, although both of these functions are helpful in understanding what inclusive education may involve. The concept of activity as developed by Vygotsky also offers an explanation for human consciousness and higher mental processes (Kozulin, 2005). The dependence of learning on particular sorts of activity, communication and tool-use raises the paradoxical possibility that inclusive learning needs to be happening before we can properly understand what it is.

In this chapter I consider some alternative ways of understanding learning in the classroom context. A social constructivist perspective is applied to inclusion by focusing on the collective experience of classroom learning, with particular reference to how the processes of cognition and communication can be conceived as 'situated', 'distributed', 'dialogic' and 'multimodal'. This draws attention to certain aspects of learning that may be undervalued in approaches which promote inclusion mainly through the description of individual pupils' special educational needs, the planning of differentiated classroom tasks, and the use of additional adult support for pupils and teachers. A more explicit interest in learning processes focuses attention on how children engage with learning activities, respond to teaching and develop knowledge, skills and understanding across the curriculum. The central importance of the classroom environment, the sharing of knowledge, and the different forms of communication between teacher and pupils emerges particularly strongly. The implications are that children's educational needs and progress should be assessed in relation to how well they employ the resources in the classroom environment, contribute to classroom conversation and knowledge-building, and engage in different ways of communicating (assuming, crucially, that the teacher is facilitating and also developing in these areas). Looking at classroom learning in this way helps to reinforce the value of ensuring that the knowledge base of inclusive education includes what we know psychologically about how children learn.

Learning in classrooms

Teaching approaches which seem intrinsic to inclusive learning are already represented in many classrooms where emphasis is placed on pupils' dialogue, collaboration, choice, exploration and learning to learn, and where it is assumed that all pupils are capable of learning (Hart *et al.*, 2004). The concept of the inclusive classroom implies that the teacher's decision-making about classroom activities and the whole learning environment is embedded in a thoughtful, active and positive attention to the children as individuals and groups of pupils, who themselves support and extend each other's learning. However, Jackson (1968: 10) famously remarks that classrooms are intrinsically about 'crowds, praise and power', reminding us that attempts to create inclusive learning environments have to face up to the fact that most formal school activities take place with or in the presence of others who are not there by choice or preference. What children say and do is constantly evaluated and there are hierarchies of power and responsibility which may shift to some extent (over time or in different contexts) but which do not tend to favour the children in any significant and consistent sense. These and other characteristics of schools seem to work against the responsiveness, respect and flexibility intrinsic to inclusion, but there are many accounts of learning and teaching which succeed in demonstrating how the values and beliefs associated with inclusion may appear in classroom practice. For instance, the teachers involved in Hart *et al.*'s (2004) learning without limits project are seen to have a common belief in the 'transformability of learning capacity' (p. 192) which contrasts with the fatalism of defining fixed ability levels or assuming that classroom conditions cannot change. Specific teaching principles emerge which underpin their classroom practice, including notions of 'co-agency' and power-sharing, acting in the interests of everybody, and trusting the pupils to learn when the conditions are right for them. This is a perspective on inclusive learning that acknowledges the classroom context as a potentially supportive reality for the pupils involved if certain principles and values are explicitly in place.

As Doll *et al.* (2004: 15) discuss, it is the classroom rather than the child which can be seen to become more resilient when strategies are embedded for promoting pupils' autonomy, self-regulation and self-efficacy alongside an emphasis on caring and connected relationships between teachers and pupils, peers and the home and school. In considering the inclusion of children identified with learning disabilities, Keogh and Speece (1996) draw attention to certain classroom features, including the relevance of the teaching method, the curricular content, the management of learning activities in time and space, the use of resources, and the interactions between peers and teachers – all being experienced differently by individuals and groups of pupils. Some recent approaches to educational research have aimed to tackle the complexity of classroom life, including Könings *et al.* (2005) who consider the whole learning environment in terms of the reciprocal relationships between the perceptions, preferences and activities of students, teachers and educational designers; and Wortham (2006) who investigates the connections between pupils' academic learning and their changing social identification, using the techniques of linguistics and anthropology.

At the heart of any approach to classroom research is a view of what learning is, and it is important to be explicit about this when concerns arise about the children whose academic progress is erratic, limited or worryingly slow compared to their peers. Psychological conceptions of learning have traditionally focused separately on changes at behavioural, cognitive and neural levels – these representing broadly behaviourist, constructivist and neuroscientific schools of thought. The associated mechanisms or processes of learning range from simple behaviourist stimulus-response associations and rote learning to more complex accounts of information handling, language use and meaning making, the workings of the brain and neural connectionism. Each of these different psychological perspectives on learning, whether behavioural, cognitive or neuroscientific, also potentially says something useful about specific educational tactics – for instance, how to reinforce desired behaviour, how to make certain material more memorable, how to support the transfer of learning between different situations and build on previous learning.

Yet one of the problems in gaining a coherent view of children's full experience of learning in school is that the psychological perspectives outlined above are not simply operating at different levels of analysis in which, for example, changes at behavioural level are 'explained' by cognitive changes which in turn are 'explained' by brain functions. Within these alternative models the human learner's knowledge is seen primarily in terms of *either* behavioural responses, *or* mental schemata *or* biological effects, and researchers in each tradition do not necessarily seek connections between them. This splitting of research into different strands may be due in part to the use of metaphors which underlie different accounts of learning. For instance, Sfard (1998) distinguishes the 'acquisition metaphor' and the 'participation metaphor'. The former identifies learning in terms of the accumulation of knowledge and concepts by reception or active construction, '… gaining ownership over some kind of self-sustained entity' (p. 5). The latter, in contrast, focuses on the ongoing learning activity which involves becoming a member of a particular community with its own language and norms, i.e. understanding participation in terms of becoming 'part of a greater whole' (p. 6).

Sfard remarks on the meaning and promise of the participation metaphor: 'the vocabulary of participation brings the message of togetherness, solidarity and collaboration … The new metaphor promotes an interest in people in action rather than in people "as such"' (p. 8). This apparent affinity between the participation metaphor and inclusion seems to open up the possibilities for reframing pedagogy as a more inclusive process. Yet Sfard (1998: 11) warns against the hazards of allowing a single metaphor to dictate in educational discourse and debate about what learning is, and McGuinness (2005) similarly rejects the use of overly simple metaphors in the light of her analysis of the UK teaching and learning research programme projects. In relation to inclusion, the crucial point seems to be not about the specific nature of learning metaphors, but about the implications of their plural existence in our thinking and conversation. As

Gallimore (1996: 232) remarks, '…(w)hat's in the head of participants in a particular setting contributes to the "reality" that is perceived and responded to'. In working towards inclusion, it seems to be very useful to see that disagreements may rest as much on different ways of understanding learning as they do on opposing beliefs about, say, human rights, politics and economic decision-making.

The need to acknowledge and respond to people's different ways of understanding learning applies as much to the learner as to the teachers. Marton and Booth (1997) use evidence from their interviews with young people and adults to identify the different ways in which learning may be experienced. For instance they contrast 'learning as memorizing and reproducing' with 'learning as understanding' or 'learning as changing as a person'. They remark on the motivational implications of associated 'surface' or 'deep' approaches which may be adopted: 'the former focusing on the tasks themselves and the latter going beyond the tasks to what the tasks signify' (p. 38). Marton and Booth go on to argue that 'the approach to learning adopted by an individual … in a particular situation is a combination of the way in which that person experiences learning and the way that he or she experiences the situation' (p. 47). Carr and Claxton (2004) make a similar point about individuals' tendencies to respond or learn in certain ways. Their view is that personal learning dispositions such as resilience and playfulness are closely linked to the perceived opportunities and constraints in each new setting.

This moves us towards a position in which an understanding of classroom learning requires attention to a complex range of psychological factors including the learner's experience, other people's beliefs and the nature of the task and situation, together with certain processes which are not consciously available, such as the workings of the brain. Not least there is the crucial element of how we talk about all of these. This set of interconnecting factors is not easily encompassed in one theoretical framework. However, this is not to say that alternative views of learning cannot be weighed up against each other to check for complements and contradictions in their teaching implications and the underlying aims and values which they embody. For instance, behaviourist approaches work very well in enabling the acquisition of certain skills and factual knowledge in a step-by-step way, but they cannot be used exclusively in an education system which also values social participation, creativity, critical reflection and understanding as learning outcomes.

Social constructivist views of learning acknowledge the cultural value given to different educational outcomes as well as focusing on the interplay between the individual and the group that leads to cognitive growth and cultural affiliation (Bruner, 1996: 153). Engeström's (2005) often cited analysis of the activity system highlights the relations between not only the participants, the immediate focus of the activity, the goals, motives and the tools in use, but also the wider community, the division of labour, and the social rules, norms and values. There is a need also to understand interacting activity systems and the multiple voices and dialogues evident in these networks, bearing in mind that consensus is unlikely and even undesirable for learning and progress to take place. As Wells (1999: 235) points out, this model of culturally embedded activity draws attention to possible points of leverage in the attempt to overcome the encapsulated nature of schooling. For example, changing the nature of the rules that prescribe the sorts of 'actions' that participants engage in and their intended outcomes, modifying the division of labor, or valuing other semiotic tools in addition to written texts, all create quite different 'activity systems,' and ones that may encourage rather than resist student initiative and creativity.

This perspective gives a powerful and constructive way of thinking about inclusive learning and teaching as intimately to do with the ways in which educational activity is conceived, the perceptions of opportunities and constraints in the school setting, and the employment of particular tools and operations which allow participants to achieve the desired educational goals. Wells' reference (p. 233) to the activity theory distinction between conscious 'actions' and automatic, well-practised 'operations' is also important if practices that have become routine are serving to confirm the marginalisation and exclusion of particular pupils. In this case conscious rethinking is required for teachers to extend the teaching and learning repertoire, drawing not only on a personal commitment to inclusion but also explicit support within the school and beyond.

The collective experience of classroom cognition, communication and learning: a situated, distributed, multimodal and dialogic process

In the light of the social constructivist perspective outlined above, classroom learning has both cognitive and communicative elements (integrated with other facets of learning, such as the nature of motivation, classroom relationships and emotional processes). These will be discussed next in terms of the overlapping concepts of 'situated cognition', 'distributed intelligence', 'dialogic teaching' and 'multimodal communication'. No claims can be made in this chapter to cover these areas of research and thinking in the detail that they deserve, and the terms themselves are used in different ways in the literature. The aim is rather to present some significant examples of writing in each area as a basis for establishing how these strands of thinking might both represent and promote inclusive learning and teaching.

Situated cognition

'Situated cognition' expresses the idea that, as Donaldson (1978) showed in relation to Piagetian assessments of children's cognitive development, some aspects of knowledge and certain cognitive strategies are closely connected to the situation in which they are learned, used and assessed. A familiar educational example is Nunes *et al.*'s (1993) research on the mathematical skills of Brazilian street children, who showed far greater powers of calculation in the everyday activities of buying and selling than they did with the same type of mathematical problem in the formal school setting. Ceci (1996) refers to the different types of anthropological and experimental research evidence about cognitive performance in different contexts, making a case for challenging IQ-related models of fixed intelligence.

The educational implications of situated cognition tend to focus on the value of placing classroom tasks in a 'real context', however this is not just to do with glossing, say, an abstract mathematical problem in terms of an imaginary shopping activity. The point is to exploit situated cognition by using real-world and purposeful activities to engage pupils, to employ what they may have learned in different contexts, and in this way to develop higher level cognitive skills like reasoning and problem-solving. This involves enabling children's active engagement in the real-life experience of project work directly connected to the concerns of the pupils, school and local community. Particular opportunities for this may fall within certain cross-curricular areas such as the arts, environmental studies, sports activities and citizenship.

The implications of situated cognition also extend to the physical and social context of learning. Fuhrer (2004) describes how children cultivate particular behaviour settings which allow them to interact in ways that support their self-growth, and he presents some empirical evidence of adolescents' preferences for leisure time settings of medium physical variability combined with high openness and choice of activity. Most schools would score low on both physical variability and programme openness, therefore affording less opportunity for children's active self-development. However, in any academic context learners inevitably exploit environmental resources to reduce the mental effort required for extended problem-solving and knowledge acquisition (Pea, 1996: 63). In addition to the help of other people and typical classroom resources like pencil and paper for note-taking, the classroom may also include representations of symbolic tools like algorithms, scripts and rules in the form of classroom displays, textbooks and other written reminders of previous learning. Both the physical features of the classroom and the beliefs about what is allowed and expected in that context are important for learning (Kershner, 2000). The point is that the classroom itself may be designed in a way that helps or hinders learning, according to its perceived 'affordances' (Norman, 1998; Gibson, 1979), i.e. the opportunities and constraints it appears to provide which enable individual pupils both to engage in productive learning activities and to demonstrate what they already know.

Distributed intelligence

Closely connected to situated cognition is the notion of 'distributed intelligence'. This emphasises the social and 'distributed' nature of learning and intelligence, in which thinking and learning is seen as a partnership between the individual, other people involved and the cultural tools in use, including language (Bruner, 1996). Situated cognition is primarily descriptive in showing how thinking is tied to the social and physical environment, but distributed intelligence indicates the implications of this for human activity. Pea (1996) conceives distributed intelligence as a phenomenon that emerges from people's desires and motivations to achieve certain goals. Intelligence is therefore seen as a process of people in action rather than an individual capacity for learning, i.e. it is '… accomplished rather than possessed' (p. 50). This involves calling on the resources in the environment to help with tasks like remembering, reasoning, problem-solving and creating. As noted above, the social and physical environment offers tools which help to offload and enhance the thinking involved. The important human element is that tools that have been designed or adapted for use '… literally carry intelligence in them, in that they represent some individual's or some community's decision that the means thus offered should be reified, made stable, as a quasi-permanent form, for use by others' (p. 53). Therefore a child's use of a computer, for instance, offers a sophisticated means of engaging with the knowledge and experience of the original designer in addition to the immediate support and mediation of the teacher and classroom peers.

The idea that intelligence and knowledge can be distributed across space and time does not mean that all thinking is distributed and that individuals lack any 'in-the-head' cognitive repertoire – a sort of 'situational determinism' (Salomon, 1996: 133). The social constructivist premise is that children and teachers collectively contribute to the building of knowledge in the immediate classroom setting and subsequently in the future activities and contexts to which they disperse. Salomon (pp. 122–3) describes the reciprocal relations between the individual learner and the shared thinking evident in collective activities. He argues that classroom activities like the use of computer writing-guidance programs (which incidentally incorporate the thinking of the software designer) not only enhance the quality of an individual pupil's work in particular lessons; the experience also leaves 'cognitive residues' in the individual learner's mind which can be brought to the next writing task in a spiralling process of development. This opens up the possibility of everyone (including the teacher) learning something new simply by participating together in classroom activities, and individual contributions to knowledge may not be identifiable. Distributed intelligence, as with other psychological models of intelligence has both a conceptual and metaphorical importance, and the related implications for teaching and assessment are considerable.

Dialogic teaching

The detailed analysis of teacher–pupil dialogue is central to sociocultural views of learning, and it has proved useful in developing interactive, responsive teaching for pupils identified with specific 'learning disabilities' (Kraker, 2000) and pupils in general (Mercer, 2000; Wells, 1999). One example of a broad pedagogical approach which focuses on classroom talk is Alexander's (2005) notion of 'dialogic teaching'. The central principle developed by Alexander is that children's talk is at the heart of their thinking and learning. However its apparent ease and familiarity for most people, and its transitory nature, can result in it being given less reflection, attention and educational status than writing. Alexander's point is that talk is not simply an element of the curriculum, but it has a pedagogical role which reaches across the curriculum. Alexander draws on different types of evidence to justify this position, including psychological views about the dynamic connections between thought and language, as exemplified by Vygotsky's work, together with more recent indications from neuroscientific studies of early brain development. Sociological research has provided evidence of the kinds of language used in different contexts, and the associated patterns of relationship and power: '… if we want children to talk to learn – as well as learn to talk – then what they say probably matters more than what teachers say' (Alexander, 2005: 24).

The teacher's role is to draw out and support children in their talking, using techniques to help the children to express and develop their ideas. Alexander points out that this is a dialectic process in which the teacher genuinely engages in conversation with children and takes some responsibility for explaining his or her own views as well as guiding the children to sustain their own arguments. To summarise, Alexander's argument is that dialogic teaching advances children's learning, confidence and engagement in the classroom. It is:

- collective – teachers and children address learning tasks together, whether as a group or a class, rather than in isolation;
- reciprocal – teachers and children listen to each other, share ideas and consider alternative viewpoints;
- supportive – children articulate their ideas freely, without fear of embarrassment over 'wrong' answers; and they help each other to reach common understandings;
- cumulative – teachers and children build on their own and others' ideas and chain them into coherent lines of thinking and enquiry;
- purposeful – teachers plan and facilitate dialogic teaching with particular educational goals in view (p. 26).

A further point made by Alexander, which has particular relevance to inclusive education, is that the skills that children develop through their experience of dialogic teaching – listening, attending, responding to others, articulating questions, presenting and evaluating ideas, arguing and justifying points of view – are central to citizenship. So the dialogic teaching approach is not 'content free' in the sense that it is simply a way of teaching anything. It rather embodies a way of thinking about education and an associated set of principles and values which may not only typify inclusive learning but also require and promote it – bearing in mind the affective processes also involved (Skidmore, 2006).

Multimodal communication

The focus on teacher–pupil dialogue can be usefully extended to include other modes of communication in classroom activity. Kress *et al.* (2001), focusing on the science classroom, propose that language is '… simply one of several modes through which the business of science is done, by the teacher or by the students' (p. 1). They conceive the various modes – language, image, gesture and action – as affording different opportunities for active meaning-making. Their detailed analyses of science lessons shed light on how different pupils who have apparently experienced the same lesson may draw on different communicative resources to produce texts with images and writing which demonstrate distinctly different understandings of the science learning in which they are engaged.

This approach to analysing the multimodal aspects of communication and knowledge representation may help to deal constructively with the question of whether pupils have particular 'cognitive styles' or 'learning preferences' which can and should be accommodated by adapting and individualising the teaching approach. The idea that children may be 'visual', 'auditory' or 'kinaesthetic' learners, for instance, translates the mutual process of dynamic, multimodal communication to a fixed characteristic and capacity of each child involved. The broad idea that different learning styles exist has recently had a powerful influence in education, with programmes being developed to support teaching responses (e.g. Smith *et al.*, 2003). The approach has even been extended to apply to whole groups of children such as boys and girls, although the evidence suggests that caution is needed. For example, in their research on school-based strategies for raising boys' achievement, Younger and Warrington (2005) found difficulties in the precise measurement of preferred learning styles, which in any case seem to change over time and in different contexts. Classroom activities cannot easily be identified as one style or another, and the teacher's intentions may not be experienced similarly by the pupils. However it was clear in this project that focusing on 'learning styles' to talk about learning did have positive effects on pupils' motivation, confidence and self-awareness, and on teachers' creative planning, teaching and assessment.

Coffield *et al.* (2004) discuss both the appeal of the learning styles model and the objections to it, based on their extensive survey of the available literature and evidence relating to the post-16 sector. Some of the main appeal lies in the promise the notion of learning style offers to practitioners faced with the complex task of teaching diverse groups of students, and the associated possibility of redefining 'learning difficulties' as the results of a mismatched approach to teaching. Coffield *et al.* also note that learning styles have been used as the basis for constructive dialogues about learning between teachers and learners, enhancing the motivation and metacognitive understanding of both. Coffield *et al.* divide the critics of 'learning styles' into two main camps: those who accept the basic premises of attempting to measure individual learning styles but find current models inadequate according to accepted psychometric criteria, and those who reject all the assumptions about the very possibility of quantitative measurement based on subjective, general and decontextualised judgements using self-report questionnaires which have become overcommercialised in test materials and training. Practically there are dangers in labelling learners as falling into certain types, in spite of warnings from the original theorists and test designers. One of

Coffield *et al.*'s main contentions is that most learning style models are limited to teaching rather than to pedagogy – the latter being a notion which '… encompasses the performance of teaching together with the theories, beliefs, policies and controversies that inform and shape it' (Alexander, 2000: 540). However in spite of the confusion and lack of consensus in the learning styles field, Coffield *et al.* do not call for it to be abandoned. They identify a need for further research on certain promising models identified in their evaluation – a process which, as they point out, would involve bringing together different concepts and traditions of research in psychology, sociology and education.

Conclusion: teaching and learning in inclusive classrooms

To summarise, there is a growing body of psychological evidence which suggests that certain processes of thinking and learning are embedded or situated in particular contexts and activities. In school, knowledge is shared between pupils and teachers, supported by the lines of communication and other tools available in the classroom learning environment. The emerging challenge for inclusive learning and teaching is to explore the educational relevance of particular mutual influences and 'transactions' (cf. Sameroff, 1995) which take place over time involving an interplay between factors relating to the child, the school and the wider social and cultural context. This mirrors the 'bio-psycho-social' frameworks which have been applied to understand phenomena like attention deficit/hyperactivity disorder diagnoses, in which environmental and experiential factors mediate between a biological predisposition and the behavioural manifestations in particular settings (Cooper, 2005: 128). Sociocultural thinking as outlined above suggests that children and adults participate in many different activity systems, bringing their knowledge and experience to each new encounter. Learning, in turn, creates new knowledge amongst the participants and changes the knowledge that each takes away. This is a dynamic system in which disturbances and contradictions are both common and necessary to maintain activity and the development of knowledge.

This perspective on learning potentially supports the development of inclusive education, when efforts are made to provide children with access, welcome and cognitive support and to ensure that the pupils also perceive it in these ways. However, as mentioned earlier in the chapter, there are some tensions between the shared and individual aspects of classroom learning. In practice teachers' priorities necessarily shift between responding to the changing needs of individuals and to whole groups of pupils, as emerged clearly in studies of gender and special school teaching for example (Kershner, 2005). So how do individual pupils learn to shift identities, transfer their knowledge between different activities and contexts, and contribute to the development of new ideas and skills with other people? The apparent 'fixing' of certain children's intellectual capabilities is one of the main barriers to inclusion, so flexibility is required if inclusive learning is to have power and sustainability beyond the immediate classroom environment.

Oversimplified understandings of situated and distributed perspectives on thinking and learning are in danger of losing sight of the individual learner as a developing person with metacognitive self-awareness and self-regulation, agency, control, and transferable knowledge and skills. If learning is too closely tied to the situation, to other people and to the mode in which information is communicated then we might wonder what the individual learner can take forward to the next activity and learning challenge, especially if carrying an experience of failure with them. It is hard to imagine a version of inclusion that does not also aim to support individual pupils' growing independence and autonomy as lifelong learners in and out of school. This is where the importance of talking about learning emerges strongly, as does the use of combinations of teaching strategies for specific purposes. For instance, Gersten *et al.* (2001) describe how the transfer of learning can be supported by the explicit teaching of concepts and procedures alongside the introduction of relevant and purposeful activities that engage pupils. This combined approach also applies to complex tasks like learning to read, with the textual demands of decoding print and understanding meaning. The use of combined teaching strategies is not unusual for teachers, but more research is needed on explicit and targeted combinations for pupils currently identified as having special educational needs (Davis and Florian, 2004).

In the end I would argue that inclusive education will benefit from a view of the classroom as a place that both embodies and supports learning for a diverse range of learners. If factors like politics, resources, organisational systems, social attitudes and personal preferences mean that certain children are excluded from participating in classroom and school activity, then the activity setting changes. The inevitable result is that the psychological processes, experiences and outcomes of teaching and learning are qualitatively different for all involved. The point is that inclusive practice does not just support marginal and potentially disaffected pupils, but that these and all the other pupils are collectively the embodiment of inclusive educational activity without which a study of inclusion cannot make sense. Schools have to develop general structures and procedures to support pupils' learning, but individual pupils bring their own knowledge, skills, preferences and motivations into each new classroom activity. This diversity contributes to a dynamic and creative process of teaching and learning that maintains the school as a healthy educational context while promoting all pupils' learning in often unpredictable ways.

References

Alexander, R. (2000) *Culture and Pedagogy: International Comparisons in Primary Education.* Oxford: Blackwell.

Alexander, R. (2005) *Towards Dialogic Teaching: Rethinking Classroom Talk*, 2nd ed. York: Dialogos UK.

Bruner, J. (1996) *The Culture of Education.* Cambridge, MA: Harvard University Press.

Carr, M. and Claxton, G. (2004) 'Tracking the development of learning dispositions', in H. Daniels and A. Edwards (eds) *The RoutledgeFalmer Reader in Psychology of Education* (pp. 106–131). London: RoutledgeFalmer. [Article originally published 2002.]

Ceci, S.J. (1996) *On Intelligence: A Bioecological Treatise on Intellectual Development*, expanded edn. Cambridge, MA: Harvard University Press.

Coffield, F., Moseley, D., Hall, E. and Ecclestone, K. (2004) *Learning Styles and Pedagogy in Post-16 Learning: A Systematic and Critical Review.* London: Learning and Skills Research Centre.

Cooper, P. (2005) 'AD/HD', in A. Lewis and B. Norwich (eds) *Special Teaching for Special Children? Pedagogies for Inclusion* (pp. 123–137). Maidenhead, Berks: Open University Press.

Davis, P. and Florian, L. (2004) *Teaching strategies and approaches for pupils with special educational needs: a scoping study,* Research Report RR516. London: Department for Education and Skills.

DfES (2004) *Removing barriers to achievement: the government's strategy for SEN.* London: Department for Education and Skills.

Doll, B., Zucker, S. and Brehm, K. (2004) *Resilient Classrooms: Creating Healthy Environments for Learning.* New York: Guilford Press.

Donaldson, M. (1978) *Children's Minds.* Glasgow: Fontana/Collins.

Engeström, Y. (2005) 'Non scolae sed vitae discimus: toward overcoming the encapsulation of school learning', in H. Daniels (ed.) *An Introduction to Vygotsky*, 2nd ed. (pp. 157–176). Abingdon, Oxon: Routledge. [Article originally published 1991.]

Fuhrer, U. (2004) *Cultivating Minds: Identity as Meaning-making Practice.* London: Routledge.

Gallimore, R. (1996) 'Classrooms are just another cultural activity', in D.L. Speece and B.K. Keogh (eds) (1996) *Research on Classroom Ecologies: Implications for Inclusion of Children with Learning Disabilities* (pp. 229–250). Mahwah, NJ: LEA.

Gersten, R., Baker, S. and Pugach, M., with Scanlon, D. and Chard, D. (2001) 'Contemporary research on special education teaching', in V. Richardson (ed.) *Handbook of Research on Teaching*, 4th ed. (pp. 695–722). Washington, DC: AERA.

Gibson, J.J. (1979) *The Ecological Approach to Visual Perception.* Boston: Houghton-Mifflin.

Hart, S., Dixon, A., Drummond, M.J. and McIntyre, D. (2004) *Learning Without Limits.* Maidenhead, Berks: Open University Press.

Ireson, J. and Hallam, S. (2001) *Ability Grouping in Education.* London: Paul Chapman Publishing.

Jackson, P.W. (1968) *Life in Classrooms.* New York: Holt, Rinehart and Winston.

Keogh, B.K. and Speece, D.L. (1996) 'Learning disabilities within the context of schooling', in D.L. Speece and B.K. Keogh (eds) *Research on Classroom Ecologies: Implications for Inclusion of Children with Learning Disabilities* (pp. 1–14). Mahwah, NJ: LEA.

Kershner, R. (2000) 'Organising the physical environment to support children's learning', in D. Whitebread (ed.) *The Psychology of Teaching and Learning in the Primary School* (pp. 17–40). London: RoutledgeFalmer.

Kershner, R. (2005) 'Gender and achievement in special schools', in M. Younger and M. Warrington (eds) *Raising Boys' Achievement in Secondary Schools: Issues, Dilemmas, Opportunities* (pp. 157–170). Maidenhead, Berks: Open University Press.

Könings, K.D., Brand-Gruwal, S. and Van Merriënboer, J.J.G. (2005) 'Towards more powerful learning environments through combining the perspectives of designers, teachers, and students'. *British Journal of Educational Psychology,* 75(4), 645–660.

Kozulin, A. (2005) 'The concept of activity in Soviet Psychology: Vygotsky, his disciples and critics' in H. Daniels (ed.) *An Introduction to Vygotsky,* 2nd ed. (pp. 101–123). Abingdon, Oxon: Routledge. [Article originally published 1986.]

Kraker, M.J. (2000) 'Classroom discourse: teaching, learning and learning disabilities'. *Teaching and Teacher Education,* 16, 295–313.

Kress, G., Jewitt, C., Ogbord, J. and Tsatsarelis, C. (2001) *Multimodal Teaching and Learning: The Rhetorics of the Science Classroom.* London: Continuum.

Marton, F. and Booth, S. (1997) *Learning and Awareness.* Mahwah, NJ: LEA.

McGuinness, C. (2005) 'Behind the acquisition metaphor: conceptions of learning and learning outcomes in TLRP school-based projects', *Curriculum Journal,* 16(1), 31–47.

Mercer, N. (2000) *Words and Minds.* London: Routledge.

Norman, D.A. (1998) *The Design of Everyday Things.* London: MIT Press. [Originally published 1988.]

Nunes, T., Schliemann, A.D. and Carraher, D.W. (1993) *Street Mathematics and School Mathematics.* Cambridge: Cambridge University Press.

Palincsar, A.S. (2005) Social constructivist perspectives on teaching and learning, in H. Daniels (ed.) *An Introduction to Vygotsky,* 2nd ed. (pp. 285–314). Abingdon, Oxon: Routledge. [Article originally published 1998.]

Pea, R.D. (1996) 'Practice of distributed intelligence and designs for education', in G. Salomon (ed.) *Distributed Cognitions: Psychological and Educational Considerations.* (pp. 47–87). Cambridge: Cambridge University Press.

Salomon, G. (1996) 'No distribution without individuals' cognition: a dynamic interactional view', in G. Salomon (ed.) *Distributed Cognitions: Psychological and Educational Considerations* (pp. 111–138). Cambridge: Cambridge University Press.

Sameroff, A.J. (1995) 'General systems theories and developmental psychopathology', in D. Cicchetti and D.J. Cohen (eds) *Developmental Psychopathology, vol. 1: Theory and Methods* (pp. 659–695). New York: Wiley.

Sfard, A. (1998) 'On two metaphors for learning and the dangers of choosing just one'. *Educational Researcher,* 27(2), 4–13.

Siegler, R.S. (1996) *Emerging Minds: The Process of Change in Children's Thinking.* New York: Oxford University Press.

Skidmore, D. (2006) 'Pedagogy and dialogue', *Cambridge Journal of Education,* 36(4), 503–514.

Smith, A., Lovatt, M. and Wise, D. (2003) *Accelerated Learning: A User's Guide.* Stafford: Network Educational Press.

Wells, G. (1999) *Dialogic Inquiry: Toward a Sociocultural Practice and Theory of Education.* Cambridge: Cambridge University Press.

Werstch, J.V. and Kanner, B.G. (1992) 'A sociocultural approach to intellectual development', in R.J. Sternberg and C.A. Berg (eds) *Intellectual Development.* Cambridge: Cambridge University Press.

Wortham, S. (2006) *Learning Identity: The Joint Emergence of Social Identification and Academic Learning.* Cambridge: Cambridge University Press.

Younger, M. and Warrington, M. with McLellan, R. (2005) *Raising Boys' Achievement in Secondary Schools: Issues, Dilemmas and Opportunities.* Maidenhead, Berks: Open University Press.

Chapter 6

The psychology of inclusion

The emotional dimension

Isobel Urquhart

Introduction

The justifications for inclusive education consistently include reference to the detrimental effects of discriminations in educating students on, for example, their self-concept, motivation and educational achievement. In this chapter, I argue that any account of inclusive practices must address the emotional dimension – that is how it *feels* to be excluded from the learning community by reason of the barriers to access and learning in that context. My own commitment to doing so is firmly related to what I perceive as the teacher's primary task: to support children's and young people's learning. An interest in emotions, therefore, is in the service of ensuring that all students gain full access to learning and achievement through inclusive educational policies and practice. As Booth and Ainscow (2002) argue, 'Learning from attempts to overcome barriers to the access and participation of particular students [contributes to] changes for the benefit of students more widely'. This view of inclusion implies its relevance to all learners and their entitlement to belong within an educational community on equal terms.

A growing number of publications offer teachers and therapists advice about counselling pupils in school contexts, and school counsellors are more widely employed by schools and some local education authorities (LEAs) than at any time in the past (Baginsky, 2004). However, this will not be the focus of the chapter, for the reason, as Daniels (2001: 113) argues, that 'successful schools are those which understand the need to integrate perspectives on cognitive and emotional development in their planning of teaching and learning'. This approach extends far beyond pathologising and then alleviating the emotional difficulties of some individual learners, and it requires us to consider the wider educational context within which the personal emotional experiences of learning and relationships of all students are embedded. In this way too, inclusion must shift from its traditional focus on responding to emotional difficulties seemingly 'presented' by the child identified with special educational needs, to encompass the development of inclusive strategies and classroom practices that acknowledge the importance of the affective dimension to learning and teaching for all (Slee, 2001). It further requires a critical understanding that inclusive school-based strategies and classroom practices are themselves compromised by aspects of current systems of education and policy. Educational systems have emotional impact – in the pedagogies and educational practices these policies afford as well as in the classroom dynamics experienced by both learners and teachers. Thus, it is essential not only to understand the individual's personal experience and its early origins and interactions with family members and children and teachers in school, but also to recognise how these are nested within wider systems. An ecological perspective on inclusion (Bronfenbrenner, 1989) allows us consider the emotional dimension at personal, interpersonal and structural levels, bearing in mind the web of interconnecting systems and mutual influences involved in linking the child, classroom, school, neighbourhood and family with the wider community. The chapter draws on psychodynamic approaches which have nowadays moved from the traditional focus on the individual psyche and interpersonal relations to extend this perspective into the public domain, including the field of education (Davou, 2002; Greenhalgh, 1994; Hughes and James, 1999; Park, 2000; Salzberger-Wittenberg *et al.*, 1983; Weiss, 2002a, 2002b). This not only reflects a welcome and growing interest in understanding and supporting the emotional lives of young learners generally, but it is also a response to increasing concerns about rising numbers of exclusions, diagnoses of childhood depression and other perceived pressures on children's mental wellbeing, with wide implications for developing inclusive educational practice.

The personal: children's learning and emotional growth

It is a truism that cognition and emotion are indivisible, an 'intricately bound developmental process' (Bell and Wolfe, 2004). As Daniels (2001: 113) points out, 'children do not think in the absence of how they feel'. Constructivist theories of learning, which emphasise the active construction of the meaningfulness of experience by individuals, acknowledge this indivisibility. Both Piaget (1952) and Vygotsky (1962/86) recognised that emotion and cognition were 'indissociable', as Piaget put it, and both acknowledged that to separate cognition from emotion gave a false impression of the cognitive process. Piaget's concept of assimilation, for example, depends upon a child having an internal organising structure that is sufficiently developed, *both cognitively and emotionally,* to incorporate unfamiliar experience. Vygotsky (1962/1986: 10) explained that the separation of cognition from emotion erroneously 'makes the thought process appear as an autonomous flow of thoughts thinking themselves, segregated from the fullness of life, from the personal needs and interests, the inclinations and impulses of the thinker'. Le Cornu and Collins (2004) have recently adopted this constructivist conceptual framework to argue that such an approach to learning provides the theoretical basis for building more opportunities for pupils and teachers to feel included within the education process, emphasising the importance of dialogue.

What is sometimes missing from such accounts, however, is the acknowledgement that these elements are not always consciously available to us for reflection (Damasio, 2002; Davou, 2002). The psychodynamic tradition, committed to the idea that not all mental functioning is conscious, constantly reminds us of the workings and impact on our behaviour of the unconscious. The unconscious or non-conscious part of our mental activity includes that which cannot be regulated because it cannot be called to mind; that is to say, it cannot be consciously reflected on or thought about. Clearly, learning depends upon being able to think, and to be conscious of one's thoughts, and one shared purpose of teaching and psychodynamic therapy is to expand the capacity of the individual learner to overcome barriers to thinking, and thus to learning. This is clearly encapsulated in Claxton's argument that the process of learning requires us to move from a place of 'knowing' through a period of not-knowing and on to a new place where we once again 'know', where he gives some indication of the emotional repercussions of this process:

> Learning of whatever kind is an adventure ... A problem exists for which there is no ready-made solution ... The effect of what one does next is uncertain ... The continuous engagement which learning requires may be dangerous. The urge to withdraw and protect yourself becomes stronger.
>
> (Claxton, 2000, cited in Murray, 2005: 4)

Educational therapists such as Murray (2005) or Greenhalgh (1994) explain that it follows that being a successful learner depends on acquiring the capacity to tolerate periods of uncertainty. Most children have had sufficient positive experiences in their early lives, especially in those earliest social interactions with their main caregiver that are the focus of attachment theory, that they can tolerate the level of anxiety involved in not knowing – they have some resilience when faced with uncertainty (Urquhart, 2000). However, some children have not had that kind of early experience and this tolerance does not develop so well. Situations that evoke uncertainty or a state of unknowing can be experienced as an intolerable threat to a child's psychic integrity. When children appear unwilling to learn, therefore, it may be not so much about a conscious rejection of learning as a wish not to have to experience the uncomfortable feelings and anxiety aroused by the learning process (Murray, 2005: 5).

Defences against learning

'Uncomfortable feelings' does nothing to convey just how intolerably anxious, hopeless or frustrated we sometimes feel, faced with a learning environment and/or a task that takes us out of the security of the certainties we are used to, whether these are social or cognitive. These feelings, which are faced by both learners and their teachers, can be completely overwhelming at times, preventing us from thinking rationally and hindering our capacity to internalise and represent experience and therefore to think about it. For some children, this is their everyday experience in school.

Psychodynamic theory suggests that the quality of one's earliest emotionally driven social interactions continues to influence later emotional growth and development, and is all the more powerful for having developed pre-verbally. When psychological anxiety, sometimes occurring in the very earliest social interactions as part of the attachment processes, becomes too much to bear, individuals protect themselves against conscious awareness of it by 'denying' it access to conscious awareness. When later experiences are non-consciously perceived as similar, however, the pattern of defensive and protective response is re-evoked: the individual again adopts behaviours and emotional responses that defend against conscious experience of the re-evoked painful and unsoothable feelings initially associated with an earlier experience. An emotional defence is thus a protective response to a situation that evokes, often at a non-conscious level, a long-standing anxiety. In the psychodynamic world, the ensuing behaviour is called 'acting out' in order to recognise its emotional origins. It is these defensive turns, not easily available to conscious reflection, that exacerbate problems with emotional well-being in the classroom, 'acted out' in behaviours that are often disturbing to the teacher and the class. One particular defence, 'projection', is worth considering in more detail because an understanding of its dynamics can help teachers to interpret and thus intervene more effectively – and therefore in a more inclusive way – when it creates barriers to learning. Projection, as a concept, attempts to describe and explain our own emotional experience of other people's acted-out defensive behaviours. For example, pupils' attention seeking and avoidance activities such as running out of the room, or forgetting homework or instructions, can be experienced by the teacher as a personally felt sense of low self-efficacy, that is, experienced as a personal evaluation of her *own* emotional state, as 'not knowing what to do' or 'not being able to teach'. Thus, she experiences the feeling of uncertainty as her own, rather than that of the learner.

Such defences keep the child at an emotional distance from other people. They preserve an illusory sense of feeling safe from the threat, but they also prevent further change, i.e. learning, either social or academic, from occurring. They can, however, be reinterpreted by the perceptive teacher as non-verbal attempts to communicate that which cannot be expressed verbally because it cannot be brought to conscious attention.

It is important to add that emotional defences and projections are not simply 'symptoms' that define the pathology of some individual children. Inclusive practice also involves understanding the reactive behaviours of any and all learners and developing our capacity to imaginatively understand how learning itself is a risk that may be exacerbated or alleviated by policies, pedagogical practices, school and classroom climate, the teacher's own resilience and self-efficacy as well as the child's capacity to own and regulate his or her emotions.

The interpersonal: teachers and learners

Most teachers take it for granted that there needs to be a positive emotional relationship between the teacher and the learner in order to build the fundamental trust necessary for any learning to occur. The capacity to empathise with the emotional experiences of learners in the classroom is an important aspect of the teacher's professional social competence, enabling him or her to not only anticipate what needs to be done to create an inclusive learning environment, but also to make ongoing fine adjustments and sensitive decisions while teaching. In this context, understanding our own feelings about learners and colleagues, how these arise and what they tell us about the learning situation and the learners themselves, is part of the emotional dimension to inclusive practice.

In their extensive review of the literature on teachers' attitudes towards integration and inclusion, Avramidis and Norwich (2002) showed that whilst attitudes were generally positive, the nature and severity of children's needs strongly influenced teachers' disposition towards inclusive practices. In a related study, Poulou and Norwich (2002: 128) found that negative feelings were negatively associated with intentions to help the children who elicit these feelings. That is, in their analysis of teachers' responses to vignettes of the behaviour of children identified with emotional and behavioural difficulties, they found that 'the more negative their feelings (anger, irritation, indifference) for these children, the less they were inclined to help them'. Poulou and Norwich go on to argue, however, that an inclusive policy can help to prevent some of the well-known effects of low teacher expectancy and self-fulfilling prophecies that such emotional reactions can elicit (Chaplain, 2003).

Poulou and Norwich suggest that while it is unrealistic to expect teachers to 'freeze' their feelings, 'it would be more desirable for them to learn to control those negative feelings and not allow them to influence their teaching role' (p. 128). Nonetheless, as the authors acknowledge and this chapter has suggested, the insight into and regulation of one's feelings is a complex process, not readily accessible to conscious awareness and thus not easy to control. In order to improve inclusive practice, therefore, teachers need some means of understanding the relationships they have with their classes and with individual students that helps them to think about, clarify and resolve how the affective dimension to learning and teaching can create barriers to inclusion, including their attitudes to certain kinds of students and educational needs. With that insight, teachers may then feel more enabled to effect changes towards a more inclusive pedagogy.

An understanding of the psychodynamic concept of 'transference' may be helpful in overcoming some of the barriers to inclusion described above. Transference can be defined as the 'experiencing of feelings ... toward a person in the present that are inappropriate to that person and are a repetition, a displacement, originating [in] significant persons of early childhood' (Greenson, 1978, cited in Weiss, 2002b: 109). As Salzberger-Wittenberg *et al.* (1983) rightly point out, this can be a positive transferential experience, as when children interact with their teachers warmly and with affection, and are able to 'use' the teacher's role in the classroom to learn effectively. However, Greenhalgh (1994: 55), describing transference in the classroom, captures the feeling of the negative transference for teachers: 'it is as if the teacher catches the flak originally associated with some-one else'. It can be a defensive process, 'providing an illusory sense of security, rather than confronting a difficulty'. In the transference situations described in educational contexts by psychodynamic theorists such as Salzberger-Wittenberg *et al.* (1983), Greenhalgh (1994), Weiss (2002a, 2002b) or Geddes (2003), people often do not 'know' what causes them to react and behave towards a situation or a person. This is so for both children and teachers in the classroom.

While a child may deal with the frustrations of learning through self-worth protection strategies that place the 'uselessness' outside oneself, e.g. 'this work is stupid', such defensive strategies may also include an unconscious transferential projection of how useless adults are for putting things right or at meeting the demands for a learning task that does not threaten his or her self-worth (e.g. by telling the teacher she or he is stupid). Teachers' implicit reactions to feeling use-less may lead them to more and more frenzied attempts to alleviate the anxious feelings aroused by this transferential demand. Such attempts could include pro-viding less and less challenging work that the pupil can accept, as just one example of a response intended to be responsive to the pupil but that is ultimately excluding in its effects.

An 'emotionally holding' environment

Greenhalgh (1994: 107) offers teachers detailed advice about managing the emo-tional impact of learning for children with emotional difficulties. He describes the provision of 'emotional holding' as:

> a set of processes that unfold over time when adults can be relied on to be sympathetically attentive to the difficult and intensely felt emotions experi-enced by children that prevent them learning and moving forward from their defensive, 'stuck' feelings and behaviours.

Without this support, vulnerable children's capacity for positive relationships, emotional growth and learning is impeded by the impact of their anxieties and emotionally defensive behaviour. However, it is my view that this process is not just part of an expert response to children with emotional difficulties but is an essential and often intuitive response on the part of teachers to mediating the emotional climate of learning. The argument of this chapter suggests that, more widely adopted and articulated as part of community knowledge, the processes of emotional holding could help to dismantle some of the barriers to inclusive prac-tice. Ideally, they form part of the ongoing, socially interactive ways in which a teacher tolerates and mediates the experience of difficult feelings for all learners and creates a learning environment that is physically and psychologically safe, with rules, rituals and routines that help to create a predictable environment (Chaplain, 2003). Furthermore, the teacher's ongoing warmth and commitment towards each individual student, her awareness of transference reactions, and her ability to enter imaginatively into the emotional experience of the pupils' learning all form part of what enables her to contain the anxiety evoked by learning, to 'hold in mind' the emotionally charged meanings that children attach to the learning process. In addition, emotional holding includes the various means of mediating the curriculum and managing classroom processes that inform her planning and responsiveness when teaching. It may also include explicit curricular teaching about and fostering of emotions, via programmes like circle time (Mosely, 1996) and nurture groups (Bennathan and Boxall, 2000).

In their study of the role of affect in learning, LeCornu and Collins (2004: 29) found that, when the social and learning environment provides a psychologically secure space, children were 'prepared to "risk themselves" by attempting to extend their knowledge and change the way they think and behave'. This emotionally holding environment necessarily requires the teacher to mediate the curriculum:

> Much depends on the teacher's skill here in establishing the sorts of classroom interactions which enable 'learning conversations' between teacher and children and amongst the children themselves. Such conversations allow for meaningful dialogue which helps children makes sense of their learning.
>
> (LeCornu and Collins, 2004)

Learning conversations among teachers

An understanding of the emotional dimension to learning and teaching necessarily includes taking teachers' emotional responses to their work and to the children seriously. When teachers were given the opportunity to share their stories of classroom experiences (Ainscow *et al.* 2003: 236) they were shown to be able to develop cooperative and creative ways of helping to make classes more inclusive. A group of teachers who work in the same school could, for example, come to appreciate how children's emotional communications reveal the impact of the learning task or learning situation on learners – resulting in more imaginative and inclusive adjustments in their school and classroom practices (Hanko, 2003; Murray, 2005).

Gerda Hanko pioneered work in setting up teachers' groups in schools, where teachers bring case examples of students who were giving cause for concern for collective consideration. She recognised, however, the need to respond to the emotional dimension that cannot be ignored when encouraging teachers who work together to share practice. The group dynamics involved in asking a group of teachers who work with each other every day to share their classroom practice with their colleagues can, even today when teaching is an increasingly visible activity, be threatening and may be subverted in all sorts of ways.

In some ways, such meetings allow the sharing of practice – and I argue the affective dimension to such practice – that might potentially meet the observation that 'in discussions of pedagogy we lack those middle level concepts with which teachers' knowledge might be shared, used and developed' (Greeno *et al.*, 1996, cited in Daniels, 2001). Daniels (2001) goes on to argue that 'if these middle level concepts are to be developed, this is most likely to occur at the sites of practice in conversations about practice'. Middle level concepts, in contrast to universalist psychological theories that a priori do not take account of sociocultural contexts, might thus be said to include detailed and theorised articulations of learning situations as communities of practice (Wenger, 1998), and of what counts as 'community knowledge'. Current interest in *conversations* draws on similar ideas about communities of practice and so relates to the work of Ainscow *et al.* (2003: 227) who argue that the development of inclusive practices involves collaborative working arrangements 'which can [encourage] engagement with various forms of evidence that *interrupt* [implicit] ways of thinking'.

The structural: educational systems

While the chapter has so far discussed some of the personally felt dilemmas aroused by learning, and the negotiation of the learning process in relation to teachers, it is important to place these processes within the larger structures of educational systems and policies and their impact on the affective dimension to teaching and learning. Children who are 'vulnerable in our education systems ... depend on the efficacy of education for their progress, in contrast to the more resilient members, who can draw on their own resources to compensate for the inadequacies in the system' (Wedell, 2005: 3). By implication, Wedell's discussion of inclusion in terms of the systems of education we put in place acknowledges an emotional dimension since the capacity for resilience to an adverse psychosocial environment is a process of emotional regulation. Given the levels of distress, anxiety and assaults to their self-esteem that children sometimes experience as a result of exclusionary practices in their schools, Wedell is right to focus our attention on why we have designed systems of education in this way. That is to say, systems which exclude the full participation of some students.

Attention to the affective impact of an education system that is inefficacious for some cannot simply be a matter of helping some children to find personal resources with which to overcome the negative emotional impact of schools and learning – what Wedell refers to as 'softening the blow'. It should lead us to focus also on what he describes as the rigidities of the educational system. A number of commentators have criticised in particular the effects of an explicitly 'performance-based' education system in terms of children's *unhappiness* – presenting either as a loss or unmet need the children's (and sometimes the teachers') emotional wellbeing within the educational experience (McNess *et al.*, 2003). Reay and Wiliam (1999), for example, found that the process of preparing for and sitting the National Curriculum Tests in a growing climate of fear and anxiety affected the confidence and performance of all the pupils in their study regardless of their achievement levels. Barton and Slee's (1999) forthright political critique of inclusion argues that policy imperatives of 'competition' and 'selection' are incompatible with inclusion.

In what may be indirect resistance to that assessment-driven education system, many in the teaching profession are turning towards ways of making the emotional dimension an explicit part of the curriculum. Increasingly, they advocate the need to teach or otherwise ensure 'emotional intelligence' (EI) or 'emotional literacy' (EL). Although the terms are widely and confidently used by schools and teachers as if they referred to some established concept, it is still somewhat premature to assume the term has construct validity or that there is firm evidence of a directional and causal relationship between academic or social performance in schools and the various interventions intended to promote such emotional intelligence. Petrides *et al.* (2004), for example, noted the need to more carefully define the construct in psychological terms, noting that conceptual distinctions between ability EI and trait EI lead to differences in measurement methods that have important consequences for operationalising the concept. Notwithstanding the problematic nature of the concept of emotional intelligence, however, it may not be necessary to embrace the full emotional literacy programme in order to include opportunities in classrooms and school for overt and specific conversation about the emotional aspects of learning. As discussed earlier, such opportunities to talk about the process of learning may enable students and their teachers to be better able to understand and tolerate the feelings and uncertainty that are an inevitable but troubling aspect of the nature of learning.

While this chapter is committed to the importance of the emotional dimension to inclusive education, we should take care to resist the romanticisation of the emotional as an automatic 'antidote' to exclusionary practices. For example, emotional intelligence programmes may raise unrealistic expectations that they are sufficient, in themselves, to ensure positive transformational effects on individual learners' attitudes to learning and subsequent motivation, behaviour and achievement. In England, the recent policy initiative, Social and Emotional Aspects of Learning (SEAL) (DfES, 2005), puts the government's imprimatur upon this new focus on the mental health of school students. Their recommendation makes it a priority that there should be formal (taught) and non-formal ways of ensuring children's 'emotional literacy' and 'mental well-being'. Nonetheless, there remains an oddly amnesiac character to the government's championing of children's emotional lives, given that the system of education that successive governments have promoted significantly contributes to a distinct lack of mental wellbeing for numbers of pupils and colleagues.

Such recommendations for formal teaching to ensure emotional literacy risk reproducing the customary barriers to inclusion, including a deficit model that finds that it is only children, and only some children, and certainly not adults or organisations, whose emotional intelligence or emotional literacy is undeveloped.

In the process, an uncritical espousal of a syllabus intended to teach or foster emotional intelligence risks narrowing into a covert attempt to regulate unwanted behaviours through 'regulating' students' emotional reactions to uncongenial learning environments experienced as unsafe or excluding.

Government exhortations and emotional literacy programmes seem unaware that many of the emotional aspects they refer to are not easily made overt or consciously available to teachers or children, and may elicit, in some, powerful defensive reactions. Before such initiatives can be safely or effectively implemented with children, it is essential that teachers are able to have opportunities to talk together in a safe and supportive context. There, they can reflect on their own experiences of the emotional dimension to learning, and to learn together how students' defences and teachers' corresponding anxieties can become entangled and defeat the primary purpose – to enable students to learn within an inclusive education system. Ainscow *et al.* (2003) emphasise that opportunities for teachers to observe one another's classroom practice were noticeably associated with developing more responsive practice, and could be adapted to provide a basis for a conversation about the affective dimension to teaching and learning. Engaging in such discussions is inevitably and essentially an emotionally charged experience, which takes skilful and sensitive care to facilitate. Nevertheless, meetings where teachers share their experiences can be highly informative, not least in the way they can replicate the experiences of children in our classrooms, both positively in terms of experiences of trust and dependency that may develop between the individual members of the group, and negatively in terms of the defensive reactions experienced.

Conclusion

No one really doubts the significance of an emotional dimension to learning. Whether it is the eagerness with which our curiosity drives us to know more, or the sense of personal satisfaction in achieving mastery, right through to the worries about how our work will be received by others or our fears about whether we are stupid, most of us I would guess have at least one memory of how powerfully our feelings have been involved in the learning process, particularly in our school days. In this chapter I have attempted to argue that an inclusive school is a learning community that takes the affective dimension seriously as a significant aspect of learning. This has been examined at three different levels of experience: the child's personal experience of the learning process, and the emotional defences that might, if not understood, exclude some children; the child within the social organisation of school, where the importance of the relationship between teachers and their students has been emphasised, and how much is invested, psychodynamically, in that relationship, for good or ill; and finally, the emotional impact of national educational systems and policies on the potential for inclusivity of the learning community, and how 'softening the blow' of these on our most vulnerable students is simply not ambitious enough if we want genuinely inclusive schools.

I have also argued that understanding key aspects of psychodynamic theory, such as the role of the unconscious, the important and long-lasting influence of early emotional experience, and the communication of feelings such as the hopes and fears around learning through non-verbal and non-conscious means and transferential relationships can help schools, teachers and others to develop inclusive schools. Further, I have suggested that the 'learning conversations' that are increasingly theorised within a sociocultural context of communities of practice are an important way forward for inclusion, particularly if they also share and talk about the feelings of learning and teaching.

Inclusion is a human rights issue that squarely focuses on the entitlement of all pupils to learn together (Booth and Ainscow, 2002). Commitment to such a value-based principle of inclusion requires educationalists to focus on common, universal and inclusive processes and interventions rather than simply identifying risk and deficit. Separate is not equal. Consistently over time, the poor and the marginalised have been over-represented in separate, special education. While separate education exists, there is always a way in which educators can avoid the imperative to bend their wills to making the learning environment welcoming, productive and constructive for *all* students. Nevertheless, while separate education is, by definition, exclusionary at structural levels, it has much to contribute in terms of the quality of its care for the interwoven development of students' social, emotional and academic achievement. For example, Barbara Cole (2004), investigating how mothers (who were also teachers) of children with SEN perceived educational inclusion, found that what counted as inclusion for these mother–teachers focused on the small and 'caring' things that professionals did to further the 'feelings' of inclusion for their children and themselves as parents. They valued the teachers who 'tried' and it was the 'good faith and effort' of the professionals that ultimately mattered to them. By contrast, structurally inclusive mainstream schools can still create barriers to learning that exclude some students and have much to learn from colleagues who work with our most vulnerable children and young people.

For all children to be genuinely included as fully participating individuals in their learning process, we need to pay more than lipservice to the challenges and opportunities that the affective context of inclusion entails. Psychodynamic practices have notoriously been criticised for simply being a distraction from tackling the real causes of distress in people's lives (Smail, 1993). Thus, listening to, giving voice to, those who are inaudible in the education systems includes the responsibility to go on to engage with and act upon what we hear from the most vulnerable and excluded students in the learning community, in order to build more inclusive educational systems.

References

Ainscow, M., Howes, A., Farrell, P. and Frankham, J. (2003) 'Making sense of the development of inclusive practices'. *European Journal of Special Needs Education*, 18(2), 227–242.

Avramidis, E. and Norwich, B. (2002) 'Mainstream teachers' attitudes towards inclusion/integration: a review of the literature'. *European Journal of Special Needs Education*, 17(2), 1–19.

Baginsky, W. (2004) *School Counselling in England, Wales and Northern Ireland: A Review*. London: NSPCC.

Barton, L. and Slee, R. (1999) 'Competition, selection and inclusive education: some observations'. *International Journal of Inclusive Education*, 3(1), 3–12.

Bell, M.A. and Wolfe, C.D. (2004) 'Emotion and cognition: an intricately bound developmental process'. *Child Development*, 75(2), 366–379.

Bennathan, M. and Boxall, M. (2000) *Effective Intervention in Primary Schools. Nurture Groups*, 2nd ed. London: David Fulton Publishers.

Booth, T. and Ainscow, M. (2002) *Index for Inclusion: Developing Learning and Participation in Schools*, revised ed. Bristol: Centre for Studies in Inclusive Education. Available online at: http://inclusion.uwe.ac.uk/csie/indexlaunch.htm, accessed on 18 July 2006.

Bronfenbrenner, U. (1989) 'Ecological systems theory'. *Annals of Child Development*, 6, 187–249.

Chaplain, R. (2003) *Teaching without Disruption in the Primary School: A Multilevel Model for Managing Pupil Behaviour in Primary Schools*. London: RoutledgeFalmer.

Claxton, G. (2000) *Wise Up: The Challenge of Lifelong Learning*. London: Bloomsbury.

Cole, B. (2004) 'Mission Impossible? Special educational needs, inclusion and the re-conceptualization of the role of the SENCO in England and Wales'. *European Journal of Special Needs Education*, 20(3), 287–307.

Damasio, A. (2002) *The Feeling of What Happens*. London: William Heinemann.

Daniels, H. (2001) 'Activity theory and knowledge production'. *Emotional and Behavioural Difficulties*, 6(2), 113–124.

Davou, B. (2002) 'Unconscious processes influencing learning'. *Psychodynamic Practice*, 8(3), 277–294.

DfES (2005) *Excellence and Enjoyment: Social and Emotional Aspects of Learning*. Available online at: www.standards.dfes.gov.uk, accessed on 18 July 2006.

Fonagy, P., Gergely, G., Jurist, E. L. and Target, M. (2002) *Affect Regulation, Mentalisation, and the Development of the Self*. New York: Other Press.

Garton, A.F. and Gringart, E. (2005) 'The development of a scale to measure empathy in 8- and 9-year-old children'. *Australian Journal of Education and Developmental Psychology*, 5, 17–25.

Geddes, H. (2003) 'Attachment and the child in school. Part 1: Attachment theory and the "dependent" child'. *Emotional and Behavioural Difficulties*, 8(3), 231–242.

Greenhalgh, P. (1994) *Emotional Growth and Learning*. London: Routledge.

Greeno, J., Collins, A. and Resnick, L. (1996) 'Cognition and learning' in D. Berliner and R. Calfee (eds) *Handbook of Educational Psychology*. New York: Macmillan.

Greenson, R. (1978) *Explorations in Psychoanalysis*. New York: International Universities Press.

Hall, K., Collins, J., Benjamin, S., Nind, M. and Sheehy, K. (2004) SATurated models of pupildom: assessment and inclusion/exclusion. *British Educational Research Journal,* 30(6), 801–817.

Hanko, G. (2003) 'Towards an inclusive school culture – but what happened to Elton's "affective curriculum"?'. *British Journal of Special Education,* 30(3), 125–131.

Hughes, M. and James, C.R. (1999) 'The inter-relationship of the roles of the headteacher and the deputy headteacher in primary schools', *School Leadership and Management* 19(1), 83–95.

Le Cornu, R. and Collins, J. (2004) 'Re-emphasizing the role of affect in learning and teaching'. *Pastoral Care,* 22(4), 27–33.

McNess, E., Broadfoot, P. and Osborn, M. (2003) 'Is the effective compromising the affective?'. *British Educational Research Journal,* 29(2), 243–257.

Mosely, J. (1996) *Quality Circle Time.* Cambridge: LDA.

Murray, A. (2005) 'The fear of learning and the fear of not being able to teach in a special school for pupils with emotional, behavioural and social difficulties (ESBD)'. *The Psychotherapist,* Winter, pp. 4–5.

Park, J. (2000) 'The dance of dialogue: thinking and feeling in education'. *Pastoral Care,* 18(3), 11–15.

Petrides, K.V., Furnham, A. and Frederickson, N. (2004) 'Emotional intelligence.' *The Psychologist,* 17(10), 574–577.

Piaget, J. (1952) *The Origins of Intelligence in Children.* London: Routledge & Kegan Paul.

Poulou, M. and Norwich, B. (2002) 'Cognitive, emotional and behavioural responses to students with emotional and behavioural difficulties: a model of decision-making'. *British Educational Research Journal,* 28(1), 111–138.

Reay, D. and Wiliam, D. (1999) 'I'll be a nothing: structure, agency and the construction of identity through assessment'. *British Educational Research Journal,* 25(3), 343–354.

Salzberger-Wittenberg, I., Williams, G. and Osborne, E. (eds) (1983) *The Emotional Experience of Learning and Teaching.* London: Routledge.

Schore, A. (2003) *Affect Regulation and the Repair of Self.* New York: W.W. Norton.

Slee, R. (2001) '"Inclusion in Practice": does practice make perfect?'. *Educational Review,* 53(2), 113–123.

Smail, D. (1993) *The Origins of Unhappiness.* London: HarperCollins.

Urquhart, I. (2000) 'Teaching children with emotional difficulties' in D. Whitebread (ed.) *The Psychology of Teaching and Learning in the Primary School.* London: RoutledgeFalmer.

Vygotsky, L.S. (1962/1986) *Thought and Language* (tr. A. Kozulin). Cambridge, MA: MIT Press.

Wedell, K. (2005) 'Dilemmas in the quest for inclusion'. *British Journal of Special Education,* 32(1), 3–11.

Weiss, S. (2002) 'How teachers' autobiographies influence their responses to children's behaviors: the psychodynamic concept of transference in classroom life. Part 1.'. *Emotional and Behavioural Difficulties,* 7(1), 9–18.

Weiss, S. (2002) 'How teachers' autobiographies influence their responses to children's behaviors: the psychodynamic concept of transference in classroom life. Part 2.'. *Emotional and Behavioural Difficulties,* 7(2), 109–127.

Wenger, E. (1998) *Communities of Practice.* Cambridge: Cambridge University Press.

Part 2

Promoting inclusive learning

Chapter 7

Cooperative learning for inclusion

JoAnne W. Putnam

Educating students with special needs in general classrooms requires instructional approaches that promote student achievement and positive social psychological outcomes. Inclusionary education implies that all students will participate in the academic and social life of the classroom. The challenge of inclusion is to balance the diverse learning needs of all students while maintaining a smoothly operating classroom that teachers can reasonably manage. When properly implemented, cooperative learning has shown positive benefits for students of diverse abilities and backgrounds, and is considered by many educational researchers and practitioners to be one of the most important educational interventions for successful inclusion (Johnson and Johnson, 1989; Kagan *et al.*, 2004; Slavin, 1995).

In the USA, federal legislation established in 1975 (P.L. 94–142) requires that, to the maximum extent appropriate, all children – including those with disabilities formerly excluded from school – be placed in the least restrictive environment (LRE). "Students with disabilities" includes 13 categories of disability, for example, autism, hearing impairments, learning disabilities, emotional disturbance, and mental retardation. The LRE is defined as the setting most like that of nondisabled students that also meets the child's educational needs. More recently, the Individuals with Disabilities Education Act, IDEA 2004 (Individuals with Disabilities Education Act, 2005) stipulates that students with disabilities must have *access to the general education curriculum* and to reforms that occur in general education at the state, district, and local school levels. Removal of a student from the general curriculum can only occur when a student's needs cannot be met with supplementary support services in the classroom. Any removal from the general curriculum must be specifically explained on the student's Individualized Education Plan. This change in US law has profound implications for students with disabilities, because they now are guaranteed access to the *curriculum* as opposed to simply access to a *place* (e.g., general classroom) or a *service* (e.g., speech therapy).

Access to the curriculum is assured for students with learning and behavioural challenges when appropriate instructional accommodations and modifications are designed specifically for the student. Two terms often used in the development of Individualized Education Plans are *accommodations* and *modifications*.

"*Accommodations*" (also referred to as adaptations) have been defined as a service or support to help a student fully access the instruction as well as validly demonstrate what he or she knows (Nolet and McLaughlin, 2005, p. 71). Alterations are made in the way instruction is delivered or how a student might respond to instruction as opposed to changes in the content or difficulty of the curriculum. For example, a student with a reading comprehension difficulty may benefit from working with peers to engage in partner reading, discussing a passage, and jointly responding to questions. When students need changes in their learning goals, including subject matter alterations or performance expectations, it is referred to as *modifying* the curriculum. For example, a student might work at a lower grade level in the same content area as his or her fellow students. Cooperative learning groups provide opportunities for students to work with their peers to accomplish learning objectives, but they do not preclude the use of individual accommodations or modifications during the lesson.

Basic principles of cooperative learning

Cooperative learning involves students working together in pairs or small groups to achieve academic goals. Researchers have demonstrated that for cooperative learning to produce high achievement and positive social and psychological outcomes, certain conditions must be maintained (Johnson and Johnson, 1989; Slavin, 1990) with key components including positive interdependence, individual accountability, cooperative skills, simultaneous interaction, and group reflection.

Positive interdependence, the feeling that group members must work together to achieve a common goal, is the essence of cooperative learning. It is a "we" as opposed to a "me" mentality, where students care about one another's performance, and where they coordinate their actions to achieve a mutual goal. Johnson *et al.* (1994) have developed strategies for achieving what they refer to as "positive interdependence," for example:

1   goal interdependence (i.e., a common goal for the group, a characteristic of all cooperative learning groups);
2   task interdependence (factory line, dividing the work in a jigsaw);
3   role interdependence (assigning roles to students, such as recorder, reader, encourager);
4   reward interdependence (working for a group reward, such as free time, extra points, a certificate, pizza party);
5   resource interdependence (sharing or dividing up materials, information);
6   identity interdependence (group name, motto, flag).

Individual accountability requires that all group members are responsible for learning the information and contributing to the group goal. A common problem with group learning is that one student does the bulk of the work or a student does not do his or her fair share. "Coasting" or "hitchhiking" on the work of others is discouraged through various strategies. For example, individual evaluation is essential in demonstrating that each student has mastered the material. This can take the form of a daily knowledge check or a weekly quiz. Randomly selecting students to report the group's answer or accomplishments or explain the material encourages accountability. Self-monitoring and reflection is another means for holding individuals accountable.

Students with learning challenges should be encouraged to be responsible for learning and contributing to the group in a manner that is consistent with their ability to learn and contribute. Murray (2002, p. 178) recommended that "the teacher must ensure that the contributions of the 'weaker' members of the group are genuinely important so that the group's success cannot be attributed merely to the work of one or two pupils." This may require accommodations or modifications to the cooperative task which do not detract from the group goal yet address individual needs of special students.

Cooperative skills are encouraged by teachers identifying needed group social skills and encouraging students to practise the skills in the context of academic activities. For cooperative groups to function well, children need social skills. More importantly, they need social skills to succeed in work and life. Teachers can provide social skill instruction by defining the skills, explaining their importance, demonstrating the skills, setting up opportunities for practising the skill and providing students with feedback on their use of the skills. Skills are matched to the developmental level and needs of students, and can be introduced throughout the academic year. Kagan encourages teachers to feature a "cooperative skill of the month" to address this critical area of development.

Simultaneous face-to-face interaction promotes positive academic and social outcomes in cooperative learning situations (Kagan, 1996). Working in small groups maximizes the opportunity for students to participate actively, discussing ideas, making decisions, and engaging in negotiations. In traditional classrooms, discussions and presentations often occur sequentially with one student speaking or presenting at a time.

Sometimes teachers mistake "individualistic learning – with talking" for cooperative learning. For example, working alone on a math problem and then discussing the answer in a group is not cooperative learning. Glasser (1986) refers to "genuine" cooperative tasks as those that lend themselves to group-work, involving interactive discussions and problem solving. If students can more easily learn the material on their own and would prefer to do so, they should work individually. The requirement for face-to-face interaction is compatible with distance learning and telecommunication systems, and is becoming more common in American schools.

Group reflection and goal setting. Students who engage in cooperative activities are encouraged to reflect on how well they functioned as a team and how well they achieved the group goal. Kagan identifies six steps of group processing:

1   Students assess their social and academic skills.
2   Students focus on the goals of the lesson.
3   Other groups' sharing provides another source of self-assessment and ideas.
4   Students work on presentation and listening skills.
5   Students reflect about their progress.
6   The teacher evaluates how well the lesson accomplished the goals.

(Kagan, 1996, p. 6)

Together, teachers and students develop understanding about why groups fare well or why they sometimes struggle and fail. Groups develop action plans for improving group functioning and to guide future learning.

When students with disabilities are included in cooperative groups, teachers design accommodations or modifications in advance. For example, a student with autism may need a keypad to type responses and social skill instruction to enhance group participation. His or her criteria for success may be altered to a lower level, such as receiving 75 percent on the test as opposed to 85 percent mastery expected of most students in the class. Performance assessments that reveal students' thinking and learning are also recommended, such as measuring comprehension through students' artwork on a brochure, by soliciting oral responses to questions, or having the students perform a skit to show understanding of the Wabanaki culture in the lesson plan example below. (See additional examples of cooperative learning lesson plans from Putnam, 1997, 1998).

Cooperative lesson plan
The Wabanakis of Maine and the Maritimes

Ms Wright's grade eight class is studying the Wabanaki tribes of Maine and the Canadian Maritime Provinces. She has planned an interdisciplinary thematic unit that incorporates study of culture, history, language, and traditional subsistence. The students are assigned to heterogeneous groups of four students, or "clans," to develop a brochure depicting their assigned Wabanaki clan. Each of the five clans will research a different Wabanaki tribe (teacher-assigned), to include the Penobscot Nation, Passamaquoddy, Maliseet, Micmac, and Abenaki tribes. Using books and other resources, including tribal members, students will prepare an informational brochure and make a class presentation.

Lesson objectives: Research the history, culture, language, and traditional subsistence of a Wabanaki tribe and create a colorful brochure. The brochure will be distributed and a class presentation will be given.

Time allotted: About one period per day for about three weeks.

Materials: Resource materials (e.g., books such as *The Wabanakis of Maine and the Maritimes* by American Friends Service Committee, 1989), internet, brochure software.

Roles: Editor, designer, illustrator, presentation manager.

Heterogeneous groups: Students are assigned to clans of four. Ms Wright uses her knowledge of students to assign individuals of various ability levels to each clan. For example, Stephen, who has autism spectrum disorder, is assigned to a clan with two students of average ability and a high achieving student. The clans are also mixed with respect to gender, cultural and ethnic background, and interpersonal skill level.

Positive interdependence: Each clan will research a Wabanaki tribe and create an informational brochure (goal interdependence). Each student in the clan will select one topic to research, such as culture, history, language, or traditional subsistence (task interdependence). A single tri-fold brochure will be produced using a computer and software (materials interdependence). Students will be assigned one of the four group roles (role or duty interdependence). Each clan will choose a name (identity interdependence), such as bear, eagle, salmon, wolf or moose.

Individual accountability: Individual students each will be graded on their contribution to the brochure. Each student will be tested individually at the end of the unit to assess knowledge and understanding. Group roles and task assignments will assure participation. Group members will rate the contributions of clan members (participation, effort, organization) as well as their own.

Criteria for success: Successful completion of a high quality brochure, class presentation, and unit test.

Cooperative skill: The cooperative skill designated for this unit is active listening. Students will be directly taught how to be an active listener through teacher-led discussion (what active listening "sounds like, looks like, feels like"), role play, and practising in their groups. Students will be formally observed by Ms Wright, who will use an observation form and provide feedback to each clan.

Adaptations for students with special needs: The clans will decide themselves who will fulfill each of the four roles. Stephen, who has autism spectrum disorder, has poor verbal and written expression skills but is an excellent artist. He has chosen to be the illustrator for the group brochure. Due to a neuromotor challenge, he uses facilitated communication to produce his part of the brochure, which entails typing on a laptop with his index finger. He is able to do this independently.

Stephen is slow to interpret social cues from others, so students in his group have met with the teacher to discuss how to explain their feelings to Stephen. Stephen is also allowed to take short breaks to assist him with emotional regulation when he is frustrated, scared, or experiences sensory overload.

Stephen is working on the social skill of staying with the group, as he is inclined to physically remove himself from activities and retreat into himself. He is also encouraged to indicate when he needs a break to assist with emotional or sensory regulation. Stephen will be expected to obtain 75 percent on the unit test, provide the illustration for the brochure, and to accompany the group during the presentation. He will operate the computer for their powerpoint presentation.

Evaluation and student reflection: Teacher monitoring with an observation form will occur to record instances of "active listening," and, for Stephen, "staying with the group." Students will be evaluated on their brochure (40 percent) individual sections of the brochure (e.g., Stephen's artwork), (30 percent), presentation (20 percent), and peer ratings (10 percent). Peer rating forms will be distributed by the teacher to students midway through and at the end of the unit.

Psychological theory and rationale for cooperative learning in inclusive education

"Cooperative learning is one of the most widespread and fruitful areas of theory, research, and practice in education" (Johnson *et al.*, 2000). Indeed, the number of studies conducted on cooperative learning has been documented at over 900 (Johnson *et al.*, 2000). Its widespread use and dissemination in schools throughout the world is due, in part, to grounding in theory and validation through research. With respect to psychological theory, cooperative learning is based in part on the cognitive developmental work of Vygotsky (1978), and the social cognitive theory of Bandura (1977).

In the 1930s Lev Vygotsky (1978) and, more recently, social constructivist theorists have emphasized the importance of the social and cultural factors in cognitive development. In contrast to Piagetian theory, which focuses attention on the inner workings of the individual in knowledge construction and learning, Vygotsky believed that children develop cognitively through social interaction with others. In school, children learn through mutual interactions with peers and teachers. Learning occurs when children are listening to, talking with, playing with, and teaching others. The *zone of proximal development*, or the distance between what a child learns on his or her own and what can be learned with the support of capable peers or adults, suggests that teachers should maximize the time students spend learning with others. Social constructivists also maintain that a child learns through the filter of culture, so that cultural beliefs, language, and skills influence the content of knowledge.

An implication of social constructivism for educators is to create engaging, culturally meaningful opportunities for children to interact with peers and teachers as they construct knowledge and understanding. Teachers assume the role of learning "facilitators" or "guides" rather than simply lecturing and providing direct instruction. Learning opportunities might include adult or peer tutoring; cognitive apprenticeships between an expert's and a novice's understanding and use of a culture's skills; and cooperative group learning.

Albert Bandura emphasized observation in his social cognitive theory of learning. Observational learning occurs when a person observes and imitates someone else's behavior. According to Bandura (1986), four specific processes involved in observational learning are: attention, retention, motor reproduction, and reinforcement or incentive conditions. He maintained that students are most likely to imitate high status models. To capitalize on the importance of high status models, teachers should consider pairing or grouping special needs students with others who are respected, socially skilled, mature, or who possess desired skills or abilities (e.g., sports, musical ability). Also, students are more likely to imitate models they perceive are similar to them and are believed to be competent (Schunk, 1987).

A complementarity exists between the theories of Bandura and Vygotsky, both of which provide the most compelling rationale for cooperative learning: the importance of social interactions to the learning process. Cooperative learning, when structured properly, is a teaching strategy that provides students with an ideal social context for actively constructing meaning as well as providing opportunities for peer observation and feedback. Students themselves are a valuable resource to one another's learning and development.

A longstanding criticism of pull-out classes and segregated programming for students with special needs has been the lack of appropriate peer models for students. In the past, students with special needs were typically grouped with other students who confront behavioral, social, and academic challenges. Positive role models were rarely available in segregated settings. Cooperative learning groups, under proper circumstances, provide an excellent context for students to observe and imitate appropriate peer behavior.

Advantages of cooperative learning for inclusion

> *"Cooperative learning is the embodiment of the inclusive philosophy."*
>
> (Kagan *et al.*, 2004)

Cooperative learning was identified as one of the most promising approaches for successful inclusion, according to research by Lipsky through the The National Center on Educational Restructuring and Inclusion (NCERI):

> The data indicate that instructional strategies and classroom practices that support inclusive education for the most part are the same ones that teachers believe are effective for students in general. They report that a precursor to inclusive programs is a belief in the benefits of heterogeneous classrooms. Of the districts reporting, cooperative learning is identified as *the most important instructional strategy supporting inclusive education.*
>
> (Lipsky, 1995)

Although there is no simple panacea to address the many challenges of including students with special academic and behavioral needs, it is critical that teachers understand the potential benefits of appropriately structured cooperative learning groups. Successful cooperative learning requires an understanding of the critical elements of cooperative learning, a commitment to making groups work over the long run, and a willingness to analyze and propose solutions for problems that inevitably occur in the groups.

The advantages of cooperative learning for students with disabilities include improved achievement, social skill development, and peer acceptance.

Achievement

Research reviews by Johnson and Johnson (1989) and Slavin (1990, 1995) indicated that cooperative learning (as compared with individualistic and competitive learning) increases the academic achievement and social acceptance of students with disabilities. Students engaged in cooperative learning groups also experienced greater interpersonal attraction between students with and without disabilities than in competitive or individualistic learning situations (Johnson and Johnson, 1989). Most of the investigations in these reviews have been conducted with students who have mild disabilities (e.g., those with learning disabilities, mental retardation, or sensory and physical impairments). The general findings of the research on cooperative learning and students with moderate and severe disabilities are also positive: greater academic gains comparable to competitive and individualistic situations, greater interpersonal attraction, and higher levels of social interaction behaviors (see Putnam, 1998 for a brief discussion).

Research on cooperative learning and students with special needs has been criticized for the preponderance of short-term studies lasting only three to six weeks (Slavin, 1990). Some researchers also question the effects on academic achievement. For example, Lloyd *et al.* (1988), while finding positive effects of cooperative learning on reducing social rejection, could not corroborate positive effects on academic achievement for students with learning disabilities. They recommended that continued research must be conducted to demonstrate that cooperative learning works better than individualized instruction or other well-established instructional approaches for students with learning disabilities. Similarly, Tateyama-Sniezek (1990), in a review of twelve studies on the effects of cooperative learning and the achievement of students with disabilities, reported that only half of the studies supported cooperative learning. Stevens *et al.* (1991) analyzed the same twelve studies in the Tateyama-Sniezek study and noted that only four of the studies included *group goals and individual accountability,* which are two of the necessary components of any cooperative learning group. Of the four studies that included the essential elements of cooperative learning, positive effects on achievement were found (effect size +.48).

More recently, McMaster and Fuchs (2002) performed a qualitative review of the research published from 1990 to 2000 to determine the effects of cooperative learning on the academic achievement of students with learning disabilities. The researchers did not address behavioral or social/psychological outcomes. Fifteen studies were grouped according to cooperative learning (CL) strategies used:

1   CL combined with computer-assisted instruction;
2   CL combined with strategy instruction;
3   CL combined with cross-age peer tutoring;
4   Cooperative homework teams;
5   The "learning together approach" (Johnson and Johnson, 1994);
6   CL as part of a schoolwide restructuring program;
7   Structured versus unstructured CL.

The researchers found achievement outcomes to be mixed, and that cooperative learning methods that employ individual accountability and group rewards have the best results. They concluded that further research is needed before we can conclude that cooperative learning is an effective strategy for improving academic achievement of students with learning disabilities.

An investigation by Jones and Carter (1994) focused on the performance of students who worked cooperatively in mixed-ability pairs in science. The study examined the relationship among students' achievement levels, peer interactions, and knowledge construction when low achieving students were paired with high achieving students or another low achieving student.

The mixed-ability pairs exhibited the most noteworthy performance in this investigation. Low ability students were better able to accomplish the task. The poor attention, poor comprehension of the task, poor self-regulation, and a tendency to focus on irrelevant details by the low achievers did not impede the performance of the high-achieving students.

> When the high and low students worked together, they each built successful, but parallel structures. The structures may not have been identical, but each achieved the goal of the builder ... The high student modeled learning behaviors, as well as taught the low student. The low student did not necessarily mimic the high student, but used his or her own tools and materials in the learning process.
>
> (Jones and Carter, 1994, p. 616)

Selecting challenging, multilevel tasks that promote learning and growth at different levels is a key to success in cooperative learning and inclusionary education. Ideally, cooperative tasks provide opportunities for all students to work at their own levels while still pursuing a common goal.

Social skill development

Cooperative learning provides an ideal context for social skill development. It is through interpersonal interactions that students observe, perform, and receive feedback on social behaviors, which makes cooperative learning particularly beneficial for students with learning and behavior problems. According to Johnson and Johnson (1989), cooperative group-work requires a coordination of efforts that involve 1) getting to know and trust one another, 2) communicating accurately, 3) accepting and supporting one another, and 4) resolving conflicts constructively. Through observing student behavior in cooperative groups, teachers can prioritize social/cooperative skills that merit attention. Systematic social skills instruction can be provided and students can practise social behaviors and receive constructive feedback.

Peer acceptance

Over forty empirical studies found that attitudes towards students with disabilities were more positive in classrooms using cooperative learning (Johnson and Johnson, 1989). (See Annotated Bibliography by Putnam and Farnsworth-Lunt, 1989). The social psychologist Deutsch (1951) theorized that individuals who facilitate the achievement of a student's goals are liked and accepted while those who frustrate their goal attainment are disliked and rejected. He noted that group members will attempt to compensate for the ineffective actions of group members, but will resent the actions of the "bumbler." This theory was rather crudely referred to as the "bumbler hypothesis." An investigation by Johnson et al. (1978) on students with disabilities in cooperative groups yielded findings that were inconsistent with Deutsch's "bumbler hypothesis." Their study showed that low-achieving students are actually liked more in cooperative situations than in competitive situations. Johnson and Johnson theorized that lower performance by a cooperative group member does not result in dislike and rejection due to the following factors:

1   In cooperative activities, students perceive low performing peers in multidimensional (as opposed to stereotypical) and dynamic (as opposed to static) ways. Low-performing students are recognized for their areas of strength, which are revealed over the course of ongoing and appropriately structured interactions.
2   Students tend to value high effort despite low ability. Therefore, if the low performer is trying hard in the group, he or she will be liked for making a good effort.
3   Students in cooperative groups have expectations that all members will help to facilitate the group's attainment of the goal. These expectations are generalized to the low-performing group member – even when that person doesn't actually contribute to success.
4   Students like to assist low-performing peers. There is a norm of helping others in our society, and helpers become personally committed to doing so. This personal commitment is hypothesized to result in greater liking of the low-performing peer.

(Johnson and Johnson, 1989, pp. 113–114)

Cooperative learning does not assure that *all* students will be accepted in the groups. However, the fact that low performers tend to be liked and valued more despite their weaknesses is a promising finding for creating inclusive classrooms that promote positive peer relations.

Teachers' perceptions of benefits

A study focusing more specifically on teacher implementation of cooperative learning with special education and remedial students was conducted by Jenkins *et al.* (2003). The researchers interviewed 21 teachers from six schools (all grade levels) to obtain their perceptions about and the efficacy of cooperative learning for special needs students. The three most frequent benefits of cooperative learning cited by teachers were 1) self esteem, 2) a safe learning environment and positive feeling that comes from being part of a group, and 3) higher success rates on classroom tasks and/or better products. Other benefits included providing students with greater voice and participation in the classroom and promoting better learning. It is noteworthy that teachers' mention of academic achievement as a benefit was ranked fifth, in contrast to most studies which focus on academic achievement as the primary outcome. Teachers also reported high participation rates for special and remedial education students, ranging from 50 percent to 100 percent. Forty-three percent of respondents felt all their special and remedial education students participated consistently in cooperative learning.

All but two of the teachers interviewed reported modifications of cooperative learning they use to facilitate the performance of students with special needs. Seven noted that they carefully select learning partners for struggling students. One teacher noted that "I usually try to put them in a group where they're going to have a chance to get some stimulation and really contribute." Another said, "For him [a special education student], I try not to have groups large enough that he can tune out, so that he's brought along." Four teachers mentioned that they modified the group task for a student with special needs. Teacher remarks included, "I'd give them an easy job ..." or "Sometimes I'll have a student do dictation to another if it's a written assignment" (Jenkins *et al.*, 2003, p. 286).

Cooperative group outcomes and proper implementation

Criticisms of cooperative learning are sometimes levied against forms of group instruction that do not meet the criteria set forth for appropriately structured cooperative learning (e.g., group goals, individual accountability). Antil *et al.* (1998) also found that a majority of teachers employ forms of cooperative learning that differed from those promoted by educational researchers and staff developers (e.g., Kagan's structures or Learning Together). Even when properly implemented, challenges occur when students work cooperatively. For example, students may misbehave, just as they do under other instructional circumstances. However, as Kagan *et al.* (2004) noted, cooperative learning doesn't create misbehavior and lack of social skills, rather, "it reveals them." Slavin's (1977) early research on students with emotional disabilities in cooperative groups showed that they were more likely to behave appropriately than students taught in a traditional format. Reviews of research indicate that cooperative learning results in increased attendance, increased on-task behavior, less disruptive behavior and greater liking of the subject matter, and greater liking of the teacher (Johnson *et al.*, 1994; Stevens *et al.*, 1991). Additional sources of difficulty with implementing cooperative learning may relate to problems associated with setting group objectives, students' lack of experience with cooperative learning, cultural differences, and problems with the task itself. Practical solutions for some of the most common problems associated with cooperative group processes are discussed in the literature (see *Assessment and Problem Solving in Cooperative Learning*, Putnam, 1997; Tiberius, 1990).

Teaching in a cooperative classroom is an adventure in finding solutions to the problems that inevitably arise. Perseverance and creative thinking are required to analyze both the causes of problems and to generate possible solutions. A study on "Cooperative Learning in Dutch Primary Schools" addressed some of the problems teachers face in implementing cooperative activities. Veenman *et al.* (2000) found that teachers reported problems with effective monitoring of the groups as they work. Monitoring includes providing clear instructions, reviewing procedures and strategies for task completion, and teaching cooperative skills.

Although the teachers interviewed indicated that they felt reasonably prepared to implement cooperative learning, one-third of them reported receiving little support. Support for teachers to gain expertise can involve collegial support groups, peer coaching, and ongoing staff development programs.

Teachers also express more general concerns about including students with disabilities in their classrooms. A meta-analysis of research on teacher perceptions of inclusion by Scruggs and Mastropieri (1996) included twenty-eight studies from 1958 to 1995. The researchers found that about two-thirds of the general education teachers surveyed supported the concept of inclusion, but they expressed concerns related to having sufficient time, skills, training, material, or personnel resources required to be successful.

Conclusion

Cooperative learning, when properly implemented, is an essential approach for the inclusive classroom. It is, of course, not a panacea for addressing all the needs of special students, but when used in combination with other well validated instructional interventions such as peer tutoring, multiple intelligence instruction, strategy instruction, and differentiated learning, it promises positive effects on academic achievement, social skill development, and peer acceptance. Researchers Slavin and Madden (1994) reported that their comprehensive reading programs, such as *Cooperative Integrated Reading and Composition,* are successful because they combine cooperative learning with other instructional elements to increase the achievement of all students in a heterogeneous class. Their studies "demonstrate that cooperative learning can be used as the primary instructional method in reading, writing, and mathematics, not just as an additional strategy to add to teachers' repertoires" (Slavin and Madden, 1994, p. 31).

Cooperative group learning is highly compatible with other special services, such as individualized instruction, reading tutorials (e.g., the *Reading Recovery* program), or direct/explicit instruction. However, educators must be cautious not to equate direct instruction or a reading tutorial with a need for segregated classrooms. The past assumption that the delivery of special services must occur primarily in a segregated setting is no longer considered to be valid. Nor is it wise to insist that children must spend every minute of the school day in a general class setting if this prevents them from receiving quality individualized instruction. "What's most important for the students is that they have multiple opportunities throughout their school careers to learn, work, and play with peers who are different from them, and that those differences are valued, accepted and appreciated" (King-Sears, 1997). We live in an era of globalization and cultural diversity that presents a formidable challenge for teachers who must address the needs of students with different ethnic and cultural backgrounds, students with disabilities, low-performing students, and socio-economically disadvantaged students. Cooperative group learning is an instructional approach that can greatly assist in providing opportunities to all learners in inclusive classrooms.

References

Antil, L.R., Jenkins, J.R., Wayne, S.K. and Vadasy, P.F. (1998) Cooperative learning: prevalence, conceptualizations, and the relation between research and practice. *American Educational Research Journal,* 35, 419–454.

Bandura, A. (1977) *Principles of Behavioral Modification.* New York: Holt, Rinehart, and Winston.

Bandura, A. (1986) *Social Foundations of Thought and Action.* Englewood Cliffs, NJ: Prentice Hall.

Deutsch, M. (1951) Social relations in the classroom and grading procedures. *Journal of Educational Research,* 45, 145–152.

Glasser, W. (1986) *Control Theory in the Classroom.* New York: Harper and Row.

Jenkins, J.R., Laurence, A.R, Wayne, S.K. and Vadasy, P.F. (2003) How cooperative learning works for special education and remedial students. *Exceptional Children,* 69(3), 279–292.

Johnson, D.W., and Johnson, R.T. (1989) *Cooperation and Competition: Theory and Research.* Edina, MN: Interaction Books.

Johnson, D.W., Johnson, R.T. and Holubec, E.J. (1994) *Cooperation in the Classroom* (rev. ed.). Edina, MN: Interaction Books.

Johnson, D.W., Johnson, R.T. and Scott, L. (1978) The effects of cooperative and individualized instruction on student attitudes and achievement. *Journal of Social Psychology,* 104, 207–216.

Johnson, D.W., Johnson, R.T. and Stanne, M.B. (2000) *Cooperative Learning Methods: A Meta-Analysis.* Minneapolis, MN: University of Minnesota. Available online at: http://www.co-operation.org/pages/cl-methods.html

Jones, M.G., and Carter, G.C. (1994) Verbal and nonverbal behavior of ability-grouped dyads. *Journal of Research in Science Teaching,* 31(6), 603–620.

Kagan, S. (1996) Cooperative learning. In H. Rimmerman (ed.) *Resources in Cooperative Learning.* San Juan Capistrano, CA: Kagan Cooperative Learning, pp. 1–9.

Kagan, S., Kyle, P. and Scott, S. (2004) *Win Win Discipline.* San Juan Capistrano, CA: Kagan Cooperative Learning.

King-Sears, M.E. (1997) Best academic practices for inclusive classrooms. *Focus on Exceptional Children,* 29, 1–27.

Lipsky, D. (1995) National Center on Educational Restructuring and Inclusion (NCERI). *National Study of Inclusive Education* (2nd ed.). New York, NY: National Center on Educational Restructuring and Inclusion (NCERI), City University of New York.

Lloyd, J.W., Crowley, E.W., Kohler, F.W. and Strain, P.S. (1998) Redefining the applied research agenda: cooperative learning, prereferral, teacher consultation and peer mediated interventions. *Journal of Learning Disabilities,* 21, 43–52.

McMaster, K.N. and Fuchs, D. (2002) Effects of cooperative learning on the academic achievement of students with learning disabilities: An update of Tateyama-Sniezek's review. *Learning Disabilities Research and Practice,* 17(2), 107–117.

Murray, F. (2002) Why understanding the theoretical basis of cooperative learning enhances teaching success. In J. Thousand, R. Villa and A. Nevin (eds) *Creativity and Collaborative Learning* (2nd ed.) (pp. 175–180). Baltimore, MD: Paul H. Brookes Publishing Co.

Nolet, V. and McLaughlin, M.J. (2005) *Accessing the General Curriculum: Including Students with Disabilities in Standards-based Reform*. Thousand Oaks, CA: Corwin Press, Inc.

Putnam, J.W. (ed.) (1998) *Cooperative Learning and Strategies for Inclusion*. Baltimore, MD: Paul H. Brookes Publishing Company.

Putnam, J.W. (1997) *Cooperative Learning in Diverse Classrooms*. Columbus, OH: Merrill/Prentice Hall.

Putnam, J.W. and Farnsworth-Lunt (1989) *Cooperative Learning and the Integration of Students with Disabilities*. Missoula, MT: University of Montana.

Schunk, D. (1987) Peer models and children's behavioral change. *Review of Educational Research,* 57, 149–174.

Scruggs, T.E. and Mastropieri, M.A. (1996) Teacher perceptions of mainstreaming/inclusion, 1958–1995: A research synthesis. *Exceptional Children,* 63(1), 77–84.

Slavin, R.E. (1977) A student team approach to teaching adolescents with special emotional and behavioral needs. *Psychology in the Schools,* 14(1), 77–84.

Slavin, R.E. (1990) *Cooperative Learning: Theory, Research and Practice*. Upper Saddle River, NJ: Prentice-Hall.

Slavin, R.E. (1995) *Cooperative Learning: Theory, Research and Practice* (2nd ed.). Boston, MA: Allyn and Bacon.

Slavin, R.E. and Madden, N.A. (1994) Team assisted individualization and cooperative integrated reading and composition. In S. Sharan (ed.) *Handbook of Cooperative Learning Methods*, pp. 20–33. Westport, CT: Greenwood Press.

Stevens, R., Slavin, R., and Madden, N. (1991) Cooperative integrated reading and composition (CIRC): Effective cooperative learning in reading and language arts. *Cooperative Learning,* 11(4), 16–18.

Tateyama-Sniezek, M. (1990) Cooperative learning: Does it improve the academic achievement of students with handicaps? *Exceptional Children,* 56, 426–437.

Tiberius, R.G. (1990) *Small group teaching: A trouble-shooting guide* (Monograph Series/22). Toronto: OISE Press, The Ontario Institute for Studies in Education.

Veenman, S., Kenter, B. and Post, K. (2000) Cooperative learning in Dutch primary classrooms. *Educational Studies,* (26)3, 281–302.

Vygotsky, L. (1978) *Mind in Society: The Development of Higher Psychological Processes*. Cambridge, MA: Harvard University Press.

Wabanaki Program of the American Friends Service Committee (1989) *The Wabanakis of Maine and the Maritimes*. Philadelphia, PA: American Friends Service Committee.

Chapter 8

Inclusive and effective schools

Challenges and tensions

Ingrid Lunt and Brahm Norwich

Introduction

A number of commentators have observed the potential tension between policies for greater 'effectiveness' and those for greater 'inclusiveness' in schools in the UK (e.g. Rouse and Florian 1997; Lunt and Norwich 1999; Ainscow *et al.* 2004; Dyson *et al.* 2004). These arise in part because of the radically changed political and economic contexts surrounding legislation which promotes a 'standards' agenda and the original more 'welfare-oriented' legislation which promoted 'integration', and in part because the two research traditions, 'school effectiveness' and 'inclusive schooling', have tended until recently to develop separately. There are also inherent value conflicts linked to a context which has changed over time, as suggested by Rouse and Florian: 'there has been a shift from legislation and policies based upon principles of equity, social progress and altruism, to new legislation underpinned by a market-place philosophy based on principles of academic excellence, choice and competition' (1997, p. 324). Although there has been a strong tradition, espoused particularly by Ainscow (1991), of 'effective schools for all', in general the evidence has suggested that schools which are successful in league tables and with school exam results tend not to be those which are successful with pupils with special educational needs (SEN) (Lunt and Norwich 1999). In this chapter we aim to consider some of the ideas concerning 'effective' and 'inclusive' schools and to present data from a study which aimed to look at a number of schools which appeared to have successfully combined 'effectiveness' with 'inclusiveness', at least as evaluated by pupil test scores and inclusion of numbers of pupils with special educational needs.

The problem

It has not been until relatively recently that consideration has been given to the possibility of 'effective schools for all' and what might be the implications of such a phrase. There have been suggestions that what might be 'effective' for some pupils might not be 'effective' for all pupils, and there have been conflicting views on the empirical relationship between high attainment and the inclusion of children with significant special educational needs. Despite recent government rhetoric promoting both high standards and inclusive practice, as suggested above, research and policy in these two areas have proceeded largely separately. Pupils with learning difficulties and disabilities were not the prime concern in early studies of school effects, and indeed there have been few studies of effectiveness relating to pupils with SEN (Lunt and Norwich 1999; Dyson *et al.* 2004).

A major issue arises from tensions between government policies and imperatives. On the one hand, the Education Act of 1981 appeared to promote a more 'inclusive' approach to SEN, through what at the time was called 'integration', while on the other hand legislation introduced by the Conservative government in 1988 and continued by successive Labour governments has created a more market-oriented environment for education, with the introduction of parental choice, raising academic standards, competition between schools, and league tables based on pupils' attainments in national tests and examinations. The current government has strengthened its commitment to more inclusive education through a revised Code of Practice (DfEE 2001), recent revision of the legislation (SENDA 2001), through its Green Paper *Every Child Matters* (DfES 2003) and the resulting 2004 Children Act, and through the SEN strategy document *Removing Barriers to Achievement* (DfES 2004). However, there is a further tension created by ambiguities about what is involved in inclusion.

While early distinctions in the Warnock report (DES 1978) between 'locational', 'social' and 'functional' integration have been superseded by discussions of the nature and extent of inclusion, the term itself has been defined in very different ways (e.g. Lunt and Norwich 1999, p. 32). This has led to widely differing views of what is implied by 'inclusive classrooms' or 'inclusive schools', and, linked with the government's own provisional commitment to neighbourhood schools for all at the same time as parental choice, has resulted in a very slow move towards greater inclusion of pupils with SEN in their neighbourhood school. Figures collected on behalf of the Centre for Studies in Inclusive Education (CSIE) (Swann 1985, 1988; Norwich 1997, 2002; Rustemier and Vaughan 2005) have demonstrated a very gradual reduction in the numbers of pupils in special schools, or in other segregated placements, though this has been accompanied by a rise in the numbers of pupils previously excluded and now placed in provision such as Pupil Referral Units because schools are unable to include them. Pressures on schools in relation to league tables have meant that they have been reluctant to take on pupils with SEN, unless they bring significant additional resources, for fear that these pupils will undermine their position in the league tables. On the face of it, there remains a clear tension between pressures to achieve high standards (measured usually by percentage of pupils scoring high GCSE results) and pressures to include pupils with SEN.

Studies of effective schools and inclusive schools

The 'school effectiveness' movement developed out of studies in the 1970s such as the ground-breaking study by Rutter *et al.* (1979) which showed not only that schools make a difference, but also that it might be possible to identify features of more effective schools. Over the past twenty years, it has become increasingly clear that this issue is highly complex and embodies multiple values, and that each school is unique within its own social context which includes its community, intake and the values articulated by staff and parents. It has also become clear that effectiveness depends on a range of different short and longer-term outcomes, and that it is not widely associated in the literature, and certainly not in the minds of policy-makers, with more 'process-oriented' outcomes such as meeting the needs of the wide diversity of learners.

Similarly, there have been a number of studies which have attempted to identify features of so-called 'inclusive' schools. Many of these general features turn out to be similar to those identified for 'effective' schools, for example collaborative teamwork, effective use of support staff, visionary leadership, effective parental involvement and curriculum adaptation (see Lipsky and Gartner 1996; Giangreco 1997; Clark *et al.* 1999). More recently, there has been a focus on 'value-added' measures, and an attempt to evaluate effectiveness in relation to a wider range of learners, or pupil intake.

Effective and inclusive schools

There are a small number of studies which have attempted to examine features of schools which combine 'inclusiveness' with 'effectiveness'. Rouse and Florian (1996) for example, asked key stakeholders in the USA and the UK what they considered to be essential characteristics of an effective and inclusive school. Features included clear policies, administrative leadership and long-term professional development, and such schools were considered to be 'diverse problem-solving organizations with a common mission that emphasizes learning for all students'. In a subsequent study, the same authors suggest that 'effectiveness can mediate the equity-excellence dilemma' (p. 333) and that 'if an effective school is characterized in part by a common mission, an inclusive school's common mission includes a philosophy of zero-reject' (Rouse and Florian 1997). As they suggest, 'it is necessary to develop a series of outcome indicators that could be used to demonstrate the benefits of inclusive education for all' (p. 334). The same authors (Florian and Rouse, 2001) suggest that 'it is the process of becoming inclusive that makes some schools better for all children and as a result a more popular choice for parents' (p. 410) and that the teachers in some of these schools have adopted a 'problem-solving approach' to inclusion. A similar theme is identified by Ainscow *et al.* (2004) whose Network strategy is 'based on the belief that the aim of raising attainment of all students is fundamentally served by ensuring that developments of policy and practice positively affect the learning of the most marginalized and at-risk students' (p. 129).

Many of these findings correspond with those of a major DfES sponsored study (Dyson *et al.* 2004) which found no evidence for a relationship, using national pupil-level data, between inclusion and attainment at local education authority (LEA) level. An LEA's policy in terms of the proportion of pupils educated in mainstream schools seems to have no bearing on overall levels of attainment in schools in that LEA, when other variables are taken into account. This study also found a very small, yet statistically significant relationship between the level of inclusivity in a school and the attainments of its pupils. Though a causal relationship could not be ruled out, it was concluded that there were reasons for this not to be likely. These reasons were the high variation in attainments in schools of similar levels of inclusivity and that case studies showed that higher and lower performing schools which were highly inclusive operated a similar model of provision. These case studies included sixteen highly 'inclusive' primary and secondary schools. The authors identified strategies that seemed likely to enhance the attainment of all pupils which included careful individual monitoring, flexible groupings, customizing provision to individual circumstances and strategies for raising achievement generally. The findings of this study, which included 'high attaining' inclusive schools and 'lower attaining' inclusive schools suggested that attainment was largely independent of levels of inclusivity. The researchers suggested that the commitment to inclusion meant wanting to 'do the best' for all children, and that this was reflected in the school ethos. The idea here is that somehow the process of becoming more inclusive may help schools to become more effective, though this calls into question traditional measures of effectiveness, and in particular those associated with the government's drive to raise standards.

Inclusive effective schools: DfES data

An analysis of official DfES data on secondary schools carried out by the authors (Lunt and Norwich 1999) showed that in general those schools which scored highly in relation to academic performance (one, albeit crude, measure of effectiveness) tended not to score highly on the number of pupils on roll with SEN (one, albeit crude, measure of inclusiveness); as schools became higher GCSE attainers, they tended to have lower percentages of pupils with SEN for each of three SEN indicators. In fact, the average percentage of pupils with statements tended to increase as the attainment level of the group of schools decreased, and the inverse correlation between GCSE attainment and percentage of pupils with SEN was even more pronounced when the number of pupils on stages of the Code of Practice were considered. Although these data need to be interpreted with caution, in particular since they are school-level rather than pupil-level data and they reflected two years only rather than trends over time, they provide a useful indication of some of the challenges created for schools by the potential contradictions of the current policy context.

Of the 3,151 secondary schools under consideration in this analysis, there was a small number (42) which appeared to combine 'high effectiveness', as measured by high GCSE average point scores, with 'high inclusiveness', as measured by high percentages of pupils with SEN. Of these 42 schools none was in London or other major urban conurbations, only 1 was in a new unitary LEA while 4 were in metropolitan areas. The remaining 37 were in county LEAs. These schools were almost equally dispersed in county LEAs in the east of the country (10), the northwest (10) and the southwest (8), and are likely to contain demographic features which might have contributed to their achievements as 'effective' and 'inclusive' schools.

Questionnaire survey

Questionnaires were sent to these 42 schools, focusing on (i) the school organization (deputy headteacher), (ii) the pastoral system (pastoral deputy headteacher or head of year), (iii) the SEN organization (SENCO) (see appendix). A total of 32 out of the possible 42 schools responded with returned questionnaires.

A mean of 17.2 per cent of pupils across the 32 schools were on the Code of Practice stages, with a mean of 4 per cent with Statements. This is well above the mean of 2.8 per cent for all secondary schools in 1999 and confirms the selection of these schools as having well above average proportions of pupils with Statements on roll. This high percentage of pupils with Statements is also reflected in 13 out of 32 or 41 per cent of the sample schools being additionally resourced for SEN. Of the 32 schools, 13 gave details which indicated that these schools had special units or resource centres covering the following areas of SEN: 3 for multiple learning disabilities (MLD), 2 for specific learning difficulties, 5 for hearing impairment or hearing and visual impairment, 2 for physical disabilities, 2 for language and communication difficulties and 2 for emotional and behavioural difficulties. Several schools covered more than one area of SEN, with 5 of the 13 schools providing details.

The questionnaires revealed some common features which included the fact that the majority had School Councils (94 per cent), and Parent–Teacher Associations (94 per cent). In 94 per cent of the schools (30) SEN coordination was organized by one person and this person was a member of the senior management team in 66 per cent of the schools (21). In the great majority of cases, the SENCO received between 2 and 4 additional points for taking on this responsibility. In one school a deputy head was responsible for SEN coordination.

In 59 per cent of the schools, there were subject department SEN representatives, with different patterns of links over SEN matters. In some of these schools the SEN subject representatives met termly, half-termly and even monthly at a SEN meeting or forum. In some, though not all, schools the representative was responsible for developing faculty or department SEN policies and practices. However, sometimes, it was the heads of departments who met over SEN matters which were then raised at their heads of department meetings. One school had a cross-curriculum working group with representatives across subject departments.

Although the questionnaires highlighted some general shared characteristics, there was considerable diversity across the 42 schools, and the questionnaire did not permit more detailed consideration of features and processes which might have facilitated their success in GCSE results and their inclusion of pupils with SEN. More in-depth case studies were therefore carried out in seven of the schools.

Case study schools

The case studies carried out in an opportunity sample of seven of the 42 schools were intended to explore in greater depth some of the features of these schools. The seven schools were located in county LEAs in the southwest, the Midlands and the southeast of the country. Each case study investigation was carried out by a different member of an educational psychology training course under supervision of one of the authors. A common format was adopted. This involved each researcher spending about three to four days in the school carrying out observations in lessons and around the school, interviews with the headteacher, other teachers, the SENCO, one or two parents, one or more pupils (preferably one on the SEN Register, one not), a school governor, the school's educational psychologist (EP) or support service teacher, and consideration of OFSTED reports and relevant documentation produced by the school. Four of the case studies are reported here.

The following themes were explored:

- leadership and structure of management;
- staff development;
- parents' views and role of governing body;
- resourcing;
- teachers' attitudes to effectiveness and inclusiveness;
- local context;
- 'culture' as manifested by the physical environment, communication and policies.

Case study findings

The **Abbey School** is located in a very rural county, has about 750 students on roll and has special provision for pupil with physical disabilities. The school was awarded Beacon School status and has a reputation for 'academic excellence'; its prospectus is explicit that 'the education of every child is of equal value'. There is a relatively stable staff, with a new headteacher following a predecessor who was there for 24 years.

Whitehaven School is located in a generally prosperous county with a mix of rural and some towns along the coast, has 1,509 students on roll and has a Specific Learning Difficulties Unit on site. The school has a reputation for academic excellence; its primary aim is to 'develop the school as a caring community'.

The Village School is a community school located in a large county in the southeast of the country, has 950 pupils on roll, and hosts the Hearing and Language

Impairment Centre, the Centre for Pupils with Emotional and Behavioural Difficulties and a provision for pupils with Specific Learning Difficulties.

Greenfields School is located in an affluent and rural part of a large county in the southeast, has 630 pupils, and a stable staff. The school has a reputation for being 'very academic' and for having high expectations of students and staff.

(i) Leadership and structure of management

The four schools showed 'strong leadership' with headteachers who had a 'vision' for the school, and a cohesive senior management team (SMT). **Greenfields School** was said to be 'forward looking' and the headteacher was bidding for it to become an Initial Teacher Training Centre, a 'research school' and to develop a mental health centre for the village on site. In the **Village School**, leadership seemed to be a crucial factor to the success of the school; the head had been in post for 13 years, was very approachable and had an 'open door' policy, and appeared to have built up a clear understanding of the school's aims, which were communicated to staff and emerged in interviews with staff. In this school, the deputy head was also the SENCO, a fact made explicit in the School's SEN policy: 'The provision for students with SEN is overseen by the deputy head. This gives this aspect of the school a high profile and ensures that it is recognized as a key area'. The headteacher of **Whitehaven School** had been in post for 14 years and appeared to have built up a shared vision both within the SMT and the staff as a whole. Several interviewees commented on 'the united view of SMT of how children should be treated' and a 'cohesive and transparent' SMT. Although **Abbey School** had a new headteacher at the time of the study two staff members said 'we are very fortunate here, we have strong leadership'; the SMT communicated almost daily and there was a system to ensure wider communication across the school.

(ii) Staff development

Staff in all four schools were encouraged to undertake staff development, and to set goals for development as part of their performance review. **Whitehaven**, which had IiP status, had a policy of 'peer mentoring' for new and newly qualified staff which involved peer observation, and prided itself on 'responding to the needs of the school and the individual'. Staff in **Abbey School** were encouraged and supported to develop 'a particular expertise', while the **Village School** and **Greenfields** also made a strong commitment to the development of staff. All four schools regarded 'responding to pupil needs' as a priority for staff development.

(iii) Parents

All four schools had Parent Teacher Associations and had positive relationships with parents, as observed by OFSTED reports and through interviews. The high academic reputation enjoyed by the four schools and the high expectations articulated by the schools contributed to the parental support and involvement.

(iv) Resourcing

Three of the schools had units designated for pupils with SEN, and all four had a larger than average number of students on the SEN Register and with Statements. They tended to use the additional resources to support mainstream classroom provision, for example differentiation and learning support, rather than making individual provision, although in all four schools pupils had an education plan tailored to their individual needs. Two of the schools had facilities enabling wheelchair access. All the schools had a clear and transparent policy for resourcing pupils with SEN, and teachers and parents were aware of the nature of the policy and the way that resources were allocated.

(v) Teachers' attitudes to effectiveness and inclusiveness

Teachers interviewed in the schools considered that an 'effective' school was one that enabled each individual to reach their maximum potential, and one that was working towards shared goals. In the **Abbey School**, mention was made of 'teachers cooperating'. **Whitehaven** staff talked about the importance of 'valuing every pupil for who they are', and this view seemed to permeate the school.

(vi) Local context

Staff in all four schools considered that the LEA was supportive and that there was a positive context in which to develop. However, mention was also made of the decreasing support from the LEA with increasing school management, a double-edged sword. All four schools had strong community links and functions. The **Abbey**'s catchment area was said to be 'favourable', and the school had strong links with a local special school, while **Whitehaven** school served as a crucial focus within the community, and the **Village School** maintained very strong links with its community. **Greenfields School**, which is said to be the 'hub' of the village and the community, takes pupils from four feeder primary schools with which it maintains very strong relationships. The local context for all four schools reflected strong LEA support, relatively stable communities, and strong parent support.

(vii) Culture

In the **Abbey School** a 'strong ethos' was identified by over half the adults interviewed, especially for pastoral support, its reputation for academic excellence (an outstanding school OFSTED report), and the belief that 'success breeds success'; parents and staff had high expectations of pupils, there was strong pupil involvement through the School Council, low exclusion rate, and shared values with a focus on mutual respect for all individuals. **Whitehaven** shared a reputation for academic excellence, its students were very positive about school, there was a strong sense of social and moral responsibility, and frequent mention was made of the 'good relationships'. **Greenfields School** was described as 'child centred' with the 'pastoral' as important as 'the academic'. It had a strong culture of support which underpinned a commitment to 'personal excellence' regardless of ability. This relatively small school created a community in which pupils and staff knew each other and could develop a flexible and caring ethos. A striking feature of the **Village School** was the open and constructive communication both between staff and between staff and students, with staff briefings every morning which enabled information about staff and students, of any kind, to be shared to encourage a caring community.

In all four schools SEN appeared to be a 'high status' issue, taken seriously by all staff, and enabling shared provision and shared expertise to be made across classrooms and across the school.

Discussion

The small-scale case studies confirm the findings of many of the studies which have sought to identify features of inclusive or of 'inclusive and effective' schools. These include characteristics such as 'visionary leadership', 'collaboration' and 'effective parental involvement' (Lipsky and Gartner 1996), 'collaborative teamwork', 'developing a shared framework', 'involving families', and 'effective use of support staff' (Giangreco 1997), and there is now some agreement as to general features which characterize certain schools. However, as is now well known, the challenge of developing schools involves acknowledgement of the complexity of this task, and the fact that multiple and frequently conflicting value positions are involved. Identification of features of more 'successful' schools cannot provide a recipe for developing schools which are so fundamentally dependent both on their local political and financial context, the nature of their catchment area, and the priorities driven by wider incentives created by national legislation. The imperatives of choice and competition, along with the drive to raise standards (particularly of the more able pupils) continue to sit uneasily alongside the values of equity and collaboration, and the commitment required to ensure that all pupils are enabled to fulfil their potential and to receive relevant opportunities for learning.

Since the analysis carried out by Lunt and Norwich, the recent introduction of the National Pupil Database (NPD) and the Pupil Level Annual Schools Census (PLASC) makes it possible to carry out much more sophisticated, detailed and fine-grained analysis through multilevel modeling and to gain 'value added' information concerning individual pupils and schools (Florian *et al.* 2004). This could, in theory at least, begin to identify the processes at the level of curriculum, pedagogy and school organization which are facilitating pupil progress, and contribute to an understanding of the complex interaction of school level processes and different pupil outcomes. The 2002 NPD was used in the DfES study referred to above (Dyson *et al.* 2004) to look in some detail at the relationship between inclusion and attainment at school level.

The case studies described above illustrate the complexity of the processes involved in schools being able to meet the needs of a wide range of diverse learners. We should note that the schools tended to be in counties and not in urban conurbations, and thus had a greater likelihood of a stable pupil population. This demographic finding is consistent with European-wide research which has shown that the proportion of special schools is greater in areas of greater population density, when Europe is analysed in regional rather than national terms (Meijer 2000). It could be that pupils' traveling distance to school is a factor in mainstream schools making provision for children with more significant SEN in rural areas and would be even greater for special schools. This interpretation is consistent with the historic establishment of additionally resourced mainstream schools rather than special schools in Cornwall well before the advent of strong government policies for more inclusion. This point is also connected to the finding in our survey of high attaining schools that many had such additionally resourced special provision. We should also note the importance of strong and committed leadership and of what has been described by Dyson *et al.* as an 'ecology' of inclusion. We should also note the importance of the *process* of becoming more inclusive and the strategies involved in this, rather than focusing entirely on outcomes or *products*.

Conclusions

The study described here makes some contribution to our understanding of the challenges faced by schools in being 'effective', i.e. having high attainment levels for all pupils in terms of test scores and/or value-added progress, and being 'inclusive' at the same time. It is notable that the recent Dyson *et al.* case studies do not show 'full inclusion' in the sense of 'full participation by all pupils in common classrooms and shared learning experiences' (p. 5). Nor do they deal in detail with the question of pupils who significantly disrupt the learning of other children. It could be that the tensions between raising standards and inclusion are easier to manage and resolve for those with less complex and multiple disabilities (those identified as having severe and profound and multiple learning difficulties) and those involved in severe levels of behaviour difficulties (those with severe emotional and behaviour difficulties). The research on teacher attitudes to inclusion indicates that these are two areas where attitudes to inclusion are less positive (Avramidis and Norwich 2002). It follows that there is a need for further, more detailed studies of specific areas of special educational needs and how provision is organized at school and pupil levels for these more challenging sub-groups.

What this chapter suggests is that there is more to inclusive education than setting out generic school-level strategies for SEN in general. The findings also emphasize the need for interdisciplinary approaches to the study of 'inclusive' and 'effective' schools. Approaches derived from individual and organisational psychology have made a major contribution to our understanding of SEN and schools as organisations, yet the complexity of this field demands input from other disciplines. From our original training as educational psychologists we have attempted to broaden our base for enquiry and to embrace theoretical perspectives from other social science disciplines.

References

Ainscow M. (ed) (1991) *Effective Schools for All.* London: David Fulton.

Ainscow M., Booth T. and Dyson A. (2004) Understanding and developing inclusive practices in schools: a collaborative action research network. *International Journal of Inclusive Education* 8(2), 125–139.

Avramidis E. and Norwich B. (2002) Teachers' attitudes towards integration/inclusion: a review of the literature. *European Journal of Special Needs Education* 17(2), 129–147.

Clark C., Dyson A., Millward A. and Robson S. (1999) Inclusive education and schools as organisations. *International Journal of Inclusive Education* 3(1), 37–51.

DES (1978) The Warnock Report. London: HMSO.

DES (1981) Education Act. London: HMSO.

DfES (2001) Special Educational Needs. Code of Practice. Annesley, Notts: DfES Publications.

DfES (2003) Every Child Matters – The Green Paper. Annesley, Notts: DfES Publications.

DfES (2004) Removing Barriers to Achievement. The Government's Strategy for SEN. Annesley, Notts: DfES Publications.

Dyson A. and Millward A. (2000) *Schools and Special Needs: Issues of Innovation and Inclusion.* London: Paul Chapman Publishing.

Dyson A., Farrell P., Polat F., Hutcheson G. and Gallanaugh F. (2004) *Inclusion and Pupil Achievement.* London: DfES RR578.

Farrell P. and Ainscow M. (eds) (2002) *Making Special Education Inclusive.* London: David Fulton Publishers.

Florian L. and Rouse M. (2001) Inclusive practice in English secondary schools: lessons learned. *Cambridge Journal of Education* 31(3), 399–412.

Florian L., Rouse M., Black-Hawkins K. and Jull S. (2004) What can national data sets tell us about inclusion and pupil achievement? *British Journal of Special Education* 31(3), 115–121.

Giangreco M. (1997) Key lessons learned about inclusive education: summary of the 1996 Schonell Memorial Lecture. *International Journal of Disability, Development and Education* 44(3), 193–114.

HMSO (2001) Special Educational Needs and Disability Act 2001. London: HMSO.

Lipsky D.K. and Gartner A. (1996) Inclusion, school restructuring and the remaking of American society. *Harvard Educational Review* 66(4), 762–795.

Lunt I. and Norwich B. (1999) *Can Effective Schools be Inclusive Schools?* London: Institute of Education.

Meijer, C.J.W. (2000) Funding and inclusion, in SEN Policy Options Steering Group (eds) *Developments in Additional Resource Allocation to Promote Greater Inclusion.* Tamworth: NASEN.

Norwich B. (1997) A trend towards inclusion. Statistics on special school placements and pupils with statements in ordinary schools England 1992–1996. Bristol: CSIE.

Norwich B. (2002) LEA inclusion trends in England 1997–2001. Bristol: CSIE.

Rouse M. and Florian L. (1996) Effective inclusive schools: a study in two countries. *Cambridge Journal of Education* 26(1), 71–85.

Rouse M. and Florian L. (1997) Inclusive education in the market-place. *International Journal of Inclusive Education* 1(4), 323–336.

Rustemier S. and Vaughan M. (2005) Segregation trends: LEAs in England 2002–2004. Bristol: CSIE.

Rutter M., Maughan B., Moprtimore P. and Piston J. (1979) *Fifteen Thousand Hours. Secondary Schools and their Effects on Children.* London: Open Books.

Swann W. (1985) Is the integration of children with special needs happening? An analysis of recent statistics of pupils in special schools. *Oxford Review of Education* 11(1), 3–18.

Swann W. (1988) Trends in special school placement to 1986: measuring, assessing and explaining segregation. *Oxford Review of Education* 14(2), 139–161.

Chapter 9

Inclusive psychology and social transformation

Responding to the challenges of the new South Africa

Petra Engelbrecht

Introduction

A flourishing democratic society acknowledges the rights of all previously marginalised individuals and communities as full members of society and requires the recognition of diversity as reflected in the attitudes of its citizens and the nature of its institutions (Green, 2001). The past twelve years have witnessed the establishment of a democratic society with human dignity, freedom and equality entrenched in its Constitution after decades of apartheid in South Africa. There has been enormous pressure on all South Africans to focus on the future and to rejoice in the birth of a democratic society. However, the strong thrust towards reconciliation and social transformation has, in many everyday contexts, created ambivalence about recognising the impact of the past and its legacy in still-existing attitudes and inequities (Gibson, 2002). This has impacted not only on society in general but also on education and the role of psychologists within education. South Africans still find themselves in a society where apartheid policies have left a legacy of severe disparities and where the circumstances in which the majority of families live impact negatively on their capacity to create a meaningful future for their children (Biersteker and Robinson, 2000). The result has been that although inclusive education has been promoted as the educational strategy most likely to contribute to a democratic and just society (Engelbrecht, 1999), the implementation of inclusive education still remains a challenge in most schools (Engelbrecht and Oswald, 2005). Within these complex contextual influences that have shaped, and continue to shape the transformation of society in South Africa, educational psychologists have been challenged to critically review their roles and professional identities in order to play a meaningful role within a transformed society.

In order to understand social transformation in South Africa, its impact on education and the role that educational psychologists can play in a democratic society, this chapter will first of all focus on the contextual influences on society (pre- and post-1994) before the transformation of the role of psychologists in an inclusive education system will be discussed.

Contextual influences on education and psychology pre-1994

Educational transformation in South Africa should be viewed against the broader background of the political events which took place in the country. The National Party came into power in 1948 and the central feature of the period between 1948 and 1994 is the extent to which racially entrenched attitudes and the institutionalisation of discriminatory practices led to extreme disparities in all sectors of South African society, including education and psychology. From 1948 until 1994, the only contender in the production of education policy was the state, which utilised its power vested in legal complicity unhindered by a popular constitution (Jansen, 2001). The racially segregated structure of education in South Africa, which went hand in hand with marked differences in funding for education, affecting, for example teacher qualifications, the provision of education support services and teacher/learner ratios, distinguishes the development of education from that in other countries (Du Toit, 1996; Henrard, 2003). This white–black dichotomy resulted in extreme disparities in the services rendered to the various population groups, including support services in special education. As in the case of mainstream education, special education for white children with disabilities was quantitatively and qualitatively expanded, existing special schools enlarged, new ones established and courses for the training of teachers in those schools instituted at universities and teacher training colleges (Du Toit, 1996). The ways in which the inequality of provision for children with disabilities manifested itself can be illustrated for example by the fact that 37 per cent of all special schools in 1990 were in white education departments (serving 9.6 per cent of the 1990 school-going population) while only 29.6 per cent were in African education departments (serving 79.2 per cent of the 1990 school-going population) (Donald, 1996). Related to these inequalities has been a conceptualisation of special educational needs as only present in children with intrinsic deficits or disabilities. As a result, all extrinsically generated special educational needs that for structural and systemic reasons existed in South Africa for the disadvantaged majority of its citizens, were ignored (Donald, 1996). The focus was on the individual, which resulted in highlighting personal inadequacies in individuals rather than in challenging social inadequacies in the system (Department of Education, 1997). As a direct consequence of inadequate conceptualisation, specialised education support services as provided by educational psychologists were conceptualised and operated predominantly in terms of cure rather than prevention. Training programmes of educational psychologists reflected a focus on an applications-only, value-neutral profession and educational psychologists strictly defined a narrow scope of practice for themselves. The theoretical emphasis focused on a biomedical paradigm that situated disability – as well as other special needs-related difficulties – within the individual rather than in society. Furthermore, adequate practical exposure in the wider society context was lacking and it was widely accepted that the practice of educational psychology in South Africa was dominated by white privileged psychologists and support reserved for an elite group of white clients (Pillay, 2003). Educational psychologists as professional support providers tended to view their services as indispensable to their clients, who it was believed did not have and could not develop the capacity to overcome or cope with life's challenges without professional assistance (Engelbrecht, 2001). The terrain of professional educational psychology was therefore characterised by a strong sense of ownership of skills. Inevitably such an a-contextual, deficient and individualistic approach ignored systemic factors and the influence of broader socio-economic and political factors in the provision of psychological support (Donald, 1996; Engelbrecht, 2004). Faced with experts who placed themselves in the position of the 'unknowing other' (Tomlinson and Swartz, 2002), communities in the early 1990s increasingly expressed their criticism about the validity and utility of professional knowledge and the resultant exclusionary practices towards learners who were experiencing diverse barriers to learning and development (Engelbrecht, 2001).

The overall social and educational situation in South Africa at the beginning of the 1990s was therefore characterised by severe disparities with the result that South Africans of all ages found themselves in a society struggling to meet the most fundamental needs of all its citizens. The disparity between the rich and the poor and the resultant inability of poverty-stricken families to meet the most basic needs of their children such as nutrition and shelter, the impact of politically related factors on high teacher-learner ratios and limited provision of educational psychological support services contributed to the stressors with which South African citizens had to cope (Biersteker and Robinson, 2000).

In view of apartheid's divide-and-rule policy, its legacy of group-based discrimination and the exclusion of the nonwhite population from political participation, negotiations in the early 1990s on how to achieve the constitution of a post-apartheid, democratic South African state, extensively emphasised equality, the need to redress previous disadvantages, democracy and nation building (Henrard, 2003).

The transformation of South African society since 1994

Understandably, as discussed earlier, the history of legally instituted and entrenched discrimination under apartheid influenced the development of a new Constitution. The principle of equality lies at the core of the Constitution and it subscribes to a particular vision of equality, one which is usually called 'substantive equality' in contrast with mere 'formal equality'. Substantive equality demands a contextual approach which takes into account differences in circumstances and supports the 'need to redress the imbalances of the past to achieve broad representation' (RSA, 1996a; Henrard, 2003). The Constitution of the Republic of South Africa Act of 1996 includes a Bill of Rights that entrenches the rights of all South Africans, regardless of race, gender, sexual orientation, disability, religion, culture or language, to basic education and access to educational institutions (RSA, 1996a). The final adoption of the Constitution of South Africa in 1996 therefore emphasised the new democratic government's commitment to restoring the human rights of all marginalised groups.

The potential for meaningful participation which the democratic elections of 1994 and the finalisation of the Constitution in 1996 made apparent to the majority of South Africans, introduced a new era of possibilities for an inclusive society in the process of developing social transformation. The need for parity in all sectors of society, including education, was thus a necessary imperative in a new democratic South Africa and the demand for parity was captured, as discussed earlier, in the commitment to equity and redress as cornerstone principles in the transformation of society and the commitment of the new government to bring South Africa in line with international standards of the recognition of human rights (Sayed, 2002; Waghid and Engelbrecht, 2002). Every education policy initiative since 1994 has therefore been founded on the democratic principles enshrined in the Constitution and Bill of Rights of 1996. The strategic goals of new policies are to ensure that the transformation of education will be implemented in keeping with a spirit of democracy, respect for human rights, justice, equality, freedom, nation-building and reconciliation – key precepts contained in the Preamble of the Constitution (RSA, 1996a; Waghid, 2004).

Key education policy documents and legislation such as the White Paper on Education and Training (Department of Education, 1995), the White Paper on an Integrated National Disability Strategy (Department of Education, 1997) and the South African Schools Act (RSA, 1996b) stress the principle of education as a basic human right as enshrined in the Constitution. This principle implies that all learners have the right to equal access to the widest possible educational opportunities and encapsulates the vision of an educational system that not only recognises the wide diversity of children's educational needs but also expects schools to meet these diverse needs (Waghid and Engelbrecht, 2002). The first clear indication, however, of a move towards acknowledging the complexity of educational needs and the role that social and political processes operating within education systems play in excluding children, was in the Report of the National Commission on Special Needs in Education and Training (NCSNET) and the National Committee on Education Support Services (NCESS) in 1997 (Department of Education, 1997). The report stressed the need for a paradigm shift from a focus on 'learners with special needs' within a biomedical framework to a systemic approach in identifying and addressing barriers to learning.

In 2001, the *White Paper 6: Special Needs Education, building an inclusive education and training system* was published (Department of Education, 2001). The White Paper acknowledged the failure of the education system to respond to the needs of a substantial number of children, not only those previously defined as having special needs. In response to the NCSNET/NCESS report (Department of Education, 1997), it acknowledged the existence of a broad range of learning needs which, if not effectively addressed, could contribute to continued failure to learn (Department of Education, 1997; Loebenstein, 2005).

This policy provides a framework for systemic change where strategies are orientated towards building the capacity of the system to respond to the full range of barriers to learning, including disabilities that exist among children in the country (Howell and Lazarus, 2003).

The development of an inclusive approach to education as a process of addressing and responding to the diverse needs of all learners by increasing participation in learning and reducing exclusion (Sandkull, 2005) resonated with the principles of rights and equity emphasised by policy makers and the Constitution in South Africa after 1994. The recommendations of the NCSNET/NCESS report (Department of Education, 1997) as a result, were largely phrased in the language of human rights, which differs radically from that of the biomedical model. It moved away from the dominant and persistent focus on individualising, professionalising and depoliticising disability by stating that barriers to learning and development from a systemic view can be located within the learner, the school, within the education system and within the broader social, economic and political context (Engelbrecht, 2001). This is in accordance with the principles of the Salamanca Statement and the reaffirmation of education as a fundamental human right at the World Education Forum in 2000 (Sandkull, 2005).

Inclusive education within the South African context is therefore framed within a human rights approach, transforming the human values of integration into the immediate rights of all excluded learners. Inclusive education, as defined in *White Paper 6*, is based on the ideal of freedom and equality, as described by the Constitution, and is seen as a single system of education dedicated to ensuring that all individuals are enabled to become competent citizens in a changing and diverse society (Department of Education, 1997; Engelbrecht, 2006).

Although these policies, including *White Paper 6*, can be viewed as state-of-the-art policy documents, developed to put in place the legal and regulatory conditions for the transformation of education, general consensus is that although they might be admirable in their sentiments, the policies generally lack detail and specificity in transforming actual conditions on the ground (Christie, 1999; Jansen 2001; Loebenstein, 2005). In spite of the fact that these policy-visions have a role to play in displacing the social engineering of apartheid, they are idealistic texts that have proved not to be rooted in the realities of schools, or responsive to complex contextual conditions on the ground (Christie, 1999).

Despite the commitment to transformation and inclusive education for example in *White Paper 6* (Department of Education, 2001), traditional conservative attitudes, socio-economic factors as well as an inadequate educational support system have prevented the establishment of an extended network of inclusive school communities. It has become increasingly clear that without analysing the pressures for exclusion that still exist within school communities, the ultimate vision of an inclusive society cannot be attained (Engelbrecht, 2006). The ways in which poverty, twelve years after the demise of apartheid, still shapes children's lives and how these patterns of daily life create patterns of participation in education that include late-coming, illnesses, repetition of grades and eventual drop-out are a major feature of life in poverty-stricken rural communities in South Africa (HSRC, 2005). The establishment of inclusive school communities in urban and poverty-stricken rural areas requires a shift from exclusion that is influenced by traditional conservative attitudes and practices, individualism and a focus on a biomedical model to an emphasis on belonging, alliances and mutual support within a community-based context. The role that professionals like educational psychologists can play to facilitate the process cannot be stressed enough.

Transforming the role of educational psychologists

The development of psychology in South Africa followed a path that closely parallels the discipline's international history. Dominated from the outset especially by North American intellectual and methodological trends, psychology underwent exponential growth and rapid professionalisation after the Second World War with clear distinctions developing between the various professional registration categories (e.g., clinical, counselling and educational psychology). According to Painter and Terre Blanche (2005) the major achievement of the psychology mainstream in South Africa was probably the tendency, despite psychology's expanding influence in various spheres of education, social research and intervention, to keep politics almost hidden from view. This was done by playing the politics of scientific neutrality and neutral professionalism. Specifically by adopting the biomedical model and by understanding their practice as value-free science, the majority of psychologists ignored issues of race and discrimination during the apartheid era. However, an increasing realisation developed that the myth of political neutrality must be cast aside in the face of the political and social realities in the country, in order to provide a critical voice that can highlight the disempowering aspects of psychologists' roles.

In the case of educational psychologists, their role within educational support services (as discussed earlier) was increasingly debated in the period leading up to the establishment of a democratic society. Policy proposals after 1994 advocated the reconstruction of education support services that are more contextually relevant and systemically sensitive (De Jong, 1996). The growing realisation that educational psychologists within support services cannot function in isolation, but are an integral part of the particular as well as wider social systems within which they function, eventually led to a reappraisal of the role of context in providing effective and empowering educational psychological support and interventions. Appreciating the continuous dynamic interaction between the multiple systems within which support takes place clarifies the challenges and opportunities facing educational psychologists within an inclusive society (Engelbrecht, 2001).

The theoretical framework within which educational psychologists function therefore moved away from the traditional biomedical model to an ecosystemic approach that is underpinned by contemporary systems and constructivist theoretical positions (De Jong, 1996). Ecosystemic values in the practice of educational psychology in South Africa – such as promoting sustainability, collaboration, partnership and cooperation within an inclusive democratic society – now define the basic parameters within which the practice of educational psychologists is being developed. Redefining their roles within this theoretical framework enables educational psychologists to provide their services in a broad array of contexts, including support in classrooms, school and community contexts, to facilitate change within organisations and to form collaborative partnerships within communities. However, a philosophy of inclusion where everyone is accepted and valued and diversity is viewed as a rich resource to support learning for all, is not yet shared by all professionals, and a participatory conception of democracy and an emphasis on participation of and accountability to learners and communities still needs to be developed amongst educational psychologists in general (Engelbrecht, 2001).

It is true that it takes courage to move away from the safety and comfort of an ideology based on the positivist assumption that the professional knows best, and adopt an approach that values socially constructed knowledge, combining the unique knowledge and skills of everyone who is involved in the development of an inclusive society. Educational psychologists are however in a potent position to contribute to the development of a sense of citizenship and a culture of thinking that embodies the inclusive and democratic values of equality, human rights and the appreciation of diversity as outlined in the Constitution (Engelbrecht, 2004).

Conclusion

In South Africa, as in many other internally divided countries, social transformation is not a neatly circumscribed set of events but is influenced by the country's history as well as individuals' history, identity, values and traditions. The development of an inclusive psychology within a young democracy in the process of social transformation, presents many challenges to psychologists, including educational psychologists, who have to try to find ways to deal with the emotional and intellectual ambivalence of recognising the impact of the past and its legacy in still existing inequities. In an inclusive educational context where there are few professional resources, educational psychologists have an extremely important role to play in crossing divides of race, class, culture, language and knowledge in inclusive community settings. By doing so they should be able to affirm the position and status of inclusive psychologists who have not only adapted successfully to change, but have been collaborative facilitators of considerable change and development within a transformed education system.

References

Biersteker, L., and Robinson, S. (2000) Socio-economic policies. In D. Donald, A. Dawes, and J. Louw (eds), *Addressing Childhood Adversity* (pp. 26–59). Cape Town: David Philip.

Christie, P. (1999) Inclusive education in South Africa: achieving equity and majority rights. In H. Daniels, and P. Garner (eds), *World Yearbook of Education* (pp. 150–168). London: Kogan Publishers.

Department of Education (1995) *White Paper on education and training in a democratic South Africa.* Pretoria: Government Printer.

Department of Education (1997) *Quality education for all: report of the National Commission for Special Needs in Education and Training (NCSNET) and the National Commission on Education Support Services (NCESS).* Pretoria: Government Printer.

Department of Education (2001) *Education White Paper 6. Special needs education. Building an inclusive education and training system.* Pretoria: Government Printer.

De Jong, T. (1996) The educational psychologist and school organization development. *South African Journal of Psychology,* 26(2), 114–122.

Donald, D. (1996) The issue of an alternative model: specialised education within an integrated model of education support services in South Africa. In P. Engelbrecht, S.M. Kriegler and M.I. Booysen (eds), *Perspectives on Learning Difficulties in South Africa* (pp. 71–85). Pretoria: Van Schaik Publishers.

Du Toit, L. (1996) An introduction to specialized education. In P. Engelbrecht, S.M. Kriegler and M.I. Booysens (eds), *Perspectives on Learning Difficulties* (pp. 1–14). Pretoria: Van Schaik Publishers.

Engelbrecht, P. (1999) A theoretical framework for inclusive education. In P. Engelbrecht, L. Green, S. Naicker and L. Engelbrecht (eds), *Inclusive Education in Action in South Africa* (pp. 3–12). Pretoria: Van Schaik Publishers.

Engelbrecht, P. (2001) Changing roles for education support professionals. In P. Engelbrecht and L. Green (eds), *Promoting Learner Development* (pp. 17–29). Pretoria: Van Schaik Publishers.

Engelbrecht, P. (2004) Changing roles for educational psychologists within inclusive education in South Africa. *School Psychology International,* 25(1), 20–29.

Engelbrecht, P. (2006) The implementation of inclusive education in South Africa after ten years of democracy. *European Journal of Psychology in Education,* xxi(3), 253–264.

Engelbrecht, P., and Oswald, M. (2005) Trailing the *INDEX FOR INCLUSION* in South African schools. Unpublished Research Report, UNESCO.

Gibson, K. (2002) Healing relationships between psychologists and communities: how can we tell them if they don't want to hear? In L. Swartz, K. Gibson and T. Gelman (eds), *Reflective Practice: Psychodynamic Ideas in the Community* (pp. 9–22). Pretoria: HSRC Publishers.

Green, L. (2001) Theoretical and contextual background. In P. Engelbrecht and L. Green (eds), *Promoting Learner Development: Preventing and Working with Barriers to Learning* (pp. 3–16). Pretoria: Van Schaik Publishers.

Henrard, K. (2003) Post-apartheid South Africa: transformation and reconciliation. *World Affairs,* 166(1), 37–55.

Howell, C. and Lazarus, S. (2003) Access and participation for students with disabilities in South African higher education: challenging accepted truths and recognising new possibilities. *Perspectives in Education,* 21(3), 59–74.

HSRC (2005) *Emerging Voices: A Report on Education in South African Rural Communities.* Pretoria: HSRC Publishers.

Jansen, J. (2001) The race for education policy after apartheid. In Y. Sayed and J. Jansen (eds), *Implementing Education Policies: The South African Experience* (pp. 12–24). Lansdowne: UCT Press.

Loebenstein, H. (2005) Support for learners with intellectual disabilities in the transition to secondary schools. Unpublished PhD Thesis. University of Stellenbosch.

Painter, D. and Terre Blanche, M. (2005) Critical psychology in South Africa: looking back and looking ahead. *South African Journal of Psychology,* 34(4), 520–543.

Pillay, J. (2003) Community psychology is all theory and no practice: training educational psychologists in community practice within the South African context. *South African Journal of Psychology,* 33(4), 261–268.

RSA (1996a) *Constitution of the Republic of South Africa.* Pretoria: Government Printer.

RSA (1996b) *South African Schools Act, Act 84 of 1996.* Pretoria: Government Printer.

Sandkull, O. (2005) Strengthening inclusive education by applying a rights-based approach to education programming. *Paper presented at ISEC Conference*, Glasgow.

Sayed, Y. (2002) Post-apartheid educational transformation: policy concerns and approaches. *Paper presented at AEKA Conference*, New Orleans.

Tomlinson, M. and Swartz, L. (2002) The 'good enough' community: power and knowledge in South African community psychology. In L. Swartz, K. Gibson and T. Gelman (eds), *Reflective Practice: Psychodynamic Ideas in the Community.* Pretoria: HSRC Publishers.

Waghid, Y. and Engelbrecht, P. (2002) Inclusive education, policy and hope: mapping democratic policy changes on inclusion in South Africa. *International Journal of Special Education,* 17(1), 20–25.

Waghid, Y. (2004) Compassion, citizenship and education in South Africa: an opportunity for transformation? *International Review of Education,* 50(5–7), 525–542.

Chapter 10

Can educational psychologists be inclusive?

Peter T. Farrell and Keith Venables

Introduction

Recent research has shown that educational psychologists can have a huge impact on the development of policy and practice towards the maintenance of segregated special education systems. For example a recent survey of educational and school psychology practice in ten countries (Jimerson *et al.*, 2004) indicates that educational psychologists (EPs) continue to have a key role in the assessment of children with special educational needs and in making recommendations for educational provision, with this being the most commonly performed task in eight of the countries that took part in the survey. In addition, over the past twenty years or so a number of surveys of teachers' and administrators' perceptions of the EP role in Europe and the USA indicate that, in the main, they expect them to carry out special education assessments (Ford and Migles, 1979; Evans and Wright, 1987; Dowling and Leibowitz, 1994; Kikas, 1999; DfEE, 2000; Gilman and Gabriel, 2004; Farrell *et al.*, 2005).

Despite this research there are indications that some EPs are striving to become more inclusive in their work. For example, in the UK there is a nationwide interest group known as 'EPs for Inclusion'. Its April 2000 newsletter said

> The current educational and political climate is encouraging many in the disability rights movement, students, teachers, academics, educational psychologists, policy makers and others to attempt to put together innovative projects and models of good inclusive practice. So, early in 1998 a number of [educational psychologists] ... began meeting to establish a mechanism to support educational psychologists who wished to promote inclusion.

This support group sought to find ways of exchanging information and good practice, both in relation to the day-to-day practice of EPs in the wider context of policy making and funding whilst supporting educational psychologists who wish to promote inclusion.

This contradictory role played by EPs, on the one hand supporting a segregated system and on the other supporting inclusion, is vividly illustrated by evidence from one local education authority (LEA) in England. In this LEA there were large variations in the number of recommendations made by different EPs for children to be placed in special schools for children with moderate learning difficulties (MLD) and emotional and behavioural difficulties (EBD). An analysis of referrals showed that half the EPs were responsible for referring 91 per cent of the children who attend special schools for children with EBD and MLD. There is no indication that the EPs who referred fewer children were working with those whose learning and behaviour problems were less severe. There does, however, appear to be a trend suggesting that more recently trained EPs tended to refer fewer children for special school. These figures are a stark reminder that, for pupils with special needs, EPs can make a big difference to the placement of these children and therefore they influence the extent to which such children can bene-fit from opportunities that inclusive education can bring. Some EPs in this LEA managed to maintain children with SEN in mainstream schools while others were happy to recommend that similar children should be placed in special schools.

This clearly has huge implications for parents and children and for the man-agers of educational psychology services. For, in this LEA, the service offered to children seemed to depend less on their needs and more on the views of the EPs as to which provision was most suitable for children with learning or behavioural problems. Decisions about placement were, it seems, something of a lottery and happened to depend on which EP the children saw. This says little for the integrity of EP practice and for the management and direction given by the principal edu-cational psychologist and his senior colleagues. Children, parents and teachers have a right to expect more uniformity of practice among the profession in this key area of work.

Of course the practice in this LEA might be unusual and therefore further research is needed to determine whether similar patterns exist in other LEAs and to explore the reasons why EPs in the same LEA can act in quite different ways with respect to recommending special schools for pupils with special needs.

Educational psychology and inclusion

The academic roots of the profession lie in the fact that all EPs have a degree in psychology, and there is a tendency for psychology courses to adopt a 'within per-son' model where explanations about behaviour and learning can, theoretically, be made by focusing on the individual. This 'within person' model, exemplified in psychology textbooks, has had a huge influence both on the way many people view the contribution that applied psychology can make to understanding devel-opment and learning, and on our practice as applied psychologists. In particular it has spawned an emphasis on studying individual differences in human mental functioning and in finding ways of measuring these differences, often using psy-chometric instruments. For the applied psychologists such instruments provide a vehicle for exploring the 'inner workings' of the mind and for arriving at explana-tions about the causes of problems in learning and behaviour. And, of course, IQ tests are the best known examples of such instruments being used widely by applied psychologists around the world.

In relation to the identification and placement of children who might have special needs, the use of IQ tests to categorize such children has had a profound impact on the development of segregated provision. The World Health Organization has perpetuated this way of thinking by publishing a table equating IQ scores with different degrees of 'mental retardation'. This table is well known and frequently quoted as providing definitive guidance on the relevance of IQ measurement (WHO, 1968). Hence the prominence given to the importance of an individual's IQ for determining the type of school, mainstream or special, that a child should attend has a long history.

And of course, if IQ tests serve this purpose, then there is a need to employ professionals to use them and this helps to explain the origins of the development of educational psychology as a profession. As Oakland (2000) stresses, the rise in the numbers of educational psychologists in different countries around the world closely mirrors the extent to which these countries have embraced the concept of intelligence and IQ testing as being indispensable in the identification of children with special needs and the legitimization of placing children, so identified, in special schools. As an emerging profession it was crucial to identify a task that could only be performed by someone from that profession and IQ testing provided the perfect example. Here was a task that was seen to be of value to schools, parents and doctors that emerged from academic psychology; individually administered IQ tests were published as 'closed' tests – i.e. only for use in clinical settings by appropriately trained applied psychologists. Hence IQ testing was something that no other professional could do – a truly distinctive task and one which therefore greatly contributed to the development and identity of the profession.

The importance of using the IQ tests to make recommendations for children to attend special schools has been given added strength in some countries, including the UK, the USA and in some states in Australia, where the role has been enshrined in legislation. Local authorities are required to employ EPs to select children for special schools and, without their involvement, the child might not receive the services that were thought to be needed. As Reschly (2000) points out, without these tasks being assigned to EPs, the profession would not have become so well established so quickly.

To many these IQ-based assessment tasks are rooted in the 'medical model', where problems are seen to be centred within the child, and can be explored through the psychologist testing the child and using the results to predict educational performance. This approach tends to ignore the contribution that the school or family, with the ongoing involvement of the EP, can make towards prevention and intervention for individuals, groups, families and communities; and, of course, the findings and implications of the psychometric tests results tend to be accepted without question.

Can schools pressure EPs to be less inclusive?

The discussion above suggests strongly that, in relation to the development of inclusion, psychology and educational psychologists in particular, are part of the problem. This is perhaps exacerbated when one considers the environment in which they work and the perceptions that others, in particular teachers, might have about their role. This is best illustrated by considering some of the factors that come into play when an EP responds to a request from a school to assess a child who is having difficulties in learning. This is perhaps the most common type of referral to an EP in the UK. By the nature of the referral process the teacher (and other colleagues) have focused on the child as the person with the problem. There is therefore pressure on the EP to see the child individually, in a separate room, and possibly to administer a number of tests, rather like a medical doctor. Interviews with the teacher and other staff tend to be for the sole purpose of getting more information that can help to explain the child's problem. Having completed the assessment the EP writes a report *on* the child and possibly makes recommendations for additional help or alternative provision. Throughout this process the school and its teachers may have a vested interest in arriving at explanations about the problem that are placed firmly *within* the child. And of course a low IQ score provides a perfect mechanism for doing this, for it exonerates the teachers from any responsibility that they may have for causing the learning problem. The child is 'unintelligent' and therefore it's not the teacher's fault that he or she cannot learn. Better still, perhaps, the low IQ score may result in the child being moved to another school and hence the hard-pressed class teacher will no longer have to face up to the problems of how to help him or her. Teachers, by referring the child in the first place, may expect the EP to confirm their belief that something is wrong with him or her and therefore to recommend alternative non-mainstream provision. The EP is aware of this and hence it is sometimes easier to respond to these pressures and recommend segregated provision rather than to challenge the teacher's original view.

Consider the difficulties faced by an EP who wants to promote an inclusive way of working. How does he or she respond to this referral? The first task would be to try and adopt what is sometimes referred to as a 'social model' of working. Here the emphasis is on removing barriers to learning and wellbeing where the EP is encouraged to respond to the referral by viewing the task as one of trying to understand the classroom and school context in which the child is learning. The assessment is more holistic and focuses on the demands that are placed on the child, in finding out about the teaching techniques that are used, and in appraising the alternative sources of support that might be available within the school. Furthermore, the EP arrives at a judgment about the class teacher's willingness to adapt and change their approach to teaching and their views about the child and his or her motivation to learn. Through working in this way the focus is on the teaching and learning situation. Interviews will be held with all stakeholders, including the child, but the emphasis is on gaining a better understanding of the classroom interaction and learning situation that seem to have an impact on the child's progress. This is likely to lead to recommendations being made as to how to improve the learning and teaching environment for the child within the mainstream school – indeed how to make his or her education more inclusive.

The problems faced by EPs who wish to work in this way can be significant. Perhaps the most difficult is how to deal with the implied blame for lack of progress that can emerge if this approach is adopted. The medical model is simpler in this regard: the problem is located firmly *in* the child and this is confirmed by the test results. No 'blame' for the failure is attributed to anyone else. In the 'social model' of working the situation is more complex as the child is not the only focus of the investigation. Through exploring the environmental conditions that can impact on learning, the EP may uncover poor practices in the school that may well account for the child's failure to learn and for which the teacher may be responsible. Obviously outcomes are never quite so simple and there are usually many reasons that could explain a child's failure to learn. However EPs have to be very tactful when 'confronting' teachers whose approach may need to be modified. The child was referred by the teacher because, in their opinion, there was something *wrong* with him or her. Now the EP is suggesting that the teacher is partly to 'blame' or that the school should try something different. Given the potential problems that can arise in scenarios such as these, it is perhaps not surprising that EPs may prefer to revert to a medical model of working, test the child and place him or her in a special education facility.

Are EPs themselves reluctant to become more inclusive?

So far this chapter has suggested that the academic roots of EP practice and the context within which EPs work, act as a major pressure that prevents them from adopting more inclusive ways or working. This is in spite of the wealth of literature that is critical of the role and negative impact of IQ testing (see for example Gillham, 1978; Brown and Ferrara, 1985; Yesseldyke, 1987; Howe, 1998; Lokke *et al.*, 1997; Leadbetter, 2005); of the inappropriateness of the medical model (e.g., Sheridan and Gutkin, 2000); and of the ineffectiveness of segregated provision (e.g., Crowther *et al.*, 1998; Farrell and Ainscow, 2002). In addition, despite pleas from EPs themselves to adopt a more inclusive orientation through embracing consultation models of practice, evidence from studies referred to earlier (DfEE, 2000; Curtis *et al.*, 2004; Jimerson *et al.*, 2004) indicates that EPs still spend the bulk of their time undertaking formal special education evaluations using IQ tests (see, for example, Farrell *et al.*, 1996; Rees *et al.*, 2003; Burns, 2004; Shapiro *et al.*, 2004).

It is difficult to resolve this paradox. On the one hand most recent literature on the developing role of EPs is extremely critical of IQ testing, the medical model of working and of their gate-keeping roles in special education assessments. Yet

EPs seem reluctant to change their practice. Are we as a profession partly to blame for this? For, in order to establish our credentials as a new profession, we stressed the fact that we were the *only* people who had the expertise and training to administer IQ tests and to use the findings to make recommendations for segregated education. Are EPs, who have been brought up in this tradition, reluctant to move forward and to abandon some of their traditional practices for fear that they will be losing their professional identity and distinctive role? And, furthermore, by losing their distinctive role, schools and local authorities might no longer feel the need to employ them? Hence a fear of the consequences for the future employment of EPs of breaking away from traditional roles can represent a major barrier to change. EPs may continue to work as they do to maintain their own profession, perhaps at the expense of the children and families who they are supposed to help. This is a damning critique, explored more fully by Farrell and Woods (in press) which needs to be addressed by the profession itself and by those who employ EPs.

Educational psychologists: making a difference in inclusion

Despite the arguments presented above, there are several examples of EPs working in ways that directly promote inclusive practices in schools and local authorities. At the outset it is necessary to stress the active role taken by the professional associations, both in the UK and overseas. In England, for example, the Association of Educational Psychologists (AEP), one of the professional associations that advises the government, local authorities and EPs about the development of the profession, has provided written guidance for its members on ways to foster inclusion (AEP, 1999). Similar policy guidance has been issued in the USA by the National Association of School Psychologists (NASP, 1999). This emphasizes its continuing support for the development of inclusive programmes for all children and young people.

In addition to the inclusive policy statements from the professional associations, professional and academic journals have published numerous accounts of EPs working to support inclusive practices in schools. These include, for example, papers on helping mainstream schools to support children with behaviour problems (Barrett and Randall, 2004; Young and Holdorf, 2003; Burton, 2004; Frydenburg *et al.*, 2004; Hutchings *et al.*, 2004; Maddern *et al.*, 2004). There are also accounts of how EPs can help to support pupils with learning difficulties in mainstream schools (see for example Brooks *et al.*, 2002; Dole, 2003; Medcalf *et al.*, 2004; Hodson *et al.*, 2005). Other examples include work that EPs have done to help schools develop general policies on inclusion (for example Hayes, 2002; Roffey, 2004; Hick, 2005).

One specific example from Wakefield, in which one of the authors of this chapter was involved (Venables), was the 'SLD Inclusion Project'. This attempted to enable young people of secondary school age, who in the recent past would have gone to a special school for children with severe learning difficulties, to be effectively supported within local mainstream secondary schools. Educational psychologists offered significant staff training for those secondary schools and worked to support families and the young people themselves. In addition they helped to create a climate in the local area where voluntary groups, health, social care and education groups, alongside schools, felt confident and supported in promoting inclusion. Over a period of eighteen months, twelve students were effectively supported to remain in mainstream secondary schooling.

Conclusion

In drawing this chapter to a close it is important to be mindful of recent national initiatives that have the potential to change the climate in relation to the work of educational psychologists in supporting inclusion.

The first of these initiatives concerns the new three-year doctoral training route into educational psychology, which came into effect from September 2006. It is likely that a significant proportion of educational psychologists who qualify from 2009 onwards will not have worked as teachers. Hence they may be more likely to bring a 'medical model' approach to their work as EPs, from their academic background in psychology. They will not have had the chance to change their views through gaining teaching experience in schools; this might lead them to developing non-inclusive orientations to their work. These concerns may be unfounded, and it remains to be seen how the curricula in the new three-year doctoral programmes can orientate new entrants to the profession towards more inclusive thinking and practice. Furthermore, the assumption that teaching itself helps potential EPs to begin to think inclusively may be false. In addition, all applicants to three-year programmes will have some experience of working in educational contexts with children.

Secondly, the Children Act (Her Majesty's Government, 2004) and the implementation of the Every Child Matters agenda heralds an era of integrated services which will require educational psychologists to define their 'unique contribution to the partnerships that promote the health, safety, enjoyment and achievement, positive contribution and economic well-being of children and young people (DfES, 2004). Educational psychologists will work for newly formed Children's Services in which LEAs and social services departments merge. There is a renewed emphasis on multi-agency work, a Common Assessment Framework and an implication that EPs' work will extend beyond the school (see Farrell et al., 2006). However, it is not clear that a more integrated children's workforce will necessarily empower children and young people themselves, enhance the choices of their parents or establish inclusive schooling across the board. Hence the implications for inclusion of the Every Child Matters agenda remain unclear.

Perhaps a greater 'threat' to inclusion comes from the government's response to the recent parliamentary Select Committee Report into special educational provision. In the report the government has been severely criticized for giving unclear messages about inclusion in relation to children with SEN and there is a suggestion that, perhaps, inclusion has gone too far even though recent figures indicate that the period 1997 to 2005 has not reduced the number of children and young people in separate provision (Rustemier and Vaughn, 2005). There is a general message in the Select Committee Report that perhaps the country should take stock and hold back from making further moves towards inclusion.

Finally EPs need to be mindful of the potential impact of the Education and Inspections Act (2006) in relation to the formation of Trust schools. These schools will be beyond the reach of the Local Authority, allowing them to use their admissions policies to refuse to accept the more vulnerable and challenged students. As such, the role of the educational psychologists as promoters of inclusion could also be limited.

Many educational psychologists who seek to promote inclusion argue that at the heart of their methodology is the 'social model' of disability. This entails recognizing that impairments do not necessarily exclude, it is social barriers that need to be removed. In the current changing social context, it is not inevitable that EPs will remain limited by their academic or professional origins. It is possible 'to make a difference' by recognizing that promoting inclusion could be a way to define the role of the educational psychologist in the new millennium.

Note: For more information about Educational Psychologists for Inclusion contact P.O. Box 7164, Belper, Derbyshire, DE56 9AW.

References

AEP (1999) *Increasing Inclusion: AEP Position Paper.* Durham: The Association of Educational Psychologists.

Barrett, W. and Randall, L. (2004) 'Investigating the circle of friends approach: adaptations and implications for practice', *Educational Psychology in Practice* 20(4): 353–368.

Brooks, P., Weeks, S. and Everatt, J. (2002) 'Individualisation of learning in mainstream schoolchildren', *Educational and Child Psychology* 19(4): 63–74.

Brown, A.L. and Ferrara, R.A. (1985) Diagnosing Zones of Proximal Development, in J.V. Weitsch (ed.) *Culture Communication and Cognition: Vygotskian Perspectives.* Cambridge: Cambridge University Press.

Burns, M.K. (2004) 'Using curriculum-based assessment in consultation: a review of three levels of research', *Journal of Educational and Psychological Consultation* 15: 63–78.

Burton, S. (2004) 'Self-esteem groups for secondary pupils with dyslexia', *Educational Psychology in Practice* 20(1): 55–73.

Crowther, D., Dyson, A. and Millward, A. (1998) *Costs and Outcomes for Pupils with Moderate Learning Difficulties in Special and Mainstream Schools* (RR89, DfEE). London: HMSO.

Curtis, M.J., Chesno-Grier, J.E. and Hunley, S.A. (2004) 'The changing face of school psychology: trends in data and projections for the future', *School Psychology Review* 33: 49–67.

DfEE (2000) *Educational psychology services (England): Current role, good practice, and future directions – The research report (DfEE 0133/2000)*. Nottingham, England: Department for Education and Employment.

DfES (2004) *Every Child Matters: Change for Children*. London: HMSO.

Dole, S. (2003) 'Applying psychological theory to helping students overcome learned difficulties in mathematics: an alternative approach to intervention', *School Psychology International* 24(1): 95–114.

Dowling, J. and Leibowitz, D. (1994) 'Evaluation of educational psychology services: past and present', *Educational Psychology in Practice* 9: 241–250.

Evans, M.E. and Wright, A.K. (1987) 'The Surrey school psychological service: an evaluation through teacher perceptions', *Educational Psychology in Practice* 3: 12–20.

Farrell, P. and Ainscow, A. (eds) (2002) *Making Special Education Inclusive*. London: David Fulton.

Farrell, P., Harraghy, J. and Petrie, B. (1996) 'The statutory assessment of children with emotional and behavioural difficulties', *Educational Psychology in Practice* 12(2): 80–85.

Farrell P., Jimerson, S., Kalambouka, A. and Benoit, J. (2005) 'Teachers' perceptions of school psychologists in different countries', *School Psychology International* 26(5): 525–544.

Farrell, P., Woods, K., Lewis, S., Rooney, S., Squires, G. and O'Connor, M. (2006) *A Review of the Functions and Contribution of Educational Psychologists in England and Wales in light of 'Every Child Matters: Change for Children'*. London: HMSO.

Farrell, P. and Woods, K. (in press) 'Consultation and the role of the school psychologist: barriers and opportunities', *Journal of Educational and Psychological Consultation*.

Ford, J.D. and Migles, M. (1979) 'The role of the school psychologist: teachers' preferences as a function of personal professional characteristics', *Journal of School Psychology* 17: 372–378.

Frydenburg, E., Lewis, R., Bugalski, K., Cotta, A., McCarthy, C., Luscombe-Smith, N. and Poole, C. (2004) 'Prevention is better than cure: coping skills training for adolescents at school', *Educational Psychology in Practice* 20(2): 117–134.

Gillham, W. (ed.) (1978) *Reconstructing Educational Psychology*. London: Virago.

Gilman, R. and Gabriel, S. (2004) 'Perceptions of school psychological services by education professionals: results from a multi-state survey pilot study', *School Psychology Review* 33: 271–287.

Hayes, B. (2002) 'Community, cohesion inclusive education', *Educational and Child Psychology* 19(4): 75–90.

Her Majesty's Government (2004) The Children Act. London: Her Majesty's Stationery Office.

Hick, P. (2005) 'Supporting the development of more inclusive practices using the index for inclusion', *Educational Psychology in Practice* 21(2): 117–122.

Hodson, P., Baddeley, A., Laycock, S. and Williams, S. (2005) 'Helping secondary schools to be more inclusive of year 7 pupils with SEN', *Educational Psychology in Practice* 21(1): 53–67.

Howe, M. (1998) *IQ in Question: The Truth About Intelligence*. London: Sage.

Hutchings, J., Lane, E., Ellis Owen, R. and Gwyn, R. (2004) 'The introduction of the Webster-Stratton incredible years classroom dinosaur school programme in Gwynedd, North Wales: a pilot study', *Educational and Child Psychology* 21(4): 4–15.

Jimerson, S.R., Graydon, K., Farrell, P., Kikas, E., Hatzichristou, S., Boce, E. and Bashi, G. (2004) 'The international school psychology survey: development and data', *School Psychology International* 25: 259–286.

Kikas, E. (1999) 'School psychology in Estonia: expectations of teachers and school psychologists', *School Psychology International* 20: 352–365.

Leadbetter, J. (2005) 'Activity theory as a conceptual framework and analytical tool within the practice of educational psychology', *Educational and Child Psychology* 22(1): 18–28.

Lokke, C., Gersch, I., M'Gadzah, H. and Frederickson, N. (1997) 'The resurrection of psychometrics: fact or fiction?', *Educational Psychology in Practice* 12(4): 222–233.

Maddern, L., Franey, J., McLaughlin, V. and Cox, S. (2004) 'An evaluation of the impact of an inter-agency intervention programme to promote social skills in primary school children', *Educational Psychology in Practice* 20(2): 135–155.

Medcalf, J., Glynn, T. and Moore, D. (2004) 'Peer tutoring in writing: a school systems approach', *Educational Psychology in Practice* 20(2): 157–178.

NASP (1999) *The Role of the School Psychologist in Inclusive Education.* Available online at: http://www.naSPweb.org/information/misc/inclusion.htm, accessed 22 November 2007.

Oakland, T. (2000) International School Psychology. In Fagan, T.K. and Wise, P.S. (eds), *School Psychology: Past, Present and Future.* National Association of School Psychologists.

Rees, C., Rees, P. and Farrell, P. (2003) 'Methods used by psychologists to assess pupils with emotional and behavioural difficulties', *Educational Psychology in Practice* 19: 203–214.

Reschly, D.J. (2000) 'The present and future status of school psychology in the United States', *School Psychology Review* 29: 507–522.

Roffey, S. (2004) 'The home-school interface for behaviour: a conceptual framework for co-constructing reality', *Educational and Child Psychology* 21(4): 95–108.

Rustemier, S. and Vaughan, M. (2005) *Segregation Trends – LEAs in England 2002–2004.* Bristol: Centre for Studies on Inclusive Education.

Shapiro, E.S., Angello, L.M. and Eckert, T.L. (2004) 'Has curriculum based assessment become the staple of school psychology practice? An update and extension of knowledge, use and attitudes from 1990–2000', *School Psychology Review* 33: 249–258.

Sheridan, S.M. and Gutkin, T.B. (2000) 'The ecology of school psychology: examining and changing our paradigm for the 21st century', *School Psychology Review* 29: 485–502.

WHO (1968) *Organization of Services for the Mentally Retarded, Fifteenth Report of the WHO Expert Committee on Mental Health, WHO Technical Report,* Serial 392. Geneva: World Health Organization.

Yessledyke, J.E. (1987) 'Do tests help in teaching?' *Journal of the Association of Child Psychology and Psychiatry* 28(1): 21–25.

Young, S. and Holdorf, G. (2003) 'Using solution focused brief therapy in individual referrals for bullying', *Educational Psychology in Practice* 19(4): 271–282.

Chapter 11

Dynamic assessment for inclusive learning

Phil Stringer

Introduction

In the early summer of 2005, the news media reconfirmed reports that Baroness Warnock, whose committee of inquiry (Warnock Committee, 1978) set a course for special needs education in Britain from the 1980s to the present, had had a change of heart about inclusion. Her argument is set out in Warnock (2005). I am not going to summarise it but I am going to draw upon one significant aspect of it and its relevance for this chapter, since she appears to have been much influenced by Dyson's (2001) observations about learners. Essentially what Dyson argued is that a British response to including pupils in mainstream schools has had to cope with a 'dilemma of difference'. This dilemma is formed from the contradictory forces of wanting to treat all learners as essentially the same and recognition that, in fact, there are important individual differences between learners which require tailored approaches. Warnock's (2005) view is that the time has come to recognise that including all children in mainstream fails some learners since their needs are so different from the 'mainstream' that although they might be included in name, they are disadvantaged and effectively excluded in practice.

Clearly, Warnock's (2005) position is a challenge to the now orthodox understanding of inclusion, put most simply as an opposition to educational segregation (for example, Ware, 1995; British Psychological Society, 2002). Yet what Warnock and Dyson (2001) are highlighting is a problematic issue at the heart of inclusion that cannot be resolved by appeals to social justice and human rights alone. They remind us that amidst the ideology and rhetoric, accepting the influence of environmental factors, there are individual children with individual differences. As an applied educational psychologist (EP) working in a local authority in England, my work is defined by an interest in how individuals learn and develop. Given the role of parents and carers in assisting a child to learn, along with educators in a more formal sense, my understanding of inclusion has been orientated towards participation and inclusion in learning communities rather than specific educational sites. In other words, my understanding recognises that at some fundamental ethical level it matters less where a child is being educated. It matters most that a child is learning and developing; that a child is being provided with an appropriate cognitive challenge and receiving the support to meet and go beyond that challenge.

The way in which I define inclusion, then, has been shaped by an imperative to comprehend individual differences in learning, reduce the obstacles to learning that confront many individuals, and consider how best to promote the learning of all children, not just those who are seen to be having difficulties in learning. In this respect, then, my definition of inclusion is a practical, working definition. Certainly it is a definition based on ideals, values and principles concerning human rights. At the same time it is a definition that, ethically, relates to specific children and young people and to their specific situations, not to idealised circumstances. I have found such a definition necessary to reconcile my values and beliefs about inclusion with the tension of working within political and social infrastructures and structures that are still 'constructing inclusion' (Thomas and Loxley, 2001). In 'constructing inclusion' I have seen promoting effective, independent problem solving and learning as being the most powerful resource in this process of construction.

The field of psychology that has most influenced my work draws from Vygotsky and neo-Vygotskian psychologists (Stringer, 1998), and I will elaborate this below. Many of the accounts of inclusion that I have read make little appeal to psychology theory. It seems as if it has been easier to identify psychology theory to react against and practice to critique, including that of EPs (for example, see Thomas and Loxley, 2001; and readings from Leyden; Weatherley and Lipsky; and Swann, in Thomas and Vaughan, 2003), without identifying psychology theory that would support inclusion. Having said that, I recognise Vygotskian constructs in the Index for Inclusion (Booth and Ainscow, 2002), although there is no explicit appeal to psychology theory in the Index.

Criticism of EP practice has frequently concerned the use of psychometric tests of intelligence or ability. I have never found traditional psychometric tests of much use in answering the questions that I am asked about a learner and the questions that I think are most useful to answer. In the main such tests are based upon theories and assumptions about learning and intelligence that I do not accept. They were the theories and assumptions that Vygotsky reacted against in his formulation of learning and development, including a reaction against intelligence testing (Vygotsky, 1978). Following Vygotsky and others, notably Feuerstein and his colleagues (Feuerstein *et al.*, 2002) I believe that there is a much more effective way of assessing learning than the use of psychometric measures. The remainder of this chapter will outline my use of dynamic assessment (DA). My argument is that EPs can make a significant contribution to understanding and promoting inclusive learning through DA.

Dynamic assessment: a preliminary description

Using the term 'dynamic assessment' is misleading since it is much more than an assessment tool. In the approaches that have influenced my practice and that of other educational psychologists in Britain, it combines assessment *and* intervention in asking a series of questions about how learners learn. In particular, the purposes of the approach are to ask: what are a child's cognitive skills; what are a child's metacognitive skills; what affective and motivational factors influence that child's learning (Tzuriel *et al.*, 1988); how does that child respond to intervention in the form of mediation; and what, then, are the implications for assisting that child to become a more effective and efficient learner? Through mediation, children and young people are involved, as active learners, and in this respect can be empowered by the process, along with all those who share in a responsibility for their learning. Unlike traditional 'static' tests that simply test what has been learnt, DA invites a child on an interactive journey, the purpose of which is to assist the child in realising what it means to be an active learner through the very process of actively learning. Whilst there are specific tests that have been developed for use in DA, later I will suggest that what matters most is the theoretical model out of which the DA instruments have grown. It is this model that enables the above questions to be addressed with confidence, using a range of materials and strategies that might not necessarily have been specifically designed as DA tests. Before elaborating this model, I want to outline two case examples.

Israar

Israar, eight years old, had been withdrawn by his parents from a local authority special school for children with complex learning difficulties, where he had been placed in a group of children with profound and multiple learning difficulties. In their view he was 'depressed', because he was wrongly placed. He had cerebral palsy, which had affected all his limbs and also his ability to produce speech sounds. His difficulties in controlling his limbs meant that any physical activity was a considerable effort and, for example, being able to point with his eyes or fingers was unreliable. Previous educational psychologist involvement had led to a conclusion that he was 'impossible to assess', because of his difficulties in accessing any form of test materials that were used. He had been attending an independent special school for children with physical disabilities but staff there considered that they were not meeting his needs and eventually he transferred to the special school for children with complex learning difficulties. His parents had misgivings about this transfer, continuing to believe that he was a relatively able boy.

Educational psychologist involvement was requested by the local authority in an attempt to resolve what had become a dispute about Israar's school placement. The request had gone to a colleague of mine. Knowing my commitment to DA, she asked whether I would be willing to work with her in attempting to assess Israar's ability. Our first visit confirmed the extent of his physical and communication difficulties and the efforts his parents were willing to make to promote his learning. It also confirmed that if we were to complete any meaningful assessment, we would have to do it over time, in relatively short sessions and to use his mother as part of the assessment process to ensure that Israar could be positioned as optimally as possible. We would also have to plan carefully what we did and how we did it, to ensure that we were assessing Israar's ability to problem solve and learn and not his ability to access a test.

Over a period of some seventeen weekly sessions, using an adapted form of two of Tzuriel's tests and the principles of mediated learning (see below), we were able to demonstrate beyond doubt that Israar had developed most of the essential cognitive skills required for learning, and that he could quickly learn how to solve novel problems involving reasoning. I argued that he could be placed in a mainstream school providing he had individual support that could draw upon an understanding of learning processes and of mediation. His parents were reluctant to take this step, opting for placement in a local authority special school for children with physical difficulties. An individual support assistant was provided, and I introduced her and Israar's teacher to mediated learning.

Ellen

Ellen was twelve years old and had been at her mainstream secondary school for nearly two terms. Tina, the school's special educational needs coordinator, described her to me as having 'no memory', as not achieving, and as completely disorganised, probably 'dyspraxic'. I was told that her life at home was fraught on account of the 'messy break-up of her parents', which had happened about eighteen months previously. There were lots of 'battles' over Ellen generally fitting in with household routines, getting ready for school, doing homework and so on.

Following an initial meeting in school with Ellen, she agreed that I could invite her mother and Tina to our next meeting. I had decided to base the session on using the Complex Figure Drawing, one of the tests from the Learning Potential Assessment Device (Feuerstein et al., 1985). I find this test particularly useful for exploring those cognitive skills associated with perceptual organisation and memory and since it is a complex figure, also exploring affective and motivational factors, such as a willingness to respond to a challenge and to accept mediation. During the session I asked both Ellen's mother and Tina to do the task, something that Ellen found intriguing. Over the course of the test Ellen's performance improved dramatically.

In rehearsing what had made the difference it was evident that Ellen was able to reflect on the cognitive skills that she had used and then, quite spontaneously, she made a connection with the need to plan and sequence a whole range of activities, including getting ready for school. As I talked with Ellen about how she might more actively use the skills in school, Tina commented that she could see that there were a number of pupils that would benefit from similarly using these skills. As it happened, she taught Ellen in a maths group and suggested establishing a 'reminding myself to be an effective learner' project with the group. I followed-up Ellen for some time (until she moved from the area). Her work in school had improved and although some aspects of her home life continued to be fraught, I was interested by the extent to which the Complex Figure had become a metaphor for her. She told me that whenever things seemed to be 'getting too much' she would think about the Complex Figure and how it is possible to make sense of something that seems bewildering.

For me, both of these case examples represent different facets of including children in an appropriate learning community, and in Ellen's case, that extends to becoming better included at home. I will now elaborate my understanding and use of DA.

The roots of dynamic assessment: The psychology of learning and development

As noted above, the dynamic assessment that I use in my practice is rooted in the work of Vygotsky (for example: 1978, 1986) and the many writers that have interpreted and extended Vygotsky's ideas (for example: Kozulin, 1990, 1998; Daniels, 1993, 1996; Wertsch *et al.*, 1995), the work of Feuerstein (for example, Feuerstein *et al.*, 2002), those that have drawn upon Feuerstein's ideas and practice and, accepting the overlap, writers that have drawn together research on cognitive development (for example, Meadows, 1993; Olson and Torrance, 1996; Ashman and Conway, 1997).

Unlike Piaget (see Vygotsky, 1986), Vygotsky paid much greater attention to the social and cultural context of learning. He saw the development of 'higher mental functions' as occurring through a series of transformations that begin with the child's social interactions but which then become internalised (Vygotsky, 1978). Vygotsky (1978) was critical of how Piaget (and of Binet, for that matter, the inventor of 'the modern intelligence test', Block and Dworkin, 1977, p. 417) viewed the relationship between learning and development. Rather than the Piagetian proposition that development is a prerequisite for learning, Vygotsky viewed learning as leading to development, indeed, that the only 'good learning' is that which is in advance of development (p. 89) This difference cannot be sufficiently emphasised, not least since the Piagetian view is the one that has tended to dominate most approaches to education and assessment in the Western world. This has led to the belief that if a child has not sufficiently developed then that child will not learn, hence such notions as 'readiness' to learn (see Watson, 1996) and the possibility that intelligence tests can measure something relatively unchanging.

Vygotsky (1978, p. 90) suggested a:

> general developmental law for the higher mental functions that … can be applied in its entirety to children's learning processes. We propose that an essential feature of learning is that it creates the zone of proximal development; that is, learning awakens a variety of internal developmental processes that are able to operate only when the child is interacting with people in his or her environment and in cooperation with his or her peers … properly organised learning results in mental development and sets in motion a variety of developmental processes that would be impossible apart from learning.

As Vygotsky (1978) describes it, the zone of proximal development (ZPD) represents the difference between what a child can do unaided and what a child can with the help of a more competent other, such as an adult. The ZPD embraces cognitive functions that are emerging, 'the "buds" or "flowers" of development rather than the "fruits" of development' (p. 86). In describing the ZPD, therefore, Vygotsky makes a distinction between a child's current level of functioning and a level of functioning that they have the potential to reach. There are obvious implications for the assessment of learning and ability, which have found form in DA and, in particular, in the way in which mediation takes place.

Although Vygotsky referred to mediation (see Cole and Scribner, 1987), Feuerstein has significantly developed the concept. There are strong connections between Vygotsky and Feuerstein, as Lidz (1995), Feuerstein et al. (2002), and Sternberg and Grigorenko (2002) acknowledge. In terms of my practice and that of other educational psychologists in Britain, Feuerstein and his colleagues have been of central importance (see Elliott, Lauchlan and Stringer, 1997; Stringer, Elliott and Lauchlan, 1997), not least because their approach to learning and assessment is fundamentally inclusive. For example, it does not discriminate against children on the basis of failing to know something (that might be strongly culturally determined) asked by a test. It does not see difficulties in learning (or failing to know something) as an inherent difficulty of a child. Their approach invites us to consider how we might intervene to create the conditions that enable effective learning to take place and, in this sense, to view learning as a shared, community activity. As Sternberg and Grigorenko (2002, p. 70) write:

> The field of dynamic testing is indebted to Feuerstein for his pioneering and path-making efforts. He placed his work in a comprehensive psychological and philosophical framework; he articulated the societal need for alternative approaches to testing. He initiated practical movement away from conventional testing; and he created an elaborate theory and a corresponding methodology.

There are three key elements in Vygotsky's (1978, 1986) work that Feuerstein has taken forward. First, the dynamic nature of intelligence; second, the concept of mediation; and third, the use of interactive methods to understand the process of learning or, in effect, intelligence formation. The framework to which Sternberg and Grigorenko (2002) refer embraces these three elements in the form of structural cognitive modifiability, mediated learning experience, and a method, the cognitive map for analysing the demands of a task (Feuerstein et al., 2002). In understanding DA, it is necessary to understand these elements and how they interact. As I see it, the 'dynamic' in dynamic assessment refers to two things: a dynamic view of learning and intelligence, and the dynamic way in which an assessment is conducted. Structural cognitive modifiability represents this dynamic view of learning and intelligence. In many respects it echoes Vygotsky's view of the formation of intelligence and the zone of proximal development (Feuerstein et al., 2002 point to some differences), in signifying that through learning there are changes in neurological structures as well as in observed performance, and that humans are capable of learning from experience across a life span.

As Feuerstein *et al.* (2002, p. 62) note:

> We define intelligence as a changing state of the organism, in constant condition of change, best reflected in the propensity of the individual to use previously acquired experience to adapt to new situations. The two factors stressed in this definition are the capacity of the individual to be modified by learning and the ability of the individual to use whatever modification has occurred for future adjustments. Whilst we hold with Wesman that intelligence will be reflected in learning experiences, we add that for certain individuals, learning how to learn – that is modifying the cognitive structure responsible for the individual's mode of learning – must first be induced. In fact, the meaningfulness and pervasiveness of this modification are in themselves a reflection of intelligence.

References in that quote to 'modification', 'learning how to learn' and 'induced', are allusions to mediated learning experience (MLE), and to the dynamic way in which both learning takes place and to how an assessment is carried out. As noted above, Feuerstein extends the concept of mediation well beyond Vygotsky's references. For Feuerstein *et al.* (2002), MLE in a general way provides an account of individual differences between learners; an absence of appropriate MLE, for whatever reason, is the primary reason for observing, say, a delay in learning, rather than, say, some kind of disability or syndrome. The disability or syndrome might affect the way in which an individual can access MLE so, in this sense, it is a secondary factor in the learning delay. Further, in the way in which MLE creates 'learning how to learn', the individual that has benefited from MLE is more able to learn and problem solve independently. More specifically, Feuerstein *et al.*, have identified a set of criteria, which constitute MLE, ranging from ensuring the generalisation of a cognitive skill to promoting self-awareness of the ability to change behaviour. Thus, at one level, the theory of MLE, describes the nature of the interaction between humans (for example, child–parent, child–teacher, younger child–older child) that promotes learning and development. At another level, it provides the dynamic or interactional structure to guide and support how an assessor works with the person being assessed.

The final, essential strand of Feuerstein *et al.*'s (2002) framework is the cognitive map. This comprises a series of dimensions that are used to analyse any learning task. The series of tests that form the Learning Propensity Assessment Device (originally the Learning *Potential* Assessment Device, LPAD, Feuerstein *et al.*, 1985) are all analysed in this way. A critical aspect of the cognitive map is a list of cognitive functions that Feuerstein *et al.* see as necessary for all learning, and as holding across all cultures. Different cultures may emphasise different skills, which is one reason why differential performance in learning can be observed between individuals with different cultural experiences. These functions are the cognitive skills that are required to attend to the important features of a problem and to ignore the non-essential features, to be able to compare stimuli, to draw upon the vocabulary that will assist in solving a problem, and so on. These cognitive functions, then, cluster to enable a particular 'mental operation', such as analogical reasoning. Feuerstein *et al.* emphasise the point that even if we do not observe a cognitive function, we should not infer its absence. Rather, as a mediator, we might not have helped the learner realise the need to use that function or we might have discouraged its use because of the way in which we presented the task.

Psychometric assessment and dynamic assessment

So far, I have not contrasted traditional psychometric approaches, such as the Wechsler Intelligence Scale (WISC) or the British Ability Scales (BAS), with dynamic assessment. I do not think that it is necessary to labour the point (for a critique of the conventional view of intelligence and of psychometric tests see, for example, Block and Dworkin, 1977; Stanovich and Stanovich, 1996; Sternberg and Grigorenko, 2002; and, of course, Feuerstein *et al.*, 2002). What I have outlined is that Vygotsky and Feuerstein's perspective on learning and development is quite different from a perspective that views intelligence as unchanging and potential as fixed. What matters most for Vygotsky and Feuerstein is the process of learning not simply the product. Very rarely in my work as an EP have I been asked how much a particular child knows. Even if that is the way that a question has been posed, almost always, what the questioner wants to know is, how does this child learn and how can we help that child to be a more effective and efficient learner. These are questions best answered by DA.

By their very nature, traditional psychometric tests can only answer one question: how much does one particular child know compared to a usually relatively small number of children of the same age. By their very nature, the sampling techniques of psychometric tests exclude the majority of children that educational psychologists are asked to see. Further, if we consider the cognitive map, in many cases we cannot know for sure whether there was some facet of the test itself that caused failure. For some children this can lead to unintentionally serious consequences, as was the case for Israar. The use of a dynamic assessment approach means that there is always something to say about how a child learns, the nature of the mediation that helps them, and how they benefit from that mediation.

Approaches to dynamic assessment

Lidz (1997) has described two broad traditions in DA: approaches that are aimed at improving the psychometric qualities of an interactive test, and approaches that focus on learning processes. The development of the former has partly been driven by attempts to overcome the criticisms that have been made of the LPAD and other tests developed for 'clinical' use, that is, that they lack reliability and validity and rely too much upon assessor judgement. As Lidz (1992) points out, in effect, the questions that practitioners based, say, in educational psychology services want to ask about learning are somewhat different from the questions that researchers based in universities want to ask. Lidz suggests that attempts to meet psychometric criteria risk sacrificing the qualities of a test to provide an understanding of learner processes. As an applied psychologist, my experience leads me to agree. Whilst I can understand the value of wanting to develop interactive tests that meet criteria for validity and reliability (the case is well made, for example, in the chapters by Guthke and Beckman; Hessels; and Swanson, in Lidz and Elliott, 2000; and by Sternberg and Grigorenko, 2002), in my experience such tests do not take me much further in understanding why a child is not learning and, critically, what action might be taken to assist that child.

Largely for this reason, amongst EPs in Britain, Feuerstein *et al.*'s (2002) approach has had the greatest influence and, in particular, the way in which that approach has been drawn upon and extended by Lidz (for example, Lidz, 1991, 2000; Waters and Stringer, 1997) and Tzuriel (for example, Tzuriel, 1997, 2000, 2001). Both Lidz and Tzuriel have developed their own tests, largely for young children, from about three years of age through to about seven, although Tzuriel's more extensive range of tests can be used with much older children who are finding learning difficult. Their 'clinical' as opposed to 'experimental' approach seems more appropriate to providing an understanding of how children learn in a way that informs intervention, although Tzuriel's tests have been carefully designed to include both a clinical and experimental version. Lidz and Elliott (2000) provide a comprehensive overview of the variety of DA approaches available; their edited volume stands as the most comprehensive account of the DA field currently available.

Given the advantages of using DA and, in particular the possibilities offered for promoting inclusion, it remains that such an approach is not widespread in EP practice. Elliott (1993, 2000) and Stringer *et al.* (1997) have provided complementary accounts about why this is so. There is no doubt that the special educational needs procedures in some local authorities that rely upon the supply of psychometric data (often in the form of centiles) to allocate resources make it difficult for EPs to adopt DA. Personally, this perplexes me since, arguably, it represents a lack of belief in the criticisms of psychometric measures and an accompanying lack of confidence to throw away the security blanket provided by a psychometric test. In this respect it also represents a failure of imagination and an inability to assert a different purpose for an applied psychologist in a local authority. (On this, see also Stringer *et al.*, 2006). Access to training and test materials are also often cited as being significant reasons for the limited influence of DA. Here Lewin (1952, p. 169) is relevant, when he urged applied psychologists to realise 'that there is nothing so practical as a good theory'; Vygotsky's work and Feuerstein's 'comprehensive psychological and philosophical framework' fulfils this, as Lidz and Tzuriel and others have grasped. The fact that the LPAD tests, and those of Lidz and Tzuriel are domain free (that is, there is no obvious pre-school or school curricula content) points the way to an approach to assessment that does not necessarily require tests that have been developed specifically for DA nor any tests at all. Sometimes I find it sufficient to talk with a child about how he or she thinks that they learn, and I am no longer surprised by the insights that most children have when they are asked.

Dynamic assessment for inclusive learning

In this chapter I have interpreted inclusion in terms of learning, and the process of inclusion as being concerned with how learners can be more effectively included in learning communities. I have argued that educational psychologists can make a significant contribution to this definition of inclusion through the use of dynamic assessment. Dynamic assessment is a strategy for assessment and intervention firmly rooted in the psychology of learning and development that is associated with Vygotsky, Feuerstein and others that have drawn upon and extended their ideas and practices. This psychology does not view learning and intelligence as a fixed and relatively unchanging individual quality but as being open to change and capable of being influenced by the mediational efforts of others. Dynamic assessment focuses upon how children learn and what interventions can help them learn more effectively. In this respect DA, in its philosophy and psychology, is orientated towards including learners through empowering the child as a learner along with those in that child's life that share a responsibility for his or her learning.

References

Ashman, A.F. and Conway, R.N.F. (1997) *An Introduction to Cognitive Education: Theory and Applications.* London: Routledge.

Block, N. and Dworkin, G. (eds) (1977) *The IQ Controversy.* London: Quartet.

Booth, T. and Ainscow, M. (2002) *Index for Inclusion.* Bristol: CSIE.

British Psychological Society (2002) *Inclusive Education – A Position Paper.* Leicester: British Psychological Society.

Cole, M. and Scribner, S. (1978) Introduction. In L.S. Vygotsky, *Mind in Society.* Cambridge, MA: Harvard University Press.

Daniels, H. (ed.) (1993) *Charting the Agenda: Educational Activity after Vygotsky.* London: Routledge.

Daniels, H. (ed.) (1996) *An Introduction to Vygotsky.* London: Routledge.

Dyson, A. (2001) Special needs in the twenty-first century: Where we've been and where we're going. *British Journal of Special Education,* 28(1), 24–29.

Elliott, J.G. (1993) Interactive assessment: If it is so 'dynamic' why is it so rarely employed? *Educational and Child Psychology,* 10, 48–58.

Elliott, J.G. (2000) Dynamic assessment in educational contexts: purpose and promise. In C.S. Lidz and J.G. Elliott (eds) *Dynamic Assessment: Prevailing Models and Applications.* New York: JAI.

Elliott, J.G., Lauchlan, F. and Stringer, P. (1996) Dynamic assessment and its potential for educational psychologists: Part 1 – Theory and Practice. *Educational Psychology in Practice,* 12(3), 152–160.

Feuerstein, R., Feuerstein, R.S., Falik, L.H. and Rand, Y. (2002) *The Dynamic Assessment of Cognitive Modifiability.* Jerusalem, Israel: ICELP Press.

Feuerstein, R., Rand, Y., Haywood, H.C., Hoffman, M.B. and Jensen, M. (1985) *The Learning Potential Assessment Device. Examiners' Manual.* Jerusalem, Israel: Hadassah-Wizo-Canada Research Institute.

Kozulin, A. (1990) *Vygotsky's Psychology.* Cambridge, MA: Harvard University Press.

Kozulin, A. (1998) *Psychological Tools.* Cambridge, MA: Harvard University Press.

Lewin, K. (1952) *Field Theory in Social Science.* London: Tavistock.

Lidz, C.S. (1991) *Practitioner's Guide to Dynamic Assessment.* New York: Guilford.

Lidz, C.S. (1992) Dynamic assessment: Some thoughts on the model, the medium and the message. In J.S. Carlson (ed.) *Advances in Cognition and Educational Practice, Vol. 1, Theoretical Issues: Intelligence, Cognition and Assessment.* Greenwich, CT: JAI Press.

Lidz, C.S. (1995) Dynamic assessment and the legacy of L.S. Vygotsky. *School Psychology International,* 16, 143–153.

Lidz, C.S. (1997) Dynamic assessment approaches. In D.P. Flanagan, J.L. Genshaft and P.L. Harrison (eds) *Contemporary Intellectual Assessment: Theories, Tests and Issues.* New York: Guilford.

Lidz, C.S. (2000) The Application of Cognitive Functions Scale (ACFS): An example of curriculum-based dynamic assessment. In C.S. Lidz and J.G. Elliott (eds) *Dynamic assessment: Prevailing Models and Applications.* New York: JAI.

Lidz, C.S. and Elliott, J.G. (eds) (2000) *Dynamic Assessment: Prevailing Models and Applications.* New York: JAI.

Meadows, S. (1993) *The Child as Thinker.* London: Routledge.

Olson, D.R. and Torrance, N. (eds) (1996) *The Handbook of Education and Human Development.* Oxford: Blackwell.

Stanovich, K.E. and Stanovich, P.J. (1996) 'Rethinking the concept of learning disabilities: the demise of aptitude/achievement discrepancy'. In Olson, D. and Torrance, N. (eds) *Handbook of Education and Learning Development: New Models of Learning, Teaching, and Schooling.* Cambridge, MA: Blackwell Publishers.

Sternberg, R.J. and Grigorenko, E.L. (2002) *Dynamic Testing.* Cambridge: Cambridge University Press.

Stringer, P. (1998) One night Vygotsky had a dream: 'Children learning to think …' and implications for educational psychologists. *Educational and Child Psychology,* 15(2), 14–20.

Stringer, P., Elliott, J.G. and Lauchlan, F. (1997) Dynamic assessment and its potential for educational psychologists: Part 2 – The zone of next development. *Educational Psychology in Practice,* 12(4), 234–239.

Stringer, P., Powell, J. and Burton, S. (2006) Developing a community psychology orientation in an educational psychology service. *Educational and Child Psychology,* 23(1), 59–67.

Thomas, G. and Loxley, A. (2001) *Deconstructing Special Education and Constructing Inclusion.* Buckingham: Open University Press.

Thomas, G. and Vaughan, M. (2003) *Inclusive Education: Readings and Reflections.* Buckingham: Open University Press.

Tzuriel, D. (1997) A novel dynamic assessment approach for young children: Major dimensions and current research. *Educational and Child Psychology,* 14, 83–108.

Tzuriel, D. (2000) The Cognitive Modifiability Battery. In C.S. Lidz and J.G. Elliott (eds) *Dynamic Assessment: Prevailing Models and Applications.* New York: JAI.

Tzuriel, D. (ed.) (2001) *Dynamic Assessment of Young Children.* New York: Kluwer Academic/Plenum Publishers.

Tzuriel, D., Samuels, M.T. and Feuerstein, R. (1988) Nonintellective factors in dynamic assessment. In R.M. Gupta and P. Coxhead (eds) *Dynamic Assessment: An Interactional Approach to Evaluating Learning Potential.* New York: Guilford.

Vygotsky, L.S. (1978) *Mind in Society.* Cambridge, MA: Harvard University Press.

Vygotsky, L.S. (1986) *Thought and Language.* Cambridge, MA: MIT Press.

Ware, L. (1995) The aftermath of the articulate debate: The invention of inclusive education. In C. Clark, A. Dyson and A. Millward (eds) *Towards Inclusive Schools?* London: David Fulton.

Warnock Committee (1978) *Special Educational Needs: The Warnock Report.* London: Department of Education and Science.

Warnock, M. (2005) Special educational needs: A new look. *Impact,* 11. London: Philosophy Society of Great Britain.

Waters, J. and Stringer, P. (1997) The Bunny Bag: A dynamic approach to the assessment of pre-school children. *Educational and Child Psychology,* 14(4), 33–45.

Watson, R. (1996) Rethinking readiness for learning. In D.R. Olson. and N. Torrance (eds) *The Handbook of Education and Human Development.* Oxford: Blackwell.

Wertsch, J.V., del Rio, P. and Alvarez, A. (eds) (1995) *Sociocultural Studies of Mind.* Cambridge: Cambridge University Press.

Chapter 12

Collaborative consultation

Psychologists and teachers working together

Ian McNab

Education in the United Kingdom has changed a lot in the last twenty-five years. Developments in education policy have gradually made mainstream schools – rather than local government authorities – responsible for children's education. Mainstream schools control ever more of the resources for addressing children's special educational needs, and are charged with ensuring the educational progress of the vulnerable. Inclusive schooling now has a place in the government's programme of wholesale reform of public services that includes the reorganisation into 'Children's Services' of health, education and social care, in which schools are seen as a locus and vehicle of service delivery (DfES 2004).

Schools now have to find ways of changing what they do so that all children can participate fully, irrespective of their personal characteristics. In other words, teachers have to be creative so that children who are unusual in some way should not be excluded on that account. How educational psychologists (EPs) participate in this work is the subject of this chapter; but first, we need to look briefly at the UK context.

The outlines of the new way of working appeared in the UK's statutory guidance about addressing special educational needs in schools (SEN Code of Practice, DfES 2001). This set out a process of 'assessment and intervention', first by the school alone (which the Code calls 'School Action'), and then by the school and external agencies ('School Action Plus'). A misleading shorthand became current, describing children as being 'at School Action' or 'at School Action Plus'.

But it is not really the children who are 'at School Action' or 'at School Action Plus'; rather, it is the work that the adults are doing that is at School Action or School Action Plus. As soon as we see the Code of Practice from this angle, we start to think of it in terms of inclusion: what do we need to do so that this child, with his or her particular attributes, can learn and succeed in this classroom, with this teacher and these peers? The Code becomes a description of how teachers get support with solving the problems they experience when attempting to carry out their responsibilities for teaching and managing children in ordinary classrooms.

That the adult's 'problem' is what matters is, of course, not a consequence of the Code of Practice: it has always been inherent in the very nature of a 'referral to the psychologist':

Children do not themselves ask for help from a psychologist. Whatever issues or difficulties they may or may not have attributed to them, it is an adult, who by making a referral, is asking for help. It follows, therefore, that a referral is related to the constructions that a referrer is putting on the events that constitute the child and his actions and, at the same time, is also related to the referrer's construction of himself.

(Ravenette 1988)

In general, teachers refer children when they themselves feel stuck. The significance of this fact is fundamentally important to understanding the Code of Practice from the teacher's point of view. It is about teachers changing what they are doing so that their routine classroom practices once again include the children about whom they were feeling stuck.

But the Code recognises that this is not easy, and that teachers need, and have a right to, support. So the SEN Code's procedures are a system whereby teachers engage wider and wider circles of support for their efforts to manage children's needs inclusively. Figure 12.1 represents this visually. The teacher with the concern is in the centre, alongside the child for which she is responsible. If the teacher feels stuck because her normal ways of teaching and managing – her 'routine practices' – do not seem to work, she starts to try things

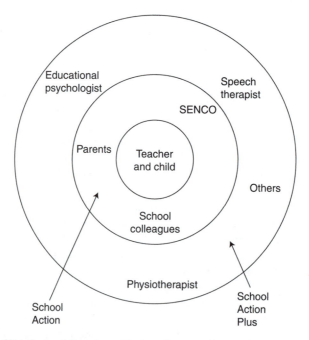

Figure 12.1 SEN Code of Practice – Circles of support for teachers

that are not quite so routine, which is what the term 'differentiation' describes. This is normal classroom work, and not part of the SEN Code.

But if the teacher's concerns are not resolved, she may start to use the Code's procedures. She first engages her 'School Action' team, which consists of the child, the parents, the SENCO, and any specialist teachers in school who normally participate when called on. Together they set about investigating the situation to identify relevant information and to invent some possible solutions that the teacher can try out – like doing a sort of experiment. This is what an 'individual educational plan' is: a small experiment in checking what might work to get the 'teaching and learning' process going again.

But if this does not do the trick, the teacher and her School Action team call upon a wider circle of professionals to come and join them. This 'School Action Plus team' consists of the existing School Action team – teacher, child, parents, SENCO and others from within the school – *plus* whatever outside professionals seem relevant to the search for a solution: advisory teacher, speech and language therapist, educational psychologist, occupational therapist, social worker, or whoever might be appropriate.

Thus to describe a child as 'at School Action Plus' is, in a very important sense, a misleading shorthand: it is the process – i.e., the work – that is at School Action Plus. It is also clear that external professionals do not take over the responsibility for children's education and development. Rather, they work collaboratively with those responsible for children's education – the school staff and the parents.

If the work has come this far, and the teacher needs the collaboration of a School Action Plus team, there is unlikely to be a 'quick fix'. A solution is likely to need a lot of hard work by everyone concerned; and no single member of the team is likely to arrive with an 'off-the-shelf' solution to donate. Inherently, such situations call for collaborative work that builds on the different kinds of knowledge and expertise that the participants bring. The teacher and those working alongside her consult about possible solutions, so that they may construct something that the teacher will actually be able to use, given her particular skills and resources, her particular classroom circumstances, and the other constraints and realities of her actual situation. This is inclusion in practice.

EPs have tried to find a name for this relatively new way of working: 'joint work'; 'consultation'; 'collaboration'. There is no perfect description, so we may call it 'collaborative consultation', to try to capture the sense of working together with the teacher as a team on the teacher's difficult problem of finding solutions to teaching or managing children when she has tried everything she can think of, and things still seem stuck. The main business of this chapter is to examine this process in more detail, to try to describe some of its essential features.

Collaborative consultation

EPs have been refining their understanding of this collaborative way of working for some years now. Turner *et al.* (1996) described how an EP team set about changing to this way of working and a group of seminal articles appeared in *Educational Psychology in Practice* (Watkins 2000). More recently, Farrell and Woods (in press) provided a detailed discussion of the issues that have emerged about this approach.

This was certainly not the style of work prevalent twenty or thirty years ago, when the school would send completed referral forms to the EP. In due course, the EP would visit the school, confining his or her contribution almost exclusively to work personally with individual children – largely administering tests – followed by an often all-too-brief chat with the teacher about what the tests purported to reveal. The EP would later send a report about the child, along with some advice about what the teacher should do. The problem for many teachers (and if we're honest, many EPs!) was in trying to make a connection between what was in these reports and what teachers could actually do in the everyday reality of their classrooms.

Unfortunately, the term 'consultation', commonly used to describe a different way of working, has developed at least three different meanings. For some EPs, it is simply a modified form of referral. Instead of getting the work via a referral form, the EP visits the school and discusses children with the teachers, to prioritise the concerns; the work then proceeds in much the same way as the traditional model.

The next variant of consultation is seen as one item on a menu of things that the EP does. The menu often comprises a list of types of work, something like the following (though with all sorts of local variations):

1   individual work (sometimes called 'case work');
2   consultation;
3   group work;
4   INSET;
5   project work;
6   etc.

Thus, consultation is thought of as distinct 'type' of work, different from 'individual work' and the rest. In particular, a view has developed that 'doing consultation' implies that the EP does not work with the child personally, but talks only to the teacher, parents and other adults. The notion that consultation is a special type of work has generated a somewhat arid debate among some EPs about the relative merits and demerits of consultation versus 'individual work'.

The third meaning transcends this spurious distinction; we may use the term 'collaborative consultation' to mark this essential difference. In this developed form collaborative consultation is not a particular kind of activity, but of a way of going about all the work that the EP does – it is a comprehensive model of EP practice.

Three things seem to characterise this way of working: the relationships between the participants; some key ideas that underlie the approach; and the fact

that the approach applies reflexively to the EP's own practice. These three characteristics need some further consideration. To keep things simple the discussion
will mostly consider work on concerns associated with individual school-aged
children (though, as implied above, the principles apply to all EP work).

Relationships

Collaborative consultation is a process that two or more people engage in. They
undertake some activities together so that some changes will take place to resolve
the concern that occasioned the work – at least enough for those with the concern
not to be troubled about it any more. There are important considerations here
about ownership and power that affect and engender relationships of a particular
kind. The process being described here is founded on, and produces, relationships
that are essentially *voluntary*, *respectful* and *collaborative* (ideas that permeate
the literature on post-modern psychotherapy, whose concepts we will come back
to in the next section).

It is essential to this work that participation is *voluntary*. No one is forced or
required to participate. This applies particularly to children and parents. The reason
is that the people who have the concern – usually one or more teachers – own the
problem. The parents may also experience a problem, though it may not be precisely
the same as the school's; but it is rare for pupils themselves to feel they have the
problem the adults express. Of course, the child may have various personal characteristics, qualities or attributes which the adults use in order to make sense of their
own problem with teaching or management (attributions such as 'slow learning',
'attention seeking', 'poorly coordinated', 'EBD', etc). However, children rarely
describe themselves as 'slow learning', 'attention seeking', etc (though they sometimes use the adults' language to give accounts of themselves that adults can accept:
'I have a lot of trouble with my work because I'm dyslexic, you know'). But many
children do experience themselves as having their own problem: having to find
ways of dealing with how the adults are treating them because the adults feel stuck,
anxious or exasperated, and construe the child as the cause of *their* problem. It is
therefore essential that the process should address the actual problem that each participant experiences, rather than the one that other participants attribute to them.
This is particularly important for the child, since other, more powerful participants –
especially teachers or parents – may tend to formulate their own problem in terms of
the child, and seek a solution in terms of changes the child must make.

But it is not just the child who can feel excluded in this way: the parents, the
teacher, the social worker, the learning support assistant – anyone involved may
feel that their concerns are not being addressed by the process, and that it is being
dominated by others involved. It is in this sense that the relationships have to be
respectful: the process has to be permeated with respect for what each of the participants is actually experiencing as problematic; it is *not* about persuading one or
more of them to adopt the construction of the problem (and a corresponding
'solution') determined by other more powerful or more vociferous participants.

This kind of respect is important if everyone is to participate willingly and actively in the difficult process of change that will bring about a solution: if you see yourself as benefiting from the work by getting *your* concerns addressed, you are more likely to work towards the collaboratively constructed solution than if you're simply required to do what someone else wants so that their needs are met.

Again, children, parents and teachers also feel genuinely respected when their particular expertise, skills, resources and knowledge are incorporated with equal regard. The different kind of expertise that each person brings is simply that – different: none is more important than another. Some participants, such as the speech therapist or the educational psychologist, bring conceptual models, technical information and particular skills that may be useful in helping the teacher, parents, child or other owner of a problem to construct solutions. But this kind of professional contribution does not have a necessary primacy: it, too, is useful only in so far as it contributes to helping the people directly involved construct a solution that they themselves can realise and maintain after all the 'experts' have gone home.

In this sense, the process of collaborative consultation demystifies 'expert authority' by seeking to create relationships between the participants that are truly collaborative and equal. This is difficult to achieve, particularly for the professional 'helpers' (the advisory teachers, educational psychologists, and health professionals). Such colleagues have a weight of professional socialisation – and some a lifetime of professional experience – that make them believe it is *their* job to solve everyone's problems. And some teachers, parents and others may, for various reasons, want to maintain them in this view. Those of us in a professional helper role have to work very hard, sometimes against a lot of contrary pressure, to allow real collaboration to develop. But when the work of the School Action Plus team becomes truly voluntary, respectful, collaborative and equal, it can transform those participants who originally felt stuck in their problem. For them the process becomes an affirmation of their strengths, resources and good qualities that builds their confidence, and enables them to apply and develop their creativity.

Conceptual orientation

It may be apparent that these descriptions of the relationships that characterise collaborative consultation as a transformational process are part of a wider conceptual orientation called 'Post-Modernism'. A particularly revealing description of the general attitude that post-modern workers have towards clients is 'respectful not-knowing': they respect the reality of their clients' experience and their unique strengths and resources; and they do not presume to know what clients' preferred future, and their way to realise it, will look like. Rather, they seek to work alongside people to help them clarify what they want, to become aware of their own strengths and resources, and to build their own solutions so that they can start to live their preferred future. They are particularly interested in the times

– however brief – when clients are or have been effective and successful; and they do not donate their own solutions out of a belief that these describe how clients ought to behave.

Another important idea is that our experienced reality is 'socially constructed'. The 'problem' – what we experience as upsetting and unpleasant – does not exist physically in external people, objects, or events; rather we experience distress because we give particular meanings to these external things and to ourselves in relation to them; and these meanings are constructed largely in the social interactions between people. For example, a teenage boy does not hand in his homework, and is abusive when asked where it is. Suppose we know he was at a party all last night: how do we make sense of, and respond to, his behaviour? But suppose instead we learn that his dad was killed in a car crash last week: what difference does this make to us? Or what if he simply won't talk to us? The seemingly 'objective' facts – no homework, abusive language – are only a small part of the sense we make of what faces us. And it is not the 'facts' but the sense we make of them that leads us to act in one way rather than another.

Key features of collaborative consultation

The practice of collaborative consultation grows out of the relationships and conceptual orientation outlined above. First, the process fundamentally respects the teacher's expertise, and, like the Code of Practice and the philosophy of Inclusion, adopts the view that the teacher is the professional central to the child's education. The teacher's knowledge and willingness to investigate and experiment lies at the heart of the process, as no one else is so well placed to effect the changes that will enable the child to be successful in a classroom irrespective of the personal attributes that in the wrong circumstances might become obstacles to learning.

Second, parents are essential partners in the process. They are not passive recipients of advice, recommendations or information from specialists and professionals. Rather, their unique knowledge and experience about their own child's development and ways of behaving and learning adds a dimension to any piece of collaborative work that no one else can contribute. Their active engagement and emotional commitment can energise the other members of the team.

Third, collaborative consultation involves pupils as voluntary and active partners, by seeking to clarify and respect their goals (as distinct from the goals attributed to them or imposed on them by the adults), and include their goals integrally in the process. This is obviously of particular importance where older children – especially adolescents – are participants, and where the behaviour of the adults and the young person towards each other are the matter of concern.

The next key area in which practice should reflect principles is that of responsibility. The ownership of the problem and the responsibility for its solution stays with the consultees. The relationships are predicated on the implicit premise that those who have a concern are, as it were, saying to the professionals, 'I have a problem I feel stuck about; I want to find a solution, and I'd like you to help me to do this'. They may not, of course, express themselves in this way initially. Indeed, the stress or emotional upset surrounding the difficulty often leads those immediately involved to feel that they just want someone to come and take the problem away and give them some relief.

However, the point is that the process of collaborative consultation inherently avoids that obscuring of the proper location of responsibilities that can insidiously disempower those who should be supported. It does this by seeking to respect and affirm the correct location of responsibility in the very procedures and activities of the process itself. For example, EP services that work through collaborative consultation tend not to operate a referral system. The very notion of 'referral' implies the transfer of responsibility from the referrer to the receiving agency, a transfer sometimes made explicit when a referral form is delivered personally, with a remark such as, 'Here's another one for you!' The reality is that the external professionals whose help teachers seek are rarely if ever in a position to effect the changes necessary for a solution: only those in day-to-day personal contact with the situation where the concern happens can do this. So the EP is responsible for doing tasks or pieces of work in collaborative consultation; but they do not 'accept referrals' or 'take up cases'. An aspect of being clear about responsibility is the need to be clear about the purpose of the EP's activity: whatever work the EP undertakes, its essential purpose is to further the collaborative process in support of the construction of solutions. We will have more to say about this in due course.

The process of collaborative consultation

Collaborative consultation consists in a special kind of conversation: one which facilitates solutions. This conversation is itself the mechanism that gives rise to solutions as its outcome. It is therefore not merely a chat, or merely 'telling', or any of the other modes of interaction that might characterise other forms of conversation that have different purposes.

The means by which such a conversation may support the kinds of change that constitute a solution have been extensively investigated in those areas of applied psychology used in therapeutic practice. The application of skills from therapeutic practice is becoming increasingly common among EPs working through collaborative consultation. They seek to develop these skills by training in, for example, Solution Focused Brief Therapy, Personal Construct Psychology, Narrative Therapy, or Cognitive Behaviour Therapy.

This is not to suggest that teachers requesting help are in need of therapy. But much of the psychology of change in a therapeutic setting can be transferred to other situations and provide a means for change there, too. De Jong and Berg (2002) give a particularly useful and practical exposition of the skills and techniques of one widely used method and Metcalf (1999) describes its applications to work in schools.

De Jong and Berg elucidate the attitude of 'respectful not-knowing' adopted in much 'post-modern' therapy. This has an important place in the process of collaborative consultation. Respect is evident in the fact that the EP appreciates and acknowledges the participants' experience of difficulty, of feeling 'stuck' or exasperated, angry or hopeless. It seeks to work on solutions to the participants' own problems. The aspect of 'not-knowing' is perhaps more subtle. It does not mean that the EP has no specialist knowledge, but that he or she cannot know what strengths and resources the participants have been drawing on to keep going in spite of the problem, nor what form their solution will take in their daily reality. Any truly workable solution has to be one that the participants can realise in their own lives, and the process therefore has to find and build on the participants' own resources and strengths. The EP simply cannot know in advance what these are – perhaps even the participants are not initially aware of their strengths and resources, or of the relevance of skills they have in another area of their lives to the concern at hand. The process has to discover these relevant strengths.

Furthermore, the elements of potential solutions lie in those moments – however fragmentary or fleeting – when the problem is *not* happening, or is happening less. Again, the EP cannot guess what these may be: collaborative consultation seeks to identify, investigate, and build on these 'exceptions'.

It follows that the EP would be unwise to donate or impose his or her own solutions, but rather must help those involved to build their own. Perhaps some readers who are EPs may be wondering, 'Where is the psychology in all this?' The EP is a participant who exercises his or her skills to 'host' the collaborative process. This is quintessentially psychology in action: it requires the EP to learn and creatively deploy a range of skills in the special kind of conversation that supports the building of solutions – in other words, the creation of change. Anderson and Goolishian (1988) called such a person a 'master conversational artist'.

Similar skill is also needed in situations where there has been a great deal of conflict and anger. The EP may help reconcile the participants so that they can work constructively together on making the situation better in whatever terms they variously envision that improvement.

The EP also brings to the process a breadth of specialist 'technical' knowledge, particularly in the form of sophisticated psychological models that may help to make sense of the puzzling and disparate information brought by the other participants. This psychological knowledge and the models that organise it may help to loosen fixed ways of thinking about the problem that are themselves part of the 'stuckness' and perplexity that everyone is feeling. The psychologist may help to 'reframe' the information available so as to give the participants a chance to make sense of it in new ways that may transform the expectations and consequent actions that have had a part in maintaining the situation. The EP offers interpretations of the available data that invite the participants to create new meanings for their experience. But this is not a matter of *telling* others what they should think and do. Rather, the EP is genuinely *offering* alternative constructions that the participants may or may not incorporate into understandings that are more helpful to their solution-building.

What is important, therefore, is the manner in which the EP contributes specialist knowledge, interpretation, or suggestions. The EP invites people to look at other options; but these should always be tentative and preferably multiple – to ensure that the participants are able to exercise their own judgement and choice about what to incorporate – if anything – into their solutions.

Teachers have described the experience of receiving information, interpretations and suggestions (Landsberg, cited by Gillies (2000)). If the 'expert' demonstrated, donated advice, or told teachers what to do or how, they tended to feel belittled, inferior, inadequate or useless. If, on the other hand, the worker asked questions (showing genuine curiosity), paraphrased the teachers' words, or offered suggestions tentatively, the teachers tended to feel valued, listened to and empowered.

What, then, does the EP do in the process of collaborative consultation? Put simply, the EP deploys any aspect of applied psychology that (a) has a clear and agreed purpose within the collaborative process; and (b) will be useful to further the process. So the EP may collect data or information, ascertain the child's views, teach the adults some skills, or use any skill, technique, activity or method – as long as (a) and (b) apply.

The idea of collaborative consultation sounds very simple, yet EPs who try to work alongside teachers and parents in this way will tell you that it is not easy. It is hard in the straightforward sense that teachers and parents tend to call in outside professionals only when they feel faced with a problem that is difficult to solve; and that usually means they have already tried all the solutions they can think of, and these do not seem to be working. There is not going to be a quick and easy resolution.

But it is also hard in the more 'psychological' sense that the problem exists in what the participants are currently doing – the actions of people involved and the responses of the others in the situation – and in the fact that these actions and reactions seem to be a repeating cycle that is hard to break out of. The solution, of course, lies in doing something different: but something different is exactly what the exasperated participants cannot seem to discover. The process of collaborative consultation – and the skill of the EP who may be hosting this kind of conversation – is about initiating the small changes the participants will build on to unblock these stuck patterns; and this means that one or other or all of them will discover within themselves the resources, the confidence, and most importantly the willingness to start to do something different.

Benefits of collaborative consultation

The way of working described above is about people working together to find ways of solving problems so that teaching and learning can go on successfully where the teacher and child are now – in this classroom, in this school. It therefore inherently fosters inclusion. But it is also itself profoundly inclusive: it is predicated on, and engenders, participation and respect among all the participants. It is also concerned with helping the adults, and especially the teachers, to find solutions to problems in teaching and learning that were causing them to feel stuck. It is therefore intrinsically a process of self-improvement that aligns readily with a school's other efforts for improvements that increase its capacity to provide for any and every child who comes through the door.

Thus the benefits of using this approach are not only to be seen in specific 'successful outcomes'. At its best, the process is also a developmental experience for everyone involved. And it engenders respect, and identifies and builds on the participants' resources and strengths: it values, affirms, and empowers teachers; and it values, affirms, and empowers children and parents.

Because all the relevant professionals participate in the teacher's School Action Plus team, multi-agency work ceases to be a matter of cross-referring children; instead, it allows the professionals to coordinate their activities from the outset as part of the initial and ongoing planning, and ensures parents and pupils real partnership with them in the process. And the involvement of parents and pupils is not just a nice idea: the process of multi-agency collaborative consultation is far more likely to succeed when parents and children are included in the team as partners and their own needs *as they themselves define them* are considered and addressed. This is inclusive practice that leads to inclusive solutions.

References

Anderson, H. and Goolishian, H.A. (1988) Human systems as linguistic systems: preliminary and evolving ideas about the implications for clinical theory. *Family Process*, 27: 371–391.

De Jong, P. and Berg, I.K. (2002) *Interviewing for Solutions* (2nd ed.). Pacific Grove, CA: Brooks/Cole.

DfES (2001) *Special Educational Needs Code of Practice*. London: Department for Education and Skills.

DfES (2004) *Removing Barriers to Achievement: The Government's Strategy for SEN*. London: Department for Education and Skills.

Farrell, P. and Woods, K. (in press) Consultation and the role of the school psychologist: barriers and opportunities. *Journal of Educational and Psychological Consultation*.

Gillies, E. (2000) Developing consultation partnerships. *Educational Psychology in Practice*, 16(1): 31–37.

Metcalf, L. (1999) *Teaching Towards Solutions*. New York: The Center for Applied Research in Education.

Ravenette, T. (1988) Personal construct psychology in the practice of an educational psychologist. In Dunnett, G. (ed.) *Working with People: Clinical Uses of Personal Construct Psychology*. London: Routledge.

Turner, S., Robbins, H. and Doran, C. (1996) Developing a model of consultancy practice. *Educational Psychology in Practice*, 1(2): 86–93.

Watkins, C. (2000) Introduction to the articles on consultation. *Educational Psychology in Practice*, 16(1): 5–8.

Part 3

Challenges and possibilities

Chapter 13

Towards an interdisciplinary research agenda for inclusive education

Alan Dyson and Andrew Howes

The inclusion 'movement' has both drawn upon and stimulated a wide range of education scholarship and research. This range embraces: attempts to refine the conceptualisation of inclusive education; studies which aim to identify the characteristics and determinants of inclusive schools and classrooms; comparative and detailed studies of practice which reveal features of inclusive practice in relation to specific groups of learners; studies of the educational and other outcomes of inclusive provision; and collaborative action research aiming to learn about and promote the changes in practice entailed in schools becoming more inclusive. Reviewing this range, Clough (2000) has usefully proposed a tentative 'framework of perspectives', with five main elements that map broadly onto related historical developments in the UK over the preceding fifty years. He has suggested that each perspective generally dominated a decade since the 1950s, having had its roots in earlier times and having consequences which in many cases continue into the present. So we have:

- the psycho-medical legacy;
- the sociological response;
- curricular approaches;
- school improvement strategies;
- and the disability studies critique.

Whilst these different perspectives indicate the richness of research and scholarship in this field, they also point to a considerable degree of fragmentation. It is our view that the relationships amongst these perspectives have not, by and large, been characterised by productive dialogue. For the most part, indeed, there has been no relationship at all, and research within any one perspective has proceeded as though the other perspectives simply did not exist. To use our own work as an example, one of us (Dyson) completed a study of the impact on the attainments of other students of the inclusion in mainstream schools of students identified as having special educational needs (Dyson *et al.*, 2004). The study operates with the familiar techniques of school effectiveness and school improvement research – analyses of student outcomes, aggregation of those outcomes at school level, and case studies of more and less 'inclusive', and more and less 'effective', schools. Its conceptualisation of inclusion is limited and traditional: the idea that students can be divided meaningfully and usefully into those with and without special educational needs is accepted; inclusion is seen as being about the placement of the former group in mainstream schools; and the worthwhileness of inclusion is to be judged simply by its impacts on the attainments of other students. Whilst the study was designed in this way for what we continue to believe are good reasons, and whilst – as good research should – it acknowledges its own limitations, it remains the case that it owes little if anything to the other perspectives which have been so productive elsewhere in inclusion research. We suggest, however, that similar criticisms could be levelled at many other studies in this field.

Moreover, where there has been engagement between different types of research and scholarship, this has often taken the form of critique rather than dialogue. At its extreme, this has involved hostile exchanges (one thinks of one writer famously describing the work of others as 'intellectual masturbation' (Oliver, 1992, for instance). However, there has been an underlying dynamic in relationships between perspectives which is usefully captured in Thomas and Loxley's (2001) phrase – 'deconstructing special education and constructing inclusion'. In essence, educational responses to student difference which are seen by inclusion advocates as marginalising are held to emanate from faulty constructions of difference. Such constructions locate the cause of marginalisation in the characteristics of individuals and groups rather than in the ideologies, structures and practices of the education system and of wider society. They are embodied in and legitimised by traditional forms of scholarly and practitioner knowledge – notably, psychology, medicine and the practices of special education. It is, therefore, necessary to engage in a process of what Corbett and Slee (2000) call 'cultural vigilantism', whereby these knowledges are deconstructed, and a new 'inclusive' way of knowing is constructed, out of which new practices and new forms of provision can emerge.

This process of deconstruction and reconstruction produces sometimes quite masterly reviews of the field – Thomas and Loxley's work is a case in point, as are Skrtic's essays on the crisis of professional knowledge (Skrtic, 1991a, 1991b, 1995). However, it is essentially a process which is based on critique. Inclusion comes to be defined in opposition to other scholarly perspectives which claim to generate knowledge about similar sets of issues in relation to similar groups of learners. This is particularly true of Clough's (2000) 'psycho-medical legacy'. The claims made by this perspective relate primarily to the understanding of differences between individuals and groups of learners in terms of the characteristics of those individuals and groups. As such, they offer a prime target for deconstruction by those who wish to foreground other understandings of difference – in terms, say, of the dynamics of social practices or the operation of power and interest in education and wider social systems. It is no surprise, therefore, that the psychological and medical understandings of learners which played such a crucial part in the development of special education have, for so long, been in the front line of the deconstruction-construction process. Indeed, it is indicative that Clough talks of the psychomedical 'legacy', as though such a perspective lost its vibrancy and validity at some time in the past.

One response to this situation is to seek to blur the distinctions between the different perspectives which do, or might, contribute to the development of inclusive education. It is no coincidence, for instance, that educational psychology, from its front-line position, has engaged in successive attempts to 'reconstruct' itself (Gillham, 1978) in ways which take account of the critiques to which it has been subject. Of particular note in recent years has been the work of Norwich (and collaborators) in arguing against caricatured representations of psycho-medical knowledge, and in exploring the interrelationship between 'medical' and 'social' models of difference and the 'connectivity' between the knowledge embodied in special and inclusive educational practices (see, for instance, Norwich, 2000b, 2002; Norwich and Lewis, 2001 and also Farrell and Venables in this volume). It is significant in this respect that Norwich sees this work as originating from an inter-disciplinary starting point:

> The book that really changed my views I [first] read as an A-level student, *Sane Society* by Fromm, a Marxian psychoanalyst. Erich Fromm took an interdisciplinary view combining psychodynamic and social-economic conflict models. He did not deny the importance of the intrapsychic, or of character or personality or macro-social factors ... So in a sense I thought 'I want to be like him ...'
>
> (Norwich, 2000a: 108)

The importance of such an interdisciplinary perspective is an issue to which we shall shortly return. However, it is important at this point to note that the divisions which beset research and scholarship in inclusive education are not accidental, and that forging links between them is not likely to be simple. If there is an oppositional dynamic within this field, it is in part because there is no coherent 'field' of inclusive education at all. As Thomas and O'Hanlon argue:

> 'Inclusion' has become something of an international buzz-word. It is difficult to trace its provenance or the growth in its use over the last two decades, but what is certain is that it is now de rigueur for policy documents, mission statements and political speeches. It has become a slogan – almost obligatory in the discourse of all right-thinking people.
>
> (2002: vii)

The result, as we have seen, is that quite different understandings of difference and quite different claims to knowledge operate in the same intellectual space. Different writers may use the language of inclusion to refer to quite different phenomena; some may arrogate that language exclusively in support of their own views, denying it to those with different perspectives; others may see themselves as working outside the field of inclusion when in fact they are concerned with much the same issues as those who identify themselves as belonging to that field.

The situation is aggravated by the peculiar role of values in inclusion scholarship and research. For many in this putative field, inclusion is: 'based on a value system that welcomes and celebrates diversity arising from gender, nationality, race, language of origin, social background, educational achievement or disability' (Mittler, 2000: 10). Such scholars might well argue that all research is based on value positions of some kind, and that it is much better to make these values explicit and a matter for open debate than to conceal them beneath a cloak of scientific objectivity. However, commitment of this kind injects new complexities into the interactions between different perspectives in this field. Competing constructions of difference come to seem not only more or less robust, but also more or less preferable in ethical terms. Under these circumstances, it becomes difficult to recognise what might be helpful, illuminating and legitimately challenging in these other perspectives. The scholarly task of questioning assumptions and testing evidence becomes conflated with the ethical task of struggling to establish better (i.e. morally better) ways of thinking.

Beneath these complexities lies an even greater problem. Building on work by Norwich (1993), Berlak and Berlak (1981) and others, one of us (Dyson) has argued that educational responses to learner difference can usefully be understood in terms of dilemmas and contradictions (Clark *et al.*, 1998; Dyson, 1999; Dyson and Millward, 2000). Put simply, mass education systems such as those of the UK are based on a contradiction inherent in the aim of offering large numbers of learners – who differ from each other in significant ways – an education which is common to all. Educators and education policy makers are thus faced with the dilemma of how to respond simultaneously to differences and commonalities between learners. This dilemma is resolved in different ways at different times and in different places. The point is, however, that, as a dilemma, it may be resolved but can never be solved. In other words, there is no way of making the tension between the two 'horns' of the dilemma disappear.

Viewed in this way, what we have called the 'field' of inclusion might more accurately be characterised as the field within which resolutions of this 'dilemma of difference' emerge. Various attempts to develop inclusive education are thus recast as attempts at resolution which emphasise the commonality pole of that dilemma. Several amongst Clough's five perspectives are equally concerned with commonality, but emphasise different aspects of what it is that learners have in common. For instance, the 'disability studies critique' tends to focus on the rights of disabled learners as citizens, while the 'school improvement approach' tends to focus on the common school organisational framework within which education is delivered. Other perspectives tend to generate resolutions which pay more attention to difference than to commonality. The 'psycho-medical legacy' in particular has, as we observed earlier, focused substantially on what makes individuals and groups different from each other.

In one sense, viewing these perspectives through the lens of dilemmas and the resolution of dilemmas changes nothing. It is still the case that different resolutions embody different understandings of difference and different value positions. They originate from, embody and serve to reproduce particular socio-political positions and therefore tend to favour some interests over others. They are not simply interchangeable or equally preferable from any given standpoint. On the other hand, precisely because resolutions are not solutions, neither is any of them in the privileged position of being able to refute any other. Each resolution is necessarily both optional and provisional. It is adopted for certain purposes and on the basis of certain assumptions and values. As other purposes arise and other assumptions and values are foregrounded, other resolutions are always likely to emerge. The dynamic within the field of inclusive education, therefore, is not one in which 'superior' (more robust, or more ethically desirable) positions critique and dispose of 'inferior' positions. Rather, the process of deconstruction and reconstruction is a continuing one in which new circumstances call for new resolutions – which will in their turn be replaced by newer resolutions.

This has important implications for the nature of research in this field and for the relationship between different types and traditions of research. As Clough (2000) suggests, the history of this field is one in which successive 'perspectives' come to dominate research at particular points in time. In establishing themselves and struggling for dominance, it is inevitable that writers within one perspective will try to present their own work as offering comprehensive and rigorous explanations and will, from time to time, critique the assumptions of preceding and competing perspectives. Such moves, we suggest, are essential for elaborating new perspectives, demonstrating their robustness, and differentiating them from their competitors. So, for instance, Tomlinson's ground-breaking *A Sociology of Special Education* (1982) was ground-breaking precisely because it undertook a comprehensive and robust exposition of this kind, and because it pointed to limitations in the preceding 'psycho-medical perspective'. That is why it remains an important book for students of the field to this day.

However, it is important to realise that Tomlinson's work did not invalidate the psycho-medical perspective, any more than, say, the subsequent rise of the 'school improvement' perspective invalidated the somewhat deterministic views that she herself espoused. Rather, critiques and expositions of this kind identify the founding assumptions of other perspectives, point to the limitations ('boundaries' might be better) which those assumptions inevitably entail, and set out alternative sets of assumptions on which the new perspective is based. In the politically charged and value-laden field of inclusive education, it is difficult not to see this process as one of conflict in which there has to be an outright winner. An alternative, however, is to see it as one of clarification, in which work within different perspectives becomes more transparent and intelligible as its assumptions and boundaries are exposed. If this process uncovers what a particular body of work fails to do and the issues it fails to address, it also reveals more clearly what it does do and where its value might lie.

Again, it might be useful to think in terms of specific examples. For many years, there have been controversies around 'non-normative' disabilities – dyslexia, attention deficit disorder, autism and so on – where the nature and usefulness of diagnostic criteria are contested and where competing explanations of learners' difficulties are available. From a psycho-medical perspective, it is important to test out the usefulness of the label for intervention purposes, to clarify diagnostic criteria, and to explore the sorts of interventions that might make a difference to individuals who 'have' these conditions. From a 'school improvement' perspective, the diagnosis and label are less important than finding teaching and organisational strategies to work with these learners. From a 'sociological' perspective, the issue is how and in whose interests such conditions are constructed when alternative constructs are readily available. However, these different accounts do not invalidate each other. It may be, for instance, that attention deficit disorder is a construct that serves to buttress the position of psychologists and (especially) medics, and to take pressure off schools and families alike. This does not mean that the label is necessarily unable to lead to interventions helpful to the learner, nor that schools need not organise themselves to respond to such learners.

In the light of this, we suggest that it is possible for productive relationships between research perspectives to be fostered in at least three ways. First, the process of critique can be made more systematic and robust, and, equally important, can be applied in an even-handed way. Systematicity and robustness come, we believe, from interrogating research in terms of a common set of questions. Some of these are the sorts of standard questions about rigour and trustworthiness which might be applied to any research – are the research questions clear, is the design appropriate, are conclusions based on the evidence, is the argumentation internally coherent and so on. Others, however, refer more to the issues raised in this chapter – what 'perspective' the research works within, in terms of the assumptions that are built into it; what values are built into that perspective; what resolutions are proposed of the 'dilemma of difference'; who is advocating these resolutions; and what interests are furthered or baulked by these resolutions. These are not questions that can be applied mechanically to every piece of research, but they do provide a common framework within which research studies can be critiqued and understood.

Even-handedness in this process comes from applying this framework to all research in the field, including research within one's own favoured perspective. As we have argued, there is a tendency for work within this field to set about disposing of other kinds of research and scholarship as fatally flawed, to seize the high moral ground by foregrounding its values, and, in some cases to argue that it is more capable than other work of challenging the marginalisation, exclusion or oppression of disadvantaged learners. Claims of this kind deserve to be taken seriously and can often be substantiated. However, this does not free such work from the obligation of being interrogated in terms of our common framework. Work which presents itself as being based on highly inclusive values and assumptions, or which explicitly aligns itself with oppressed people nonetheless has implicit assumptions which need to be explored, is nonetheless produced by particular individuals and groups, and nonetheless promotes certain interests at the expense of others. In this respect, it is as well to remember that much of the work which is now consigned to the 'psycho-medical legacy' and seen as serving the vested interests of professional groups and an exclusive education system was itself at one time offered as the best hope for marginalised learners.

The second strategy for fostering productive relationships between perspectives is to build such relationships into the design of research. To some extent, this can be done at the level of individual studies, though the close relationship between the design of studies and their founding assumptions makes it difficult to build different starting assumptions into the same study. It is much easier at the levels of programmes of research, where a series of studies can explore a particular issue from a range of perspectives. This would require a number of conditions to be in place. It would, for instance, be necessary to devote time and energy to the designing of programmes as opposed to studies, and to the business of synthesising the findings of individual studies. It is also worth noting that synthesising in this sense is about something much more complex than simply aggregating findings, since it also involves the sort of critical interrogation of assumptions which we have described above. Programmatic research of this kind also requires the creation of multi-perspectival (if not multidisciplinary) research teams and access to stable, relatively long-term, funding. It is well known, however, that such conditions are difficult to find in a research system which is fragmented and favours small- or medium-scale research on the basis of relatively low levels of time-limited funding (Hillage *et al.*, 1998). In terms of the inclusion field, particularly, it is probably true to say that most research is undertaken by lone researchers or small teams, usually based in a single institution, and usually working together precisely because of their shared perspective rather than because of any productive differences.

The third strategy is perhaps a little less problematic in current circumstances. We drew attention earlier to Norwich's attempt to locate his work in an interdisciplinary context and to his interest in exploring the boundaries between perspectives. This points to the possibility of what we might call bridge-building research and scholarship, where the explicit aim is to clarify misunderstandings between different perspectives and to explore the common ground that they might share. The UK is fortunate in that the organisation of higher education and of the school systems, and the culture of academic and professional life, erects fewer perspectival barriers than is the case in many other countries. Although some barriers undoubtedly exist, it remains the case that education researchers of all persuasions tend to work in the same relatively small departments, while educational psychologists, special educators and mainstream teachers tend to have similar academic backgrounds and to have at least some opportunities for shared training. For this reason, many researchers in the inclusion field are able to work across perspectival boundaries as the need arises. To take an example more or less at random, Lindsay and colleagues have recently undertaken a study of the under- and over-representation of different ethnic groups in the English special needs education system (Lindsay *et al.*, 2006). Such a study crosses the boundaries of the 'psycho-medical' perspective, the 'school improvement' perspective and the 'sociological' perspective, in that it requires the research team to understand the technicalities of diagnosis and labelling, the relationship between these processes and school dynamics, and the issues of power and interest with which these processes are shot through. Such boundary-crossing may seem relatively unremarkable in this country but it would not, we suggest, seem so everywhere. While we do not suggest that every study could or should cross boundaries in this way, we do argue that the capacity to do this is more valuable than we often realise and should be nurtured.

A case study of our own

We wish to conclude this chapter by undertaking a critical examination of a research study which locates itself in the field of inclusive education. We wish to show how the interrogative framework we have outlined might be used in respect of this study, consider how far the study was designed and developed in accordance with the principles set out above, and explore how this work might have been (or might still be) taken further in the light of these principles. To avoid selecting one researcher's work above others for scrutiny of this kind, the study we will analyse is a piece of work in which we ourselves have been involved.

The study in question is the 'Understanding and developing inclusive practices in schools' project, funded by the Teaching and Learning Research Programme of the Economic and Social Research Council (award no. L139 25 1001). The study was led by Mel Ainscow at Manchester, Tony Booth at Christ Church University College Canterbury, and Alan Dyson (then) of Newcastle, was funded between 2000 and 2003, and has been extensively reported elsewhere (see, particularly, Ainscow *et al.*, 2004, 2006a, 2006b). It involved engagement in twenty-five schools in three local authority areas over the period of three years. The schools were invited, in negotiation with the university researchers, to identify some aspect of their practice which they wished to develop in a more inclusive direction. They then worked with the university teams in a process of collaborative action research whereby they made changes in their practice, monitored the impacts of those changes, and undertook further cycles of change and monitoring as necessary. Relationships between teachers, local authority officers and university staff were developed and maintained over this time through a series of events, regular workshops, and increasingly through collaborative research visits between participating schools, where teachers acted as research partners for their colleagues in another school.

It is difficult to meaningfully and briefly summarise all the findings from this extensive network. But in one local education authority (LEA), for example, we conceptualised the difficulties of addressing issues of inclusion as resulting from the social boundaries that exist within schools, and between schools and their wider communities. We found that such boundaries were sometimes supported by the personal assumptions of staff, linked to personal histories and relationships within the school. They also received support where they aligned with common ways of interpreting tensions and dilemmas, such as with respect to assumptions about ethnicity and socio-economic status, for example. These boundaries, we observed, were largely taken for granted; they became for us a way of conceptualising how values, preconceptions, relationships and norms affect what is possible within institutions.

There are some aspects of this study that are closely aligned with the principles we set out above. By the (limited) standards of education research, this was a relatively long-term and large-scale study, undertaken by a relatively large team of researchers based in three institutions. The team was created specifically for this study and deliberately embraced, if not differences of perspective then at least differences of emphasis within a broadly shared perspective. Indeed, much debate took place within the project team about whether it would be possible to come up with agreed findings or whether it would be more honest to report three perspectives on a common set of issues. Most members of research teams resisted locating their work within a single disciplinary perspective and felt reasonably comfortable with at least a limited amount of boundary crossing. However, there was also a good deal of common ground between team members and the study is located more or or less squarely within the 'school improvement' perspective. While it is true that the team was put together specifically for this study, it is also true that the lead members in particular knew each other well and that social and intellectual compatibility played a large part in determining the composition of the team.

If we interrogate the study in terms of the framework we set out earlier, the nature of its focus and founding assumptions become clearer. We made much of the collaborative nature of the study in that it involved university researchers and teachers working together. This extends the participant group beyond that commonly found in educational research, but it remains the case that the study's agenda was a professional one. Productive as the teacher-researcher dialogue often was, the assumption that inclusion could be understood through such a dialogue of professionals was built into the study. Not surprisingly, therefore, the study focused on those things which professionals could most easily control – notably, school and classroom practices and the ways in which those practices could be articulated, conceptualised and discussed. If professional understandings emerged as the key to inclusion, this is hardly surprising, since a study designed and implemented by professionals focused on those understandings almost exclusively.

The values on which the study was based were, in many respects, admirably explicit. Two of the lead researchers (Ainscow and Booth) had also led the development of the *Index for Inclusion* (Booth and Ainscow, 2002; Booth *et al.*, 2000) which elaborates a set of inclusive values and gives clear indications as to what these values might look like when operationalised in schools. In broad terms, the Index privileges values of respect for difference within the common social institution of the school. The Index was used as a starting point for schools' review of the inclusiveness or otherwise of their own practices. It is worth noting that the Index is a tool to be used primarily at the level of the institution, as part of a school development process, rather than at the level of individual practice or system organisation (though it can doubtless be adapted for these purposes). Our study, too, assumed that the institutional level was the one at which inclusive developments were most likely or feasible.

When the study's values and assumptions are set out in this way, it becomes easier to see what it does and does not contribute. On the one hand, the study adds significantly to understandings of the role of the institution in the development of inclusive practice. In making sense of its findings, we explicitly considered the relationship between institutional development and the national policy context, and in so doing were required to confront issues of power and interest as they operate in that context. On the other hand, the study has little to say about power and interest in broader social structures. Its institutional focus constructs inclusion as an issue in institutional development, rather than as something which emerges (or fails to emerge) from these broader structures. Its professional focus similarly assumes that teachers are free to 'think' their way towards inclusive practices, with only limited acknowledgement that their thinking might be locked into cultural assumptions from which they cannot escape. The same emphasis on professional understanding means that the study pays little attention to understanding the sorts of differences between learners that might have interested a more psycho-medically oriented piece of research. The assumption is not that such differences do not matter, but that professionals are able to 'think' their way towards appropriate responses to such differences, and that given the opportunity, they have the commitment and capacity to do so. Moreover, the voices and values of professionals overwhelm those of learners and their families in the study. It is not that these voices are entirely silent – indeed, teachers were encouraged to collect evidence about what their students thought and wanted. However, the role of students' voices is to stimulate teacher reflection about their own practice. The assumption is that teachers, supported by university researchers, are able to understand what learners have to say, and that teachers acting in accordance with the values of the *Index* must necessarily be acting in their students' best interests. We wonder whether writers within the 'disability studies' perspective would necessarily agree with this!

We see this critique of our work not as an end in itself, but as a useful starting point for productive dialogue. It seems likely that, if we had put together a more genuinely diverse research team, some of these issues might have been addressed in the design of the research and the interpretation of its findings. Post hoc, we hope that those who work within different perspectives will themselves address these issues. There are important questions to ask about whether students share the same values as their inclusively oriented teachers and, if they do, whether they see the same aspects of practice as inclusive or exclusive. Likewise, it is important to consider how far individual teachers and institutions can escape shared social assumptions, or, more correctly, what is the nature of the interaction between understandings at the micro-level and macro-level social processes. Finally, we need to ask what the limitations are (if any) of teachers' ability to 'think' their way towards inclusive responses to difference. At what point (if any) is a different, more technical kind of knowledge useful, and at what point (if any) does the capacity of teachers to respond to difference become stretched to breaking point?

Addressing questions such as these – there are doubtless many more – would make it possible to set the findings of our (necessarily) limited study in a wider context. It would cease to be an isolated piece of research, or even a combatant in a struggle between different perspectives, and would become part of an overarching effort to explore the field of inclusive education as a whole. The differences between perspectives – and their points of incompatibility – would not disappear in such a venture, but alternative perspectives would become resources on which to draw rather than enemies to be annihilated.

References

Ainscow, M., Booth, T. and Dyson, A. (2004) Understanding and developing inclusive practices in schools: a collaborative action research network, *International Journal of Inclusive Education*, 8(2), 125–139.

Ainscow, M., Booth, T. and Dyson, A. (2006a) *Improving Schools, Developing Inclusion.* London: Routledge.

Ainscow, M., Booth, T. and Dyson, A. (2006b) Inclusion and the standards agenda: negotiating policy pressures in England, *International Journal of Inclusive Education*, 10(4–5), 295–308.

Berlak, A. and Berlak, H. (1981) *Dilemmas of Schooling: Teaching and Social Change.* London: Methuen.

Booth, T. and Ainscow, M. (2002) *Index for Inclusion: Developing Learning and Participation in Schools.* Bristol: Centre for Studies on Inclusive Education.

Booth, T., Ainscow, M., Black-Hawkins, K., Vaughan, M. and Shaw, L. (2000) *Index for Inclusion: Developing Learning and Participation in Schools.* Bristol: Centre for Studies on Inclusive Education.

Clark, C., Dyson, A. and Millward, A. (1998) Theorising special education: time to move on?, in C. Clark, A. Dyson and A. Millward (eds) *Theorising Special Education.* London: Routledge.

Clough, P. (2000) Routes to inclusion, in P. Clough and J. Corbett (eds) *Theories of Inclusive Education.* London: Sage.

Corbett, J. and Slee, R. (2000) An international conversation on inclusive education, in F. Armstrong, D. Armstrong and L. Barton (eds) *Inclusive Education: Policy Contexts and Comparative Perspectives.* London: David Fulton.

Dyson, A. (1999) Inclusion and inclusions: theories and discourses in inclusive education, in H. Daniels and P. Garner (eds) *World Yearbook of Education 1999: Inclusive Education.* London: Kogan Page.

Dyson, A., Farrell, P., Gallannaugh, F., Hutcheson, G. and Polat, F. (2004) *Inclusion and Pupil Achievement.* London: DfES.

Dyson, A. and Millward, A. (2000) *Schools and Special Needs: Issues of Innovation and Inclusion.* London: Paul Chapman Publishers.

Gillham, B. (ed.) (1978) *Reconstructing Educational Psychology*. Beckenham: Croom Helm.

Hillage, J., Pearson, R., Anderson, A. and Tamkin, P. (1998) *Excellence in Research on Schools*. DfEE Research report RR74. London: DfEE.

Lindsay, G., Pather, S. and Strand, S. (2006) *Special Educational Needs and Ethnicity: Issues of Over- and Under-Representation*. Research Report RR757. London: DfES.

Mittler, P. (2000) *Working Towards Inclusive Education: Social Contexts*. London: David Fulton.

Norwich, B. (1993) Ideological dilemmas in special needs education: practitioners' views, *Oxford Review of Education*, 19(4), 527–546.

Norwich, B. (2000a) Brahm Norwich, in P. Clough and J. Corbett (eds) *Theories of Inclusive Education: A Students' Guide*. London: Paul Chapman Publishing.

Norwich, B. (2000b) Inclusion in education: from concepts, values and critique to practice, in H. Daniels (ed.) *Special Education Re-Formed: Beyond Rhetoric?* London: Routledge.

Norwich, B. (2002) Education, inclusion and individual differences: recognising and resolving dilemmas, *British Journal of Educational Studies*, 50(4), 482–502.

Norwich, B. and Lewis, A. (2001) Mapping a pedagogy for special educational needs, *British Educational Research Journal*, 27(3), 313–330.

Oliver, M. (1992) Intellectual masturbation: a rejoinder to Soder and Booth, *European Journal of Special Needs Education*, 7(1), 20–28.

Skrtic, T.M. (1991a) *Behind Special Education: A Critical Analysis of Professional Culture and School Organization*. Denver: Love.

Skrtic, T.M. (1991b) The special education paradox: equity as the way to excellence, *Harvard Educational Review*, 61(2), 148–206.

Skrtic, T.M. (ed.) (1995) *Disability and Democracy: Reconstructing (Special) Education for Postmodernity*. New York: Teachers College Press.

Thomas, G. and Loxley, A. (2001) *Deconstructing Special Education and Constructing Inclusion*. Buckingham: Open University Press.

Thomas, G. and O'Hanlon, C. (2002) Series editors' preface, in S. Benjamin (ed.) *The Micropolitics of Inclusive Education: An Ethnography*. Buckingham: Open University Press.

Tomlinson, S. (1982) *A Sociology of Special Education*. London: Routledge & Kegan Paul.

Chapter 14

Reframing psychology for inclusive learning within social justice agendas

Peter Hick

Introduction

Psychologists from several different traditions have recently been addressing questions of inclusion. For example, a proposal for the establishment of a section of the British Psychological Society for the 'Psychology of Inclusion' came from the field of occupational psychology (Chamberlain and Meehan, 2003). The American Psychological Association has issued guidelines for 'infusing' inclusive approaches into textbooks for teaching psychology (Trimble, 2003). Abrams and Christian (2007: 215) examine social inclusion and exclusion from a social psychological perspective, proposing a 'relational dynamics' framework encompassing various dimensions of exclusion. Farrell and Venables (Chapter 10) and Hick (2005) consider educational psychologists' engagement with inclusive education, whilst Goodley and Lawthom (2006) examine the potential for engaging critical psychology with disabilities studies, both of these being fields that can bring insights to bear on inclusion in education.

The contributions that can be drawn from psychology in developing an understanding of inclusive education become clearer when an interdisciplinary frame is applied to inclusion as social justice. It is at this point, where psychology interacts with education as an interdisciplinary field, that the social context in which psychology is to be applied requires clarity about the social values on which it is based. The history of psychology's involvement in education is hardly neutral, indeed 'social and political values have a pervasive and continuing influence on the nature of psychology and its relationship with education' (Norwich, 2000: 8). Gary Thomas highlights the dangers of ignoring this issue in Chapter 1. He argues elsewhere that: 'to promote inclusion involves judgements based on values, and there is no reason to be apologetic about this' (Thomas and Glenny, 2002: 366). I adopt an orientation to promoting social justice as a starting point for understanding and developing more inclusive practices in education. The critique that such an approach is unjustifiable or unscientific is strongly countered by Brantlinger (2004). A retreat into an efficacy-based model of research in inclusive education does not avoid the question of values: 'neutrality in social justice research is ... a myth, whether or not one declares one's value system' (Blair, 1998: 20). Most importantly, the rejection of a position starting from inclusive education as social justice is based on 'the mistaken belief that one can in education unproblematically separate the disinterested from the interested, the apolitical from the ideological, the objective from the subjective, the reasoned from the irrational, the evidence-based from the arbitrary' (Thomas and Glenny, 2002: 347).

Inclusive education as social justice

As the focus of concerns encompassed by those involved in developing inclusive education has broadened, there is a sense in which the term 'inclusion' has itself become less useful. Cummings *et al.* (2003: 63) suggest that a 'significant shift in thinking ... needs to take place when the focus moves from the politics of disablement to the politics of social and economic disadvantage'. This is reflected in a tendency to use a variety of terms such as 'equity', 'enabling education', or 'inclusion and diversity', for naming research groups, textbooks or postgraduate programmes.

The trajectory of multiple discourses of inclusion in the UK has been strongly influenced by the development of policy under the New Labour government since 1997. Many observers have noted the tension, evident throughout this period, between the standards and inclusion agendas, whilst a number of studies have addressed the complexities schools face in attempting to navigate these competing pressures (Ainscow *et al.*, 2006). At the same time it is possible to discern processes of incorporating the language of inclusion, both into a welfarist 'social exclusion' agenda and in response to a powerful special needs lobby. This section discusses both of these developments before considering how psychology for inclusive education can relate to a social justice agenda.

Beyond special versus mainstream

There is a sense of unreality in the tone of moral panic framing much of the recent debate about special school closures in the UK media (e.g. *The Sunday Times*, 14 January, 2007). In fact there has not been a mass exodus of children moving from special schools into the mainstream, and there seems little prospect of this happening in the foreseeable future. The proportion of the school-age population in the special school sector remains very much the same after a decade of New Labour, and five years after the introduction of the Statutory Inclusion Framework (Ofsted, 2004; Daniels and Porter, 2007). Ofsted (2006) recently published a report signalling an attempt to move discussion forward from the 'special versus mainstream' debate. Their survey showed that 'more good or outstanding provision existed in resourced mainstream schools' than in other types of school. They criticized the 'simplistic and mistaken' view that local authority reorganizations involving special school closure meant an inevitable loss of specialist support (Ofsted, 2006: 19) Interestingly, the report pointed out that the composition of special schools is changing, so that many no longer 'specialize' in one category of special educational needs (SEN). For example schools designated as catering for students categorized as having 'moderate learning difficulties', are increasingly accommodating students described as having 'autistic spectrum disorders' and 'behavioural, emotional and social difficulties'. This development reflects recent research findings questioning the extent to which there can be said to be specialist pedagogies for particular categories of disability (see Florian, Chapter 4).

For those concerned with promoting inclusive education, a central focus remains the development of more inclusive practices within the mainstream of the education systems so that fewer children experience exclusion or marginalization (Ainscow *et al.*, 2006). Nevertheless, it is interesting to observe a tendency emerging within the special education sector to elide the concepts of mainstream and special schools. For example, the government strategy for special educational needs aims to 'break down the divide between mainstream and special schools to create a unified system where all schools and their pupils are included within the wider community of schools' (DfES, 2004: 38).

This revised meaning of inclusion reflects the contested and fluid nature of the term, and is visible in references to practices such as mixed-ability classes in special schools as a form of 'inclusion'. An appropriation of 'inclusion' as a form of special schooling gives rise to a sense of déjà vu, reminiscent of the optimism which greeted the 1970 Education Act, which marked the first legal recognition of the right to education for children described (currently) as having severe learning difficulties. As the field of inclusive education has shifted from an initial focus on placement in mainstream schools, to processes of participation and achievement, and from learners identified as having SEN to all learners, policy makers have performed an intellectual 'sleight of hand', introducing an element of double-think. The result is that 'the meaning of inclusion has been colonized' (Armstrong, 2005: 149), as 'the New Labour vision of inclusion is one that reconstructs inclusion within the traditional framework of special education and in so doing reinforces its traditional purposes' (p. 136). It is worth noting that special education emerged as a historical artifact of the development of mass compulsory schooling in late nineteenth-century capitalism, rather than in response to evidence of effective specialist pedagogy. In this process, 'the problem of school failure was reframed ... in the new field of special education, which emerged as a means to remove and contain the most recalcitrant students' (Skrtic, 1991: 152).

The marketization of inclusion and exclusion

Lunt and Norwich (Chapter 8) introduce the issue of the impact of the market reforms on inclusion in the UK education system. Much of the architecture of marketization established by the Thatcher and Major governments has been continued and extended under New Labour; from Ofsted, SATS and league tables to tuition fees, Academies and private sector partnerships. The impact of these pressures has continually 'entailed the generation of a more competitive, selective, and socially divisive series of policies and practices' (Barton, 2004: 64). Discourses of inclusion in schools become bound up in the now ubiquitous, and at times invisible, language of the market: 'There is a tendency to speak in one breath about inclusive education, but to fail to acknowledge the policy context that presses us relentlessly towards educational exclusion in the other. Here we refer to the marketisation of schooling' (Slee and Allan, 2001: 179).

Inevitably it is the disadvantaged, the minorities, and the disempowered who are the losers in the education marketplace. Unsurprisingly, students identified as having special educational needs have sustained a disproportionately high rate of disciplinary exclusion throughout this period (Hick *et al.*, 2007). Ball (1993: 8) points out that 'excluded students have their market "choice" taken away from them'. Indeed Nes (2004: 122) poses the question aptly: 'What is the market value of people with special needs?'

The relocation of inclusive education within the New Labour rhetoric of 'social exclusion' has involved a down-playing of the role of material inequality and disadvantage, in favour of an individualized and internalized discourse of 'poverty of aspiration' and self-esteem (Hick *et al.*, 2007). It has shifted the onus of social change from the institution to the individual, so that 'special educational needs continues to be a legitimating label for the failure of the system to address itself to the aspirations, dignity and human worth of so many young people' (Armstrong, 2005: 147).

Thomas and Loxley (2007) have drawn attention to the need for inclusive education to build on a broader base in social theory. Artiles *et al.* (2006) review social justice perspectives in inclusive education, identifying parallel 'justification' and 'implementation' discourses with 'individual' and 'communitarian' foci. They call for a shift from traditional approaches to social justice in theorizing inclusive education towards future transformative models that 'must embrace participatory strategies in which distribution of resources, access, and social cohesion constitutes the foundation of democratic egalitarian alternatives' (p. 267). It is this notion of transformative social justice that offers a fruitful approach to drawing on Vygotsky's legacy for psychology applied to inclusive education.

Vygotsky on social transformation, inclusive pedagogy and inclusive schooling

Of course just as there are multiple discourses of inclusion in education, so multiple interpretations are possible of the significance of Vygotsky's work today, and one should not claim one understanding or interpretation as solely authentic. It is important to recognise that recent debates around inclusion did not arise in the same form during Vygotsky's lifetime and therefore his writings cannot be neatly transposed into current contexts (Daniels, Chapter 3). The aim here is simply to review aspects of his writings that have particular relevance, and to show how central elements of his thinking can inform our understanding of inclusive learning. Vygotsky's thought remains surprisingly relevant when viewed from this perspective, on key questions such as: a sociocultural understanding of inclusive learning (Kershner, Chapter 5); inclusive and specialist pedagogies (Florian, Chapter 4); cooperative learning strategies (Putnam, Chapter 7); and the 'dynamic assessment' of learning potential as an alternative to IQ (Stringer, Chapter 11). Daniels (Chapter 3) deals in detail with terminology issues for readers who may be unfamiliar with Vygotsky's writings; clearly those who seek to understand his work will need to make allowances for references to outdated terminology. For example, given the negative resonance to contemporary ears of the language of 'defectology' it is interesting to consider how Vygotsky's description of disability as a 'social sprain' (Vygotsky 1994: 20) can be read as prefiguring a social model of disability.

Vygotsky and social transformation

In discussing Vygotsky's legacy in the context of inclusive education as transformative social justice, an obvious starting point is with the centrality of Marxism to his thought. Many scholars have pointed to the Marxist roots of Vygotsky's thinking. For example, Cole and Scribner comment that: '"A psychologically relevant application of dialectical and historical materialism" would be one accurate summary of Vygotsky's sociocultural theory of higher mental processes' (1978: 6). The influence of Marx on Vygotsky extended, for example, from his understanding of the development of thought and consciousness itself, to his vision of education in the service of social transformation. Vygotsky offers a basis for social theory that is congruent with inclusive education, by linking the social world to individual development:

> A complicated relationship between these two factors [consciousness and way of life] can be observed in a highly developed society which has acquired a complex class structure. Here the influence of the basis on the psychological superstructure of man turns out not to be direct, but mediated by a large number of very complex material and spiritual factors. But even here, the basic law of historical human development, which proclaims that human beings are created by the society in which they live and that it represents the determining factor in the formation of their personalities, remains in force.

> (1994: 176)

Tudge and Winterhoff (1999) reflect on the relations between the social world and cognitive development in the writings of Vygotsky, Piaget and Bandura, drawing attention to areas of commonality between the three. The dialectical nature of the relationship between the social and the individual is summed up by Bandura as follows: 'Personal and environmental factors do not function as independent determinants; rather, they determine each other. People create, alter and destroy environments. The changes they produce in environmental conditions, in turn, affect their behaviour and the nature of future life' (Bandura (1986: 23) in Tudge and Winterhoff (1999: 321–2)).

For Vygotsky, the dialectic of the social world and individual development was not conceived of as occurring within a static society, but as historically situated in processes of social change and transformation, in which human agency played a key part. It is important to understand the development of his ideas in the context of a period of intense creativity and innovation in art and culture in early post-revolutionary Russia (Blanck, 1990). For example Luria described his own experiences at that time:

> Life offered me the fantastically stimulating atmosphere of an active, rapidly changing society. My entire generation was infused with the energy of revolutionary change – the liberating energy people feel when they are part of a society that is able to make tremendous progress in a very short time.
>
> (Luria, 1979: 17)

We have a recent example in the new South Africa, of how psychology can respond to the challenges posed by processes of social transformation (Engelbrecht, Chapter 9). Vygotsky's vision of the role of education reflects an optimism about the possibilities for more positive social change, albeit under the difficult circumstances of his time: 'It is education which should play the central role in the transformation of man – this road of conscious social formation of new generations' (Vygotsky, 1994: 181).

Vygotsky on inclusive pedagogy

Recent research (Norwich and Lewis, 2007; Corbett and Norwich, 2005; Davis and Florian, 2004; Florian, Chapter 4) suggests that, despite traditional assumptions about special education, there is limited evidence for separate specialist pedagogies for learners described as having special educational needs. Norwich and Lewis (2007) propose a useful distinction between specialist knowledge of particular disabilities and categories of special educational need; the use of specialist teaching strategies and equipment; and whether these can be said to constitute a special pedagogy. Whilst some learners may require more intensive teaching, this doesn't necessarily amount to a fundamentally different or 'special' mode of learning. Indeed, the issue of inclusive pedagogy extends beyond learners with disabilities to all learners who may be at risk of underachieving (Dyson and Hick, 2004).

It is interesting to note how Vygotsky expressed similar views in his writings on educational psychology:

> The education of abnormal children, whether those who are impaired in some way or those who are gifted, has long been thought of as seemingly outside the field of pedagogics, as constituting a realm which the general laws of education do not reach. We have to say that that such a view is profoundly mistaken …

When they are children both the genius and person who is mentally retarded constitute just as much a subject of education as does every other child, and the general laws of pedagogics hold just as well for them as for all children of the same age. Only by proceeding on the basis of these general pedagogical laws are we able to discover correct ways of realizing the process of individualization which has to be imparted to the process of educating every child.

(1997: 3–4)

The issue of inclusive pedagogy is partially addressed within the current idea of 'personalising learning'. Here again, Vygotsky deals succinctly with what is now a topical issue:

It is false to think that the problem of individualization arises only in relation to that which goes beyond the average. On the contrary, in every individual child we confront certain forms of individualization, of course not so sharply pronounced and not so sharply expressed as in blindness, genius, deaf-muteness, or mental retardation. But a phenomenon does not cease being itself if its quantitative expression is diminished. The demand for individualization of educational methodology, therefore, also amounts to a general demand imposed on pedagogics and extends to absolutely every child.

(1997: 4)

For Vygotsky, this approach to inclusive pedagogy encompassed the question of specialist teaching strategies and approaches:

We do not deny the necessity of special instruction and training for handicapped children. On the contrary, we assert that teaching the blind to read and the deaf to develop oral speech requires special pedagogical techniques, devices and methods. On the other hand, we must not forget that, above all, it is necessary to educate a child not as a blind child but as a child. Otherwise, to educate a child as a blind or deaf child means to nurture blindness or deafness.

(1993: 83)

Harry Daniels (Chapter 3) deals in detail with Vygotsky's writings on specialized instruction, and how these relate to current debates is clearly open to interpretation. The development of pedagogies for inclusion remains a significant and unresolved challenge for research on the development of more inclusive schooling.

Vygotsky on inclusive schooling

Few, if any, of the early proponents of 'full inclusion' for children with disabilities drew significantly on Vygotsky's writings on inclusive education (Hick and Thomas, forthcoming); in fact Vygotsky's *Collected Works* were not published in English until 1993. It is only more recently that a 'sociocultural turn'

(Thomas and Loxley, 2007: 139) in understanding the socially situated nature of learning has influenced theorizing about inclusive education (Kershner, Chapter 5). Research from a sociocultural tradition addressing the social construction of difficulties in learning, tended initially to be read within a separate – if parallel – discourse from that generated by the disability inclusion movement. For example McDermott (1993: 272) gives an account of the experiences of a child described as having 'learning disabilities', showing how difficulties in learning are constructed differently in differing contexts: 'We might just as well say there is no such thing as LD [learning disability], only a social practice of displaying, noticing, documenting, remediating, and explaining it.'

Having acknowledged that alternative readings of Vygotsky are possible, it is nevertheless worth remembering what he wrote. On the question of inclusive schooling, he commented:

> Mainstreaming [lit. coeducation] with normal children has been proposed many times. Now unfortunately it can no longer remain just a question of future priority; ... our slogan [is] 'we must proceed until every elementary teacher can teach even the deaf child and, subsequently, until each elementary school becomes simultaneously a school for the deaf'.
>
> (1993: 91)

Equally, Vygotsky could be highly critical of separate special schooling:

> The special school is by its very nature antisocial and encourages antisocialism. We have not to think about isolating the blind person from life as soon as possible, but about introducing him into life as early as extensively as possible. A blind person will have to live a normal life in the seeing world; he must, therefore, learn in a general school.
>
> (1993: 85–86)

Nevertheless Daniels (Chapter 3), shows how Vygotsky's writings can equally be interpreted as supporting a case for specialized instruction for learners with disabilities, whether delivered in special or mainstream settings. He wrote: 'It is true that pupils of the auxiliary school must be introduced to these general goals by different paths; this justifies the existence of the special school, and constitutes its uniqueness' (Vygotsky, 1993: 137). Gindis (2003: 211–3) and Kozulin and Gindis (2007: 350–1) discuss the apparent change in Vygotsky's views on inclusion, from his visionary early writings, to later discussions in which he recognizes a role for special schools. They characterize his more developed position as calling for both 'integration based on positive differentiation' and 'differentiated learning environment[s]'. Judy Kugelmass suggests that:

> This development can be understood in terms of the socio-historical context of the Soviet Union in the early and mid-twentieth century. The knowledge

gained during the second half of the twentieth century regarding children's learning and development, combined with a growing understanding of the relationship between democracy, human rights and the creation of publicly supported schools for all children, have, however, created a different social context. Hopefully, the time has come for the realization of Vygotsky's vision of a radical transformation of educational processes.

(Kugelmass, 2007: 277–8)

Conclusion

The current limitations in the capacities of mainstream schools to engage diverse learners can be seen as a product of the social organization of education within our society. The limits to inclusion are socially constructed, defined and developed; and reflected in complex layers of exclusionary pressures, operating at the levels of school systems, schools and classrooms. There is a sense in which the position taken by researchers and practitioners in relation to the pressures of marketization in education is central in shaping their response to the challenge of developing more inclusive practices. For example, Linda Ware (2004: 201) concludes that adopting 'a Freirean lens allows for recognizing the importance of both hope and struggle in an interdependent fashion'. Slee and Allan (2001: 185–6) ask whether there is 'a need for a theory of activism which enables ideas about inclusion to be enacted?' They point to ways in which exclusionary practices are continually re-inscribed in policies which profess to be inclusive, then position themselves in opposition to this process: 'The partisan research ... genre to which we have signed up is one aspect of the general call to activism'. Liz Todd, an educational psychologist reflecting on ways of developing an 'enabling inclusive participative practice', calls for 'greater "political" literacy': 'The key is to interrogate and be aware of professional discourses, the models, ideas, terms ... around the systems, institutions and people with whom we work' (Todd, 2006: 153).

In conclusion then, what strategies are likely to be fruitful for those seeking to draw on psychology to develop more inclusive practices in education? The discussion in this chapter points to a need to build on approaches that are:

- explicit in aiming to promote inclusive education as a process of transformative social justice;
- less concerned to delineate and defend psychology from other domains of social theory;
- more actively engaged in developing interdisciplinary approaches in both theory and in practice.

There are a number of traditions in educational and social theory, research and practice that can be seen as congruent with such approaches. Clearly Vygotsky's work was rooted in Marxism; and recently Peter McLaren, an influential critical theorist, has noted a return to Marx in educational theory: 'the critical tradition ... has begun to reemerge in important ways – namely, as a serious engagement with Marxist analysis and the concept of social class' (2006: xiv–xv). Equally, there is much scope for developing productive alliances between the fields of sociocultural theory, critical theory and disability studies: 'The marriage of both approaches [sociocultural theory and critical theory] provides a rich foundation for examining issues of educational equity and social justice within special education' (de Valenzuela, 2007: 288). A test of such work will be its utility in informing and supporting the development of a more inclusive education system. As Newman and Holzman put it, summarizing their discussion of the role of social transformation in the development of Vygotsky's writings: 'Says Marx: "The philosophers [we must add, 'and the psychologists'] have only interpreted the world, in various ways; the point is to change it" (1973: 173). We would argue that the point is to make it' (Newman and Holzman, 1993: 145).

References

Abrams, D. and Christian, J. (2007) A relational analysis of social exclusion, in D. Abrams, J. Christian and D. Gordon (eds) *Multidisciplinary Handbook of Social Exclusion Research*, 211–232. Chichester: John Wiley & Sons.

Ainscow, M., Booth, T., and Dyson, A. with Farrell, P., Frankham, J., Gallannaugh, F., Howes, A. and Smith, R. (2006) *Improving Schools, Developing Inclusion*. London: Routledge.

Armstrong, D. (2005) Reinventing 'inclusion': New Labour and the cultural politics of special education, *Oxford Review of Education*, 31(1), 135–151.

Artiles, A.J., Harris-Murri, N., and Rostenberg, D. (2006) Inclusion as social justice: Critical notes on discourses, assumptions, and the road ahead, *Theory into Practice*, 45(3), 260–268.

Ball, S.J. (1993) Education markets, choice and social class: the market as a class strategy in the UK and the USA, *British Journal of Sociology of Education*, 14(1), 3–19.

Bandura, A. (1986) *Social Foundations of Thought and Action: A Social Cognitive Theory*. Eaglewood Cliffs, NJ: Prentice Hall. Cited in Tudge and Winterhoff, op. cit.

Barton, L. (2004) The politics of special education: a necessary or irrelevant approach?, in L. Ware (ed.) *Ideology and the Politics of (In)Exclusion*, 63–75. New York: Peter Lang.

Blair, M. (1998) The myth of neutrality in educational research, in P. Connolly. and B. Troyna (eds) *Researching Racism in Education: Politics, Theory and Practice*, 12–20. Buckingham: Open University Press.

Blanck, G. (1990) Vygotsky: The man and his cause, in L. Moll (ed.), *Vygotsky and Education: Instructional Implications and Applications of Sociohistorical Psychology*, 31–58. Cambridge: Cambridge University Press.

Brantlinger, E. (2004) Ideologies discerned, values determined: getting past the hierarchies of special education. In Ware, L. (ed.), *Ideology and the Politics of (In)Exclusion*, 11–31. New York: Peter Lang.

Chamberlain, E. and Meehan, M. (2003) A proposed section for the psychology of inclusion: letter to the editors, *Journal of Occupational Psychology, Employment and Disability*, 5(2), 11–13.

Cole, M. and Scribner, S. (1978) Introduction, in L.S. Vygotsky *Mind in Society, The Development of Higher Psychological Processes,* 1–14. London: Harvard University Press.

Corbett, J. and Norwich, B. (2005) Common or specialised pedagogy? In M. Nind, J. Rix, K. Sheehy and K. Simmons (eds) *Curriculum and Pedagogy in Inclusive Education,* 13–30. Abingdon: RoutledgeFalmer.

Cummings, C., Dyson, A., Millward, A. (2003) Participation and democracy: What's inclusion got to do with it?, in J. Allan (ed.) *Inclusion, Participation and Democracy: What is the Purpose?,* 49–66. Dordrecht: Kluwer Academic Publishers.

Daniels, H. and Porter, J. (2007) *Learning Needs and Difficulties Among Children of Primary School Age: Definition, Identification, Provision and Issues* (Primary Review Research Survey 5/2). Cambridge: University of Cambridge Faculty of Education.

Davis, P. and Florian, L. with Ainscow, M., Dyson, A., Farrell, P., Hick., P., Humphrey, N., Jenkins, P., Kaplan, I., Palmer, S., Parkinson, G., Polat, F., Reason, R., Byers, R., Dee, L., Kershner, R. and Rouse, M. (2004) *Teaching Strategies and Approaches for Pupils with Special Educational Needs: A Scoping Study,* Research Report 516. London: DfES.

DfES (2004) *Removing Barriers to Achievement: The Government's Strategy for SEN.* London: DfES.

Dyson, A. and Hick, P. (2004) Mixed difficulties, in A. Lewis and B. Norwich (eds) *Special Teaching for Special Children: A Pedagogy for Inclusion?* Maidenhead: Open University Press.

Gindis, B. (2003) Remediation through education: sociocultural theory and children with special needs, in A. Kozulin, B. Gindis, V.S. Ageyev. and S.M. Miller (eds) *Vygotsky's Educational Theory in Cultural Context,* 200–221. Cambridge: Cambridge University Press.

Goodley, D. and Lawthom, R. (2006) Disability and psychology, in *Critical Introductions and Reflections.* Basingstoke: Palgrave MacMillan.

Hick, P. (2005) Supporting the development of more inclusive practices using the index for inclusion, *Educational Psychology in Practice,* 21(2), 117–122.

Hick, P. and Thomas, G. (forthcoming) Inclusion and diversity in education: series introduction, in P. Hick and G. Thomas (eds) *Inclusion and Diversity in Education, Volume 1: Inclusive Education as Social Justice.* London: SAGE.

Hick, P., Visser, J. and MacNab, N. (2007) Education and social exclusion, in D. Abrams, J. Christian and D. Gordon (eds) *Multi-professional Handbook of Social Exclusion,* 6: 95–114. Chichester: John Wiley & Sons.

Kozulin, A. and Gindis, B. (2007) Sociocultural theory and education of children with special needs: from defectology to remedial pedagogy, in H. Daniels, M. Cole and J. Wertsch (eds) *The Cambridge Companion to Vygotsky,* 332–363. New York: Cambridge University Press.

Kugelmass, J. (2007) Constructivist views of learning: implications for inclusive education, in L. Florian (ed.) *The SAGE Handbook of Special Education,* 272–279. London: SAGE.

Luria, A.R. (1979) *The Making of Mind: A Personal Account of Soviet Psychology.* London: Harvard University Press.

McDermott, R.P. (1993) The acquisition of a child by a learning disability, in S. Chaiklin and J. Lave (eds) *Understanding Practice: Perspectives on Activity and Context,* 269–305. Cambridge: Cambridge University Press.

McLaren, P. (2006) Preface, in M. Cole (ed.) *Education, Equality and Human Rights* (2nd edn.). London: Routledge.

Marx, K. (1973) *Theses on Feuerbach* XI, in Newman and Holzman, op. cit.

Nes, K. (2004) Quality versus equality? Inclusion politics in Norway at century's end, in L. Ware (ed.) *Ideology and the Politics of (In)Exclusion,* 125–140. New York: Peter Lang.

Newman, F. and Holzman, L. (1993) *Lev Vygotsky: Revolutionary Scientist.* London: Routledge.

Norwich, B. (2000) *Education and Psychology in Interaction.* London: Routledge.

Norwich, B and Lewis, A. (2007) How specialized is teaching children with disabilities and difficulties? *Journal of Curriculum Studies,* 39(2), 127–150.

Ofsted (2004) *Special educational needs and disability: towards inclusive schools* (HMI 2276). London: Ofsted.

Ofsted (2006) *Inclusion: does it matter where pupils are taught? Provision and outcomes in different settings for pupils with learning difficulties and disabilities* (HMI 2535). London: Ofsted.

Skrtic, T.M. (1991) The special education paradox: equity as the way to excellence, *Harvard Educational Review,* 61(2), 148–206.

Slee, R. and Allan, J. (2001) Excluding the included: a reconsideration of inclusive education, *International Studies in Sociology of Education,* 11(2), 173–192.

Sunday Times (2007) 'Kelly axed 2,700 special needs places', 14 January. Accessed 30 August 2007 at: http://www.timesonline.co.uk/tol/news/politics/article586394.ece.

Thomas, G. and Glenny, G. (2002) Thinking about inclusion. Whose reason? What evidence?, *International Journal of Inclusive Education,* 6(4), 345–369.

Thomas, G. and Loxley, A. (2007) *Deconstructing Special Education and Constructing Inclusion* (2nd edn.). Maidenhead: Open University Press.

Todd, L. (2006) Enabling practice for professionals: the need for practical post-structuralist theory, in D. Goodley and R. Lawthom (eds) *Disability and Psychology,* 141–154. Basingstoke: Palgrave Macmillan.

Trimble, J.E., Stevenson, M.R. and Worell, J.P. (2003) *Toward an Inclusive Psychology: Infusing the Introductory Psychology Textbook with Diversity Content.* Washington DC: American Psychological Association.

Tudge, J.R.H. and Winterhoff, P.A. (1999) Vygotsky, Piaget and Bandura: perspectives on the relations between the social world and cognitive development, in P. Lloyd and C. Fernyhough (eds) *Lev Vygotsky: Critical Assessments, Vol. 1, Vygotsky's Theory,* 311–338. London: Routledge.

de Valenzuela, J.S. (2007) Sociocultural views of learning, in L. Florian (ed.) *The SAGE Handbook of Special Education,* 280–289. London: SAGE.

Vygotsky, L.S. (1993) in R.W. Rieber and A.S. Carton (eds), *Vygotsky, L.S., Collected Works, Vol. 2: The Fundamentals of Defectology (Abnormal Psychology and Learning Disabilities).* London: Plenum Press.

Vygotsky, L.S. (1994) The Socialist alteration of man, in R. Van Der Veer and J. Valsiner, *The Vygotsky Reader,* 175–184. Oxford, Blackwell.

Vygotsky, L.S. (1997) The problem of giftedness, *Educational Psychology,* Chapter 17. St. Lucie Press, Fl, USA. Accessed 16 December 2006 at: http://www.marxists.org/archive/vygotsky/works/1926/educational-psychology/ch17

Ware, L. (2004) The politics of ideology, in L. Ware (ed.) *Ideology and the Politics of (In)Exclusion.* New York: Peter Lang.

Index